The Politically Incorrect Guide™ to
HUNTING

The Politically Incorrect Guide™ to
HUNTING

Frank Miniter

Since 1947
REGNERY
PUBLISHING, INC.
An Eagle Publishing Company • Washington, DC

Library of Congress Cataloging-in-Publication Data
    Miniter, Frank.
    The politically incorrect guide(tm) to hunting / Frank Miniter.
    p. cm.
    Includes bibliographical references and index.
    ISBN 978-1-59698-521-6
    1. Hunting—Moral and ethical aspects. 2. Miniter, Frank—Political and social views. 3. Political correctness. I. Title. II. Title:Politically incorrect guide to hunting.
    SK14.3.M56 2007
    179'.3--dc22

                        2007029530

Published in the United States by
Regnery Publishing, Inc.
One Massachusetts Avenue, NW
Washington, DC 20001
www.regnery.com

Manufactured in the United States of America

10 9 8 7 6 5 4 3 2 1

Books are available in quantity for promotional or premium use. Write to Director of Special Sales, Regnery Publishing, Inc., One Massachusetts Avenue NW, Washington, DC 20001, for information on discounts and terms or call (202) 216-0600.

To the American hunter

CONTENTS

Hunters are wildlife's best defenders

Hunters are ducks' best friends

Conservation easements ward off suburbia

HOW TO TALK TO AN ANTI

When you edit for a hunting magazine based in Manhattan, you become acutely aware that the best-educated Americans know the least about the wild world, and you see first hand that it's fashionable—even morally desirable—in our most sophisticated circles to hypocritically disregard the realities of nature. You're bemused to learn that many urban elitists oppose logging, yet live in wood homes with fireplaces; drive gas-guzzling SUVs, yet support blanket restrictions on oil and gas development; laud clean energy, yet scream when windmills are to be placed within view of their beach homes; and oppose hunting, yet benefit from hunting every time they fly, as hunting prevents geese from taking down airliners.

And you sometimes find yourself in awkward, even scrappy, exchanges. Which is what prompted me to create a five-step program for talking to anti-hunters. For example, one warm summer evening a few years ago I attended a dinner party at a trendy New York restaurant and found myself seated across the table from a smartly dressed, prim, and priggish woman who amiably introduced herself as an attorney and asked what I did. "I edit for a hunting magazine!" I replied.

Moments later, as she speared a baby carrot with her fork, she looked me in the eye and fired. "I'm a vegetarian, you know. I'm above all that killing."

1

The first step in debating an anti-hunter is to be cordial, even if they spew invective—it keeps the dialogue rolling and tempers the emotion fueling their convictions; after all, most anti-hunters just don't know the politically incorrect truth about hunting. So I smiled.

The second step is to prompt the person to state her beliefs—contradictions and all. To induce them to explain why they've come to their conclusions on hunting. It's the Socratic method of debate and it works wonderfully with such convoluted utopianists, people who base their knowledge of nature on Walt Disney animations. So I replied with calculated surprise, "Oh, you only eat vegetables?"

"Yes."

"Why?"

"I deplore killing, the murdering of animals," she declared.

"Oh." I nodded. "Then your vegetables must come from no-animal-killing farms?"

"What are those?" she asked as her fork hovered in front of her lips.

"You look for the label that says 'no-animal-killing farm participant' when you purchase vegetables, don't you?"

"Um, no. Where does it . . . ?" She put her fork down.

"You'd better ask the waiter if this restaurant's vegetables come from a USDA-certified no-animal-killing farm."

The waiter wandered by moments later, and she actually asked, "Excuse me, I'd like to know if your produce comes from no-animal-killing farms."

His eyes flitted about uncertainly, and he stuttered, "Oh . . . I . . . I'll have to check."

He was back with a worried look. "I'm sorry, but the cooks haven't heard of that designation. But I'm sure the vegetables are safe. We get them from organic farms. They come in fresh every day."

She looked petulantly at her salad. She didn't know what to do. Then she saw me smirking and turned venomous. I felt mischievous, even a little rude, and so I apologized, "I was playing a joke, there's no such thing."

"Well, I never!"

The third step in talking to an anti-hunter to is point out her contradictions, which I'd just done in a less than civil way—a complete disregard of step one. Before she could slap me, I jumped to step four: let them know they're speaking to someone who knows, of all the dastardly things, the real facts.

"I've hunted on farms from Montana to Maine, and the farmers are always very appreciative."

"So?"

"They all have produce to defend. I haven't met a farmer yet who doesn't kill geese, rabbits, or deer to preserve his livelihood."

"And your point is?"

"Every cabbage or carrot you eat was raised by farmers who kill deer or rabbits or something so they have a crop to harvest."

She was cogitating, stumbling over her contradictions, getting agitated. It was time for the closer, step five: to provide a way out of muddled logic. This is a very important step, yet most debaters neglect it. Confronting a person with the real facts is never enough. People get rattled when you shed light on their contradictions; well-educated people never like to learn they're defending unsubstantiated biases, because that is the blindness of bigotry. If you leave them like that they'll fall back on emotion, not reason, and so they won't learn anything.

So I continued. "You shouldn't feel guilty that farmers need to protect their crops. It's only natural. Many species defend a territory and thus a food source. Wolves will kill an intruder that's not from their pack. Male lions do the same thing, as do male cougars. Even a squirrel will chase off another squirrel that's invading its territory. They have acorns to protect. They'll starve without them. Defending your food source is part of living in this world."

She scrunched her lips and agreed, "Well, I suppose that's true."

If the person will candidly debate, not become incoherently upset, then that five-step method always works. Most people just don't know the truth about hunting. Emotion gets in the way of reason. But it's not completely their fault. The mainstream media isn't telling them the whole story. Unless people have a firsthand experience, they often won't learn what hunting does for wildlife. In fact, the truth about hunting has become so politically incorrect these days that to determine if a politician is environmentally friendly the mainstream media looks no further than the "National Environmental Scorecard," a rating system concocted before each congressional election by the League of Conservation Voters (LCV), a Democratic-partisan organization whose issues revolve around global warming prevention, opposition to domestic oil and gas development, and getting legislators to pass stricter vehicle emissions standards. If a politician passes this liberal litmus test, then he's "green," if he doesn't, then he's deemed to be in league with the polluters, the environmental destroyers, and, ah, the hunters.

You see, the LCV doesn't consider critical issues such as deer management, state wildlife program funding, wetland preservation, habitat restoration, and other quantitative conservation efforts to be worthy of its environmental rating. This shuns hunters because sportsmen are the ones who implement and pay for those real-world conservation projects. As a result, a congressman might have voted to expand the Conservation Reserve Program, backed additional funding for the National Wildlife Refuge System, fought to keep the Clean Water Act strong, yet be labeled anti-environment because he or she thought it was hypocritical for the

U.S. to import oil while passing blanket restrictions on offshore oil drilling.

The mainstream media doesn't point out this disparity. The resulting media spin is so deceitful that even in these environmentally conscious times most Americans don't know that by paying special surtaxes on guns, ammunition, and other gear, hunters sent $294,691,282 to state conservation programs in 2005—or that hikers, mountain bikers, and environmentalists don't pay those conservation taxes. Most people aren't even aware that hunters' money buys critical wetland habitat and funds wildlife research in every state. Most people don't know that hunting reduces the risk of predators preying on us.

This deception is why this book was written. In these pages you'll find the straight facts that bust through the rhetoric, the anti-hunting propaganda, and the media bias on hunting. In these pages you'll hear from wildlife biologists, hunters, farmers, anti-hunters, victims of animal attacks, and many more. You'll sift through wildlife studies, animal attack records, news reports, and expert opinions on hunting. And you'll learn how the banning of hunting affects wildlife populations and conservation. This way, when you talk to an anti-hunter, or when your heart questions if hunting is right, you'll be able to give real, concrete—even if politically incorrect—answers.

Part I

THE HUMANE CASE FOR HUNTING

Chapter 1

HUNTING: WHEN KILLING IS RIGHT

I n December 2005 I went to debate some animal rights activists. They were driving in from Manhattan's Upper West Side, from Greenwich, Connecticut, and from other left-wing enclaves to protest a New Jersey bear hunt. *What a great opportunity to ask them why they think hunting is immoral*, I thought; *surely, they'll have real answers; after all, some deep reason must be prompting them to drive an hour or more to stand in the snow and chant, "Bears are our friends. Hunting is murder!"*

I arrived full of expectation at the bear check station in Wawayanda State Park—a place where hunters were required to bring in their dead bears for biologists to probe, measure, and weigh. There were a few dozen animal rights activists present. A roving mob of youthful activists all wearing ski masks, jihadist style, sprinted in to report and get new orders from an older activist, then dashed off in a mad effort to find a hunter to shadow or a wounded bear to rescue. You see, all the activists were wearing matching hunter-orange sweatshirts with the words WOUNDED BEAR RESCUE printed front and back.

But the activists were outnumbered four to one by an even more intimidating gang: America's traveling cabal of television reporters was busily organizing the activists into a single bunch, so they would look a hundred strong on the nightly news.

Guess what?

- Hunters often know more about animals and the environment and are more connected to nature than so-called environmentalists.

- Hunters aren't mindless killing machines—they truly respect and revere their prey.

I spotted an activist standing on the fringe of the melee. She didn't look as angry as the others. Instead she looked horribly disgusted, like someone had just run over her cat and sped away laughing. Despondent people are so much easier to talk to than angry ones and are often desperately honest. She was perfect. I asked her if they'd found any wounded bears to rescue yet. "No," she sighed. I jotted "all the hunters are shooting straight so far" in my notepad as if it were noteworthy, and then we began to chat about the scene buzzing around us. She was a grandmother with soft features and a gift for gab. Though she'd never seen a bear in the wild, she liked that bears were living in New Jersey's forests. It said something fine about America that bears could live so close to the suburbs of New York City, and if a few broke into homes, killed pets, even attacked people, well, that was to be expected; after all, they were bears, and that's what bears do; we have to accept bears for who they are, she explained as I dutifully jotted down in my notebook: "Activist says bear hunting is form of racism . . . or, perhaps, animalism. Believes they deserve equality."

She stopped explaining her viewpoints and asked if I agreed. I said it was indeed a fine thing that our forests have bears back in them. I told her about the bears I'd watched in the New York woods and in Alaska, Wyoming, and in other places around the world. "They are smart and enterprising, just simply amazing parts of nature. When they realize you're around, which they uncannily do, they disappear like smoke," I commented.

"I know, I know," she agreed, "it's just deplorable that some people want to shoot such wonderful creatures."

"What makes you feel so strongly that hunting is bad?" I probed, going into my five-step routine on how to talk to an anti.

"Well . . . it's just intolerable . . . that's all."

"But why? Why do you feel so passionately that bear hunting is wrong?" My pen was poised for deep thoughts.

"My heart tells me it's wrong."

"But certainly you must have reasons?" I got my pen ready again.

"What reasons do you need? Killing is just wrong."

"Even in self-defense?" I asked.

"Well . . . maybe then," she thought aloud.

"Do you have any scientific rationale for your convictions?"

"Plenty," she gasped as she pointed at the gray December forest. "Those hunters just like to kill. That's not ethical. Why can't they just go to the supermarket? These bears are our friends and neighbors. There's no scientific reason to shoot them."

"But the New Jersey Division of Wildlife doesn't agree with you," I pointed out. "How do you account for their studies?"

"Studies?" She looked confused. "They get money from hunting licenses, you know."

"That's true," I said, "but after years of research they've determined that hunting reduces human-bear conflicts by keeping bears from losing their fear of people and populations within the means of their natural habitat. They've found that it saves the state money and keeps people safer when hunting is used to control bear populations. It's not unprecedented research. Many states use bear hunting to reduce bear-human conflicts."

She gave me a quizzical look. "People have to change—not bears. We have to be tolerant. We have to show them respect, and then they'll show us respect."

"Do you really think wild animals will respect us if we don't hunt them?"

She ignored my question. She wasn't listening, not really; as I spoke, her eyes slowly popped out of her head. "You're a hunter, aren't you?"

"Yes, I am."

"How dare you!"

Well, how should I begin? I pondered, deciding not to take her question rhetorically. *Oh, I know, from the beginning*: "In 1910, President

Theodore Roosevelt wrote, 'All hunters should be nature lovers.'[1] Since then hunters have actually been wildlife's best defenders. I'll explain—"

But she interrupted. "You're a hunter! You seemed like such a nice young man. I thought you really did like bears. But you really just want to murder them!"

"*Like* them?" I replied. "I *revere* them. And hunting isn't murder. The animals aren't caged. It's simply nature's dance between predator and prey—our real connection to wild animals. You see—"

"People like you kill them!"

"Yes, hunters kill."

"Then you can't also like them!" She was angry, outraged. She'd had enough. She strode away shaking her head.

I was left wishing she'd had the maturity to debate. She seemed like such a nice activist.

I approached other activists during that long, cold morning but continued to get the same result. They were friendly until they found me out. They wouldn't debate but just walked off fuming. They were passionately irrational. One even started ranting, "YOU'RE A KILLER! YOU'RE A KILLER!" And although this tirade seemed to miss the whole point, it was, technically speaking, correct. And it is this point that every hunter needs to be able to address.

When killing is right

Yes, when hunters go into the fields and forests their aim is to kill an animal. Hunters are predators. However, they're also human, and it is human not just to feel but also to try to understand. For example, when I step into the forest before dawn and feel the cold, damp of November and smell the musty aroma of soft, new-fallen leaves, I feel alive, connected in a primal way to the natural world. The same feeling comes when hearing the whistling wings of ducks descending on a frosty morning or when listening to an elk's bugle roll down a Rocky Mountain panorama. Human hunters can and do emotionally cherish their prey, but other predators, the fox or the cougar, don't think as deeply, as personally, as the human predator does. We are moral creatures, and we must try to understand the primal urge to hunt on a moral level. As humans, we need to consider if it is morally right to kill animals.

To begin with, animals are not people. This point may not resonate with the PETA types, but almost any normal human being understands that the value of an animal's life does not compare to the value of a human's life. I could make all sorts of arguments in favor of valuing human life over animal life (humans have souls and animals do not; humans have a moral sense while animals lack one; we owe loyalty to our own species as we owe loyalty to our own families and country), but they all just muddle the self-evident fact that human life is sacred. Think about it this way: if your pet dog were drowning and a human stranger was too, would there be any doubt in your mind that you should save the human? How would society react to someone who saved Rufus instead?

The most obvious justification for killing an animal is self-defense or the defense of others. The self-preservation justification applies more broadly than you may think. Not only is it good and right to kill a bear that is threatening your family, but thinning the population of mountain lions in an area abutting a residential neighborhood is also a case of killing animals to protect humans. Indeed, considering the lethality and frequency of deer-automobile collisions, hunting deer is often a question of human preservation (even if the deer hunter doesn't see it that way). As illustrated in chapters 5 and 10, hunting is usually the most humane, effective, and affordable way to address the threats that wild animals pose to humans.

Eating is also a part of self-preservation, and another valid justification for hunting. If it's fine to let someone else—a farmer, a rancher, another hunter—kill meat for you, then it's clearly fine to kill meat yourself. In fact,

considering that my venison was happy and free until the moment of its death while my chicken was probably cooped up its whole life, it's morally *more* humane to hunt your dinner than to shop for it.

Vegetarians don't get a free ride, either: every vegetable farm in the world has to kill or trap animals to protect its crops. That soy burger your sister-in-law is eating was purchased with the blood of some hungry deer. I'll discuss this more in chapter 8.

Hunting isn't just about the pursuit of prey, it's also about building character and inculcating virtues. Hunting develops virtues in respect to the natural world that no other sport can. If this connection with nature is lost, the human race will lose a fundamental understanding of the world around us.

But just because animals are not equal to humans doesn't mean we can kill them for any reason. Indeed, it's crucial for any hunter to know there are right and wrong reasons—and right and wrong ways—to kill animals. The European agrarian society colonized America and displaced Native Americans, who farmed and hunted for sustenance, and began to "market hunt" wildlife—to kill deer, geese, moose—and sell the meat and skins commercially. As the American colonies grew and pushed west, wildlife populations, as well as the Native Americans' way of life, disappeared. After America achieved its Manifest Destiny of growing from the Atlantic to the Pacific, modern game hunting practices were devised to save species before they completely disappeared. Late in the nineteenth and early in the twentieth centuries, state and federal game departments enacted game laws to control the harvest of wildlife and to use hunting to augment wildlife populations. Money raised from hunting licenses, duck stamps, and taxes on hunting equipment began to bring back wildlife populations and to preserve habitat. Once wildlife biologists began to oversee the harvest of animals, hunting could no longer hurt a wildlife species—it's a little-known fact that since game laws were enacted *every hunted species has increased in number*. This is discussed in depth in chapter 6.

This kind of modern, sustainable-use hunting turned hunters into conservationists, and created a conservation ethic instilled in every sportsman today. As a result, there are now ethical ways for modern hunters to kill wildlife; for example, in northern states deer hunting seasons close before heavy snow forces deer to "yard up" in low-elevation areas, because it would be too easy to kill deer when they're trapped by deep snow. There are also restrictions on the type of firearm or bow used, hours that can be hunted, and the use of motor vehicles, planes, or other modern contrivances. Today's hunters are endeavoring to keep hunting fair and ethical.

Hunting is also a family activity, a cultural experience stretching deep into our primal roots. Deer camps bring generations together every fall. And the campfire conversations aren't just about who killed what. Hunters come out of the fields and forests with numb hands and frosty breath and relate tales of wildlife seen and josh each other for being outsmarted by a cock pheasant or a wily old buck. They witness dawn splashing sun over marshes, prairies, and oak groves and spend days in natural habitats, where they are more a part of the wild world than separate from its seasonal rhythms. Such connections with nature tie families together in lasting bonds that are good for people in these fast-paced times, because hunters grow through their lives with an appreciation and understanding of nature, not an idealization based on suppositions and assumptions.

Thoughtful compassion

This is part of what Theodore Roosevelt meant when he asserted: "All hunters should be nature lovers."[1] Roosevelt was fostering a human conservation ethic; he was recasting hunters as not just predators, but as cultivators of the wild—as game managers. Roosevelt wrote that statement at a time of environmental plunder in America, when deer, buffalo, elk, cougar, and more had been annihilated. He was preaching a bold concept: a melding of European game laws, where wealthy landowners possessed the animals in their woods and fields and forbade others the meat, with the American free-for-all that had decimated wildlife populations before twentieth-century game laws were enacted.

Roosevelt's vision was for the American people to be responsible stewards of the nation's animals and habitats. He wanted the populace to come around to the notion that hunting is humane and beneficial, but destroying game populations is not. He wanted us to feel shame for our excesses, to love nature, to find the mean that would enable us to celebrate nature without destroying it. Aristotle defined virtue as the mean between extremes; today's sustainable hunting virtuously embraces this mean.

In the early twentieth century, Roosevelt and other conservationists showed hunters how to weigh compassion for nature against the urge to hunt, to use scientific wildlife management to find the mean. As a result, today's hunters have both compassion and bloodlust, though it's hard for non-hunters to comprehend that hunters can harbor these seemingly at-odds feelings. But hunters do have adoration for what they hunt; for example, hunters have always written poetically about their prey. Archibald Rutledge, the author of numerous books and articles on hunting, showed he loved deer when he wrote, "No other creature seems more a shape of the moonlight than does the deer."[2] And William Faulkner showed his compassion for wildlife when he wrote in his novel *Big Woods*, "It is as if I can see the two of us—myself and the wilderness—as coevals, my own span as a hunter, a woodsman, not contemporary with my own first breath but instead transmitted to me, assumed by me gladly, humbly, with joy and pride."[3] And Ernest Hemingway wrote, "There is nothing to writing. All you do is sit down at a typewriter and bleed." He showed he felt affection for his prey in the story of one of his safaris in *Green Hills of Africa* when he "bled" out passages like: "We had come down to the Rift Valley by a sandy red road across a high plateau, then up and down through orchard-bushed hills, around a slope of forest to the top of the rift wall where we could look down and see the plain, the heavy forest below the wall, and the long, dried-up edged shine of Lake Manyara rose-colored at one end with a half-million tiny dots that were flamingoes."[4] A hunter has to love wild lands and wildlife to bleed words like that.

A Book You're Not Supposed to Read

The Greatest Hunting Stories Ever Told
by Lamar Underwood; New York:
Lyons Press, 2004.

Hunters know more about nature

Lastly, from compassion, predation, and scientific inquest comes real understanding, a sure sign that hunters temper emotion with reason. If you gave a group of animal rights activists and a group of hunters a quiz on wildlife, which would get higher marks? For an answer consider Charles Alsheimer's perspective. He's the author of a dozen books on deer and makes his living as a public speaker at hunting clubs. He does a hundred speaking engagements a year on quality deer management (QDM) and somehow he finds the time to write a book a year on QDM. He can't keep up with demand. He says, "There are eleven million whitetail deer hunters in the country, and from what I can tell 90 percent of them are into QDM. They know about buck-to-doe ratios, and what deer over-browsing does, and what percentage of protein deer need, and how managing the deer herd benefits all wildlife. They're, for lack of a less loaded word, 'environmentalists' with guns. They're managing herds scientifically and thereby helping entire ecosystems. They're active conservationists and they know all about nature's wildlife."

Non-hunters don't know such things. They don't know about deer rubs, and browse lines, and nesting cover, and gobbler strutting zones. That activist who shrugged me off had never even seen a bear. She hadn't spent countless hours under the forest's canopy watching nature, being a part of nature. She was an armchair environmentalist.

Non-hunters don't know when turkeys gobble, yelp, and putt, and how they form a pecking order. Few non-hunters understand ducks and geese, but waterfowl hunters know why they call as they do and with a glance into the sky can tell you what species the birds flying through the stratosphere are. Hunters know how geese approach a field and what they eat. Non-hunters don't know these things.

I know what cow moose sound like when they moan for mates. I know which glands bucks use to deposit scent on scrapes. I can watch rising trout and tell in an instant whether they're eating emerging insects or caddis that are riding the current as their wings dry. And, as many hunters can, I can tell when something is not right in the ecosystem. Hunters are our environmental watchdogs. They scream at state game agencies when they perceive that deer, quail, or waterfowl aren't being managed properly. They actively watch over wildlife and lobby for them. But the mainstream media never says this, because it's not politically correct to say such things.

Come to think of it, I've hunted all over North America, in Russia, Africa, and Europe, and it's always the same: hunters know more about the natural world than any environmentalist I've ever met. I've walked behind an African tracker in Namibia who could read hoof prints in the earth as we can words on a page. I once had a long discussion with a Russian hunter about how the brown bear sits on its haunches and listens for hours before approaching an outfield. I've tracked an old bull elk with an Apache on the Jicarilla Reservation and slowed as he explained we were approaching the type of place an old bull prefers to bed in. I've hunted mule deer in Montana with a guide who showed me how to slip within feet of bedded bucks. I've found turkeys' dusting and strutting areas by reading the sign left by their wings in the sand. Non-hunters can't do those things. They don't know the animals, their habits, and whims. I've found, over and over again while writing articles for various magazines, that even wildlife biologists who don't hunt often don't know what hunters know about wildlife.

Compassion and reason

The anti-hunting protesters I encountered that day in New Jersey never saw me as a nature lover. To them I was a stereotype; they refused to see me as an individual on a quest to understand their point of view. They were sure that hunters are heartless. That I "seemed like a nice young man" to the grandmother didn't equate, and so she blocked me out. When confronted by a reasonable hunter, she fled. Differences of opinion are fine, but the refusal to think, to reason, was disturbing.

To be human is to ascertain, to problem solve, I'd thought. To allow compassion to overwhelm scientific knowledge, to view all hunting, the active participation in the natural processes, as wrong simply because blood is spilled is to close your mind.

They refused to think beyond their compassion. They should be praised for their compassion; after all, would we want to be a people who feel no compassion for wildlife? That would be a denial of what's human in us. A hawk or a fox feels no compassion for a slain rabbit. To them it's meat. I once watched two coyotes catch a rabbit and then play tug-of-war with it as it squealed. Yet, though I've hunted all over the world, I've never seen an animal treated disrespectfully by a hunter. Hunters respect—often revere—their prey. Such compassion is one of our finest characteristics, but letting compassion for wildlife kick our intellect out of the picture is no better than letting bloodlust run unchecked. Our intellects, our scientific inquests, should temper our emotions.

Besides, it doesn't take an intellectual giant to comprehend that if prehistoric man had decided not to kill to survive, we wouldn't be here. To condemn hunting just because someone else is doing our killing, because as humans we've specialized to such a degree that we no longer need to personally raise vegetables and meat, is to live a lie. To say farming and ranching are okay but hunting is not is hypocritical; without hunting, or at least the killing of animals in some way, farmers would be eaten out of business. To deny people the right to earn their meat is to be blinded by misguided compassion.

Such were the things I was pondering as I confronted the activists, as I yearned to be challenged, to be honestly debated, to find out what drives the animal activist's reasoning. But there was nothing in them but raw emotion. Their viewpoint is in vogue—certainly that's true. It's how "sophisticated" people feel, or are supposed to. Yet if they're so enlightened by the knowledge of animal suffering, then why couldn't they articulate what drove them to protest? Why couldn't they rationally debate? Why isn't there a book that lucidly explains their point of view?

Myth Debunked

The Council for Wildlife Conservation and Education, Inc., a hunter-funded organization, printed a booklet called "The Hunter in Conservation" to tell the truth about hunting that the media won't relate. The booklet asserts, "Humans are animals. Like other animals, humans—even those in large cities—are dependent on one another." They printed these obvious statements because many environmental and anti-hunting groups purport that humans are not natural, and so have no business actively managing wildlife populations with hunting. Any anthropologist will tell you people have been hunting since there were people.

After all, as stereotypes go, wasn't I the Neanderthal? Wasn't I the unsophisticated savage on the scene? According to popular culture, I should have been uttering nonsensical grunts between their erudite speeches. Yet they were the irrational ones. It's rather ironic: today's hunters have wildlife biologists and so much science backing them up, and the anti-hunters have nothing but antics from PETA. Yet hunters are supposed to be rednecks with guns at best and backwoods denizens reminiscent of the cast from *Deliverance* at worst, while anti-hunters are supposed to be urban literati or something equally cosmopolitan.

I was left wondering if the activists were embarrassed to be human. Because surely it's the acknowledgment that humans have always been hunters and that we still need to kill that incenses such people; after all, accepting hunting as right, or at least as necessary, is to concede that there's a primal connection, past and present, alive in us. To hunt is to look the animal within you in the eyes—that ancient creature within all our genetics who used to tremble when wolves howled and who tore flesh from freshly killed animals and ate it with blood dripping down his chin. Accepting hunting as right is to acknowledge that despite all our sophistication, our hygiene and heredity, synthetic clothes and controlled climates, we need sustenance; we are still connected to the earth. And, just like our prey, we have disturbingly mortal bodies. Accepting hunting is to acknowledge we can be eaten too, and will be recycled by something someday. Accepting hunting is a lot of reality to shoulder, but not accepting the facts only throws you back onto simple, animalistic emotion.

Return to the natural state

Perhaps Erich Fromm went as deep as we can in evaluating the human-predatory paradox, the tug of heart and mind that separates hunters from activists, when he penned, "In the act of hunting, a man becomes, however briefly, part of nature again. He returns to the natural state, becomes one with the animal, and is freed from the existential split: to be part of nature and to transcend it by virtue of his consciousness."[5]

The fact that someone can respect and slay wildlife will always be difficult for non-hunters to grasp. But one thing is clear: without hunting, an active link with the natural world would be severed. Misconceptions would be the norm. An entire knowledge base would be lost, a link to our past annihilated. We wouldn't know or understand the natural world that is living right alongside us. Compassion would drown our better judgment. Ignorance can't lead to good things, and allowing anti-hunters to be the nation's conscience, even though they refuse to think, would be tragic for the environment and for us.

Chapter 2

WHY FLORIDA HAS KILLER GATORS

I n the mid-1980s the residents of Florida's Sanibel Island embarked on the most daring environmental experiment ever attempted. They decided to be a model of Disney-inspired pacifism. They decreed they no longer needed hunting. They officially called a truce with their island's flora and fauna, including its alligators. They wanted back into the Garden.

And why not? Situated about twenty miles south of Fort Myers, Sanibel Island is paradise. It has fifteen miles of beaches lightly dotted with windsurfers, fly fishermen, and children busily building sand castles. In 2005, about 6,100 people resided on the island, the median age was sixty, the average home value was $392,400, and the median income was $66,912. For these wealthy people living on a small tropical island, peace with nature seemed very attainable.

Welcome to Monster Island, U.S.A.

If you were to fly over Sanibel Island you'd see that it's shaped like a fishhook that comes down and hooks toward Florida's west coast. And if you were to look closely, you'd see wetlands marking a wildlife refuge on the inside portion of the hook facing the coast and houses on the sandy Gulf of Mexico side. You'd probably then ponder that all along the hook's shank

Guess what?

- On Florida's Sanibel Island, a well-intentioned policy of "live and let live" resulted in increased alligator attacks and human fatalities.

- In 2004, twice as many Florida alligators were killed for endangering people than hunters were allowed to kill.

- Louisiana's pro-hunting "Marsh to Market" program has helped ensure that there has never been a fatal alligator attack on a human in the state's history.

people and alligators live side by side. Then, if you knew that in 1985 the city managed to attain a special permit from the state allowing it to relocate (instead of kill) nuisance alligators to Sanibel Island's adjoining J. N. "Ding" Darling National Wildlife Refuge, a protected conservation area that covers half the island's seventeen square miles, you'd get goose bumps.

After all, no other Florida community has ever been granted a permit to let large alligators live after they've become aggressive. Florida had stopped relocating alligators in 1978. Experience taught the Florida Fish and Wildlife Conservation Commission (FWC) that all aggressive alligators longer than four feet need to be killed before they eat someone. But on Sanibel many of the alligators longer than four feet got a reprieve. They were allowed to stay and grow.

Meanwhile, in 1987, two years after Sanibel called a truce with nature, the U.S. Fish and Wildlife Service declared the American alligator, which was listed as an endangered species in 1972, had recovered. Today wildlife biologists estimate that there are several million alligators in the southern U.S., including over one million in Florida—though the FWC concedes that night-loving, murky-water-lurking reptiles are a little hard to count.

The 1980s and 1990s passed without a serious alligator incident on Sanibel. But by 2001, anyone paying attention could have foretold what was about to happen. Then eighty-two-year-old Robert Steele was walking his dog on a trail between two wetland areas on Sanibel when a ten-foot, nine-inch alligator shot out of the water and ripped his leg off. Steele bled to death as he screamed for help, but his horrifying death went largely unnoticed and Sanibel's mad alligator policy stayed intact because the killing occurred on September 11, 2001.

For the twelve-month period from June 2002 to May 2003, Sanibel police received 102 calls reporting aggressive alligators; then, for the following year, there were 163 calls.[1] Problems were escalating; this peaceful island was turning into Monster Island. The adult alligators, which can live for more than a hundred years, were growing. When alligators grow, their food choices change: a four-foot alligator may prey only on frogs and fish, but a twelve-foot gator may hunt deer, dogs, and even people. By 2004, many of Sanibel's alligators were over ten feet long.

Some of the reptiles had been given first names by residents—"Oh, good morning, Toothy, now don't eat the dog today, okay?" People were even feeding alligators, which is against the law in Florida, because it teaches them to associate humans with food—and sure enough, the gators did. First, shortly after 8:00 p.m. on April 21, 2004, Jane B. Keefer, a seventy-year-old Sanibel resident, was attacked by a nine-foot, seven-inch alligator in her own back yard while gardening. The gator grabbed her arm and yanked her into the water. Her husband jumped in the lake and startled the massive reptile. It miraculously let go. They were very lucky.

Keefer was transported to Health Park Medical Center in Fort Myers and was treated for relatively minor injuries to her left hand and thigh. The FWC called nuisance alligator trapper John French to the scene, where he was able to capture the offending reptile with little effort at about 10:45 that evening, which indicated that the beast had become habituated to the presence of humans. French thought it likely that the Keefers had been feeding the animal that turned on them.

Town officials were warned, but they failed to take action.

A few months later, on the afternoon of July 23, 2004, Janie Melsek, a fifty-four-year-old landscaper, was trimming vegetation near a pond on Sanibel Island when a 457-pound alligator lunged out of the water and

Books You're Not Supposed to Read

God, Guns, & Rock 'N' Roll by Ted Nugent; Washington, DC: Regnery Publishing, 2001.

The Bias Against Guns: Why Almost Everything You've Heard About Gun Control Is Wrong by John R. Lott, Jr.; Washington, DC: Regnery Publishing, 2003.

Hunting for God, Fishing for the Lord: Encountering the Sacred in the Great Outdoors by Joseph S. Classen; Huntington, IN: Our Sunday Visitor Publishing, 2006.

seized her arm. The twelve-foot gator jerked her into a pond and started to spin. Melsek screamed and flailed. The gator let go, but then it bit her thigh. She struggled and fought in the shallow water. Then it grabbed her arm again and tried take her deeper, where it could drown her. Like crocodiles, alligators kill their prey by crushing and drowning. Their jaws are made to grip. Most of the muscles in their jaws are made to close, which is why it's relatively easy to hold an alligator's mouth closed. They grab on and drag their prey to deep water. When they begin to eat, they bite onto an exposed portion of their prey and spin, thereby tearing a portion of the victim's flesh off.

Myth Debunked

Alligators are not endangered. They were taken off the endangered species list in 1987, and there are now millions of alligators living across the southern U.S.

Janie Melsek was in a battle for her life with a reptile three times her weight. Long seconds of the death struggle ticked by as the pond water turned red with her blood. Melsek was nearly drowned and her struggle over when a neighbor and police officers bravely jumped into the shallow water. In a fierce tug-of-war with the gator, they pulled Melsek and the alligator pulled her back. Finally the people yanked harder and Melsek came free from the reptile's jaws.

Minutes later, as an ambulance took her away, police shot and killed the monstrous alligator. It took four men to pull from the pond the beast residents had been feeding.

Days later, Melsek died in surgery at Lee Memorial Hospital of an infection caused by the reptile's bites. Doctors said her body simply shut down in response to the infection. She was the fourteenth person known to have been fatally attacked by a Florida alligator since official record keeping began. Two years later, in June 2006, the number had risen to twenty people killed and 351 attacked by alligators in Florida since 1948, or about thirteen attacks per year since 2000.[2] The Melsek killing, however, was the third on Sanibel in three years and the second to prove fatal.

The ensuing media hype, and the residents screaming to be saved from five-hundred-pound, meat-eating reptiles that had lost their fear of humans, forced the local community to take a rational approach to living with its reptilian residents.

After boiling-hot town meetings, the city passed an "open harvest" of all alligators over four feet on private properties. Hunters came in to save the residents of Sanibel Island from the situation their well-intentioned but wildlife-ignorant policies had created.

Lakes and ponds were searched for the monstrous carnivores. In the six months after the crackdown began, state trappers killed at least eighty large alligators, some over fourteen feet long. Under the previous policy, about five had been killed per year.

"The conservation ethic on Sanibel since the early days has been the idea that we can live in harmony with these alligators. It's part of the draw of the place," said Brad Smith, land manager of the Sanibel Conservation Foundation. "In the light of two human fatalities, perhaps that was naïve."

Sanibel's police chief, Bill Tomlinson, who was in charge of enforcing the new alligator policy, told the *St. Petersburg Times*, "Concern for human welfare has to come first. In the past six months the city has received 180 calls from residents fearful of alligators that have turned up in their yards, garages, and swimming pools. I personally couldn't live with myself if I had to tell someone down the road why their grandchild has been eaten. The motto was to live in harmony with the environment, and that's what we have done. But in doing so, we created a situation where there were too many large alligators in a small place, and I think the only failure was that people treated them like pets."

Gary Morse, public information coordinator for the FWC, says that was only one of the mistakes the residents of Sanibel made. He explained, "People who feed any kind of wildlife near the water or who interact with alligators on any level cause these creatures to lose their natural fear of people and to become dangerous."[3]

Sanibel's is an extreme case, but to a lesser extent, all of Florida has been living under the fallacy that hunting isn't a necessary wildlife-management tool.

Why Florida's gators are eating people

After an alligator walked into Candy Frey's home near Bradenton, Florida, in May 2006 and attacked her golden retriever, the forty-eight-year-old former U.S. Marine told the *Sarasota Herald-Tribune*: "I just freaked out and shot him—*boom, boom, boom, boom*."[4] A neighbor called the police and the FWC sent an officer to investigate. The officer gave Frey a warning citation for hunting without a license.

Such is the state of wildlife management in the land of Disney, where the human population is expected to top nineteen million by 2010, according to the U.S. Census Bureau, and where the alligator population many years ago passed one million. Yet in 2006 hunters were allocated only 4,406 alligator tags so they could kill a miniscule .44 percent of the state's alligator population—and some wonder why alligators are crawling into homes in search of pets.[5]

While Sanibel received its rude awakening in 2001, 2002, and 2003, the rest of Florida's wake-up call occurred in May 2006. On Wednesday, May 10, construction workers found the dismembered body of Yovy Suarez Jimenez, a female Florida Atlantic University student, in a canal near Fort Lauderdale. An autopsy revealed that she had died from an alligator's bites, not from drowning.[6] Her death was horrifyingly dramatic: she'd been stalked on land while she was out jogging. An alligator had either ambushed her on a footpath or had yanked her into the canal while she sat for a rest.

The hunt for the killer gator took several days as the national media splashed headlines like "Killer Gator Still on the Loose" across front pages and on nightly newscasts. The pressure was on Kevin Garvey's shoulders. He's an alligator trapper and the owner of Nuisance Wildlife Control. Finding the gator was personal. He patrols that very canal, between Markham County Park and State Road 84, often, and knew most of the gators that frequent the waterway. When Jimenez's body was found, he knew he would have to find this killer gator before it killed again.

For several days he lobbed his bait into the middle of the canal where Jimenez was killed. He was a hunk of pig lung with shark hooks embedded within. He caught two gators quickly, but their stomachs weren't filled with human meat; they held raccoon meat, a football, and several tennis balls. Then, when Garvey visited his trap about 8:30 Saturday morning, he saw the killer. The male reptile was blind in one eye, which could have made it more aggressive, Garvey says. It thrashed like a hooked shark as he and five others yanked it up an embankment.[7] The gator turned out to be a nine-foot, six-inch beast.

"Hopefully, this will provide some peace to the young woman's family," said Dani Moschella, a spokeswoman for the FWC. Medical examiners found two human arms in the nine-foot animal's stomach.

Early on Sunday, May 14, another body was found in a backyard canal in Oldsmar, near St. Petersburg. "I was out walking my dog. I went in the backyard and saw a pair of pants floating in the pond and I walked up closer and saw there was a pair of sneakers attached to it," said Fred Ferderber. The body was determined to be that of Judy Cooper, a forty-three-year-old homeless woman.[8]

Cooper's body had been in the water for about three days, authorities said. She'd suffered animal bites that were consistent with an alligator, according to an autopsy. Her family had not heard from her for about three months, and she had a history of drug use, her sister, Dannette Goodrich, told the *Orlando Sentinel*. Gary Goodrich, Cooper's brother-in-law, told the newspaper that officials said her purse was found near the water and drugs may have played a factor. "We don't know the condition she was in when this happened," said Goodrich.

Judy Cooper may have passed out near an alligator-infested canal. As a homeless drug user, her story wouldn't hold the headlines. But just hours after her body was discovered, Annemarie Campbell, a twenty-three-year-old woman from Paris, Tennessee, went snorkeling with three friends in a secluded recreation area in the Ocala National Forest near Lake George, about fifty miles southeast of Gainesville. The area was a popular, though remote, swimming hole.

A few minutes after Annemarie went snorkeling, her former stepfather's wife, Jackie Barrett, who had been relaxing on a sandbar, got up to check on her. When Barrett couldn't find her, she jumped in her kayak and paddled downstream but still couldn't locate her. When Barrett got back to the cabin, she saw her husband, Mark, and a family friend frantically gouging at the eyes of an alligator and prying at its jaws. The beast had Annemarie in its mouth.

The two men had walked around the side of their cabin and saw Annemarie in the gator's jaws, said Marion County Fire-Rescue captain Joe Amigliore. The two men jumped into the murky water. By jamming their fingers into the seven-foot, nine-inch alligator's eyes and trying to open its jaws, the men were able to free Annemarie and chase off the alligator, but the young woman died during the struggle. "You just don't think of your daughter dying from an alligator," said Campbell's mother.[9]

Three people had been killed in one week! Alligator experts flooded the cable news channels. There's a drought in Florida, they said, which makes alligators more desperate. It's mating season, they said; the male alligators get more aggressive when they mate in spring. They pointed out that more people are now living in close proximity to alligators—which is true. According to U.S. Census Bureau statistics, every day about 1,000 people move to Florida and 450 acres are cleared and developed. All three of those reasons have certainly increased the number of conflicts. But in the hours of news reports, in the hundreds of newspaper accounts read researching these attacks, and even when interviewing FWC officials, no one added the underlying factor that led to Florida's attacks: there are now more alligators in Florida than at any time in modern history, and they're bigger on average now than they've been since the FWC began keeping records. And as alligators get bigger, their food options broaden—to include us.

According to the FWC, the average size of alligators killed in Florida has increased from 5.93 feet in 1977 to 8.4 feet in 2004.[10] The records show a slow but steady increase over the past three decades. Florida's alligators have grown into monsters; records show that only large alligators—those over seven feet—are the ones that attack people.

In 2004, Florida alligator trappers (as opposed to hunters) were issued 15,485 permits and tags for dangerous alligators and removed 7,352 nuisance alligators from golf courses, backyards, and playgrounds. In that same year, hunters were given 5,363 tags and killed 3,237, which means that twice as many alligators are being killed because they're endangering people than hunters are allowed to kill. Hunters target the largest gators because they want them for trophies, and the large gators are the ones most likely to prey on people. Hunters can solve the problem before it occurs; trappers can take out alligators only after they've attacked a human.

Demonstrating awareness of the problem during the media hype in May 2006, the FWC took the first steps toward solving the problem when it announced: "This year, alligator season will be twice as long as last year and will span eleven consecutive weeks. Another positive change this season is that hunters may purchase multiple permits." The FWC decided it needed to start proactively using hunting as a wildlife management tool.

However, the FWC issued about 4,000 alligator harvest permits for the 2006 hunting season. The permits sold out in four hours, showing there's no lack of interest in hunting.[11] In a very restricted way, hunting has been allowed in Florida since 1988. "These special hunts provide a thrilling, hands-on, face-to-face hunting adventure unlike any other you could imagine," says the FWC's hunting brochure. Wildlife biologists set quotas for a specified number of alligators in each management unit so that they can control the number of alligators being harvested in specific regions. This is a good example of modern game management at work. This hunting system allows biologists to control animal populations based on local community safety and habitat differences. The problem with Florida's approach, however, is that it's not aggressive enough.

In 2004, Florida's hunters and trappers were collectively allowed to kill 13,124 alligators out of a population of at least one million, a harvest of a miniscule 1.3 percent of the alligator population.[12] When you add in human and alligator population growth in Florida, it's obvious that attacks will continue to rise until Florida embraces a more aggressive wildlife management approach. In fact, there is proof that hunting can stop alligator attacks.

Proof that hunting prevents gator attacks

Officials in Louisiana estimate that the state has about 1.5 million alligators (50 percent more than Florida), yet Louisiana's gators haven't killed a single human in recorded history, according to Noel Kinler, alligator program manager for the Louisiana Department of Wildlife and Fisheries. In fact, there haven't been any serious injuries from the state's 1.5 million alligators in decades.[13]

Kinler says one reason is that in Louisiana, "we use hunting to manage our alligators a lot more aggressively than Florida does." Whereas Florida's gator-safety efforts focus on public education and punishing people who feed alligators, Louisiana doesn't even have a state law forbidding the feeding of alligators. Kinler says they do ask people not to feed alligators, but they don't go any further than that. Like Florida, Louisiana has a nuisance alligator hotline. When people call the number, they don't get a government bureaucrat—they get a businessman. Louisiana's private alligator trappers respond to calls from residents threatened by gators, and they kill the gators. As an added bonus, the trapper makes his money from selling the meat and skins, not from taxes. But private hunting, without resort to the hotline, is how Louisiana mostly manages alligators.

In 2004, hunters killed 35,235 alligators in Louisiana.[14] That's ten times as many as hunters killed in Florida in the same year. Even when you add in the number killed by Florida's trappers, Louisiana's hunters killed three times as many. Meanwhile, the average size of alligators killed in Louisiana has only gone up from 6.92 feet in 1972 to 7.17 feet in 2004. In fact, the size of alligators has been very stable for decades, because the largest, boldest gators are killed and taken to the market, which is why people don't get eaten in Louisiana.

Hunters have to attain permission from a landowner before they can apply for alligator tags. "By linking the landowner with the hunter we've created an economic incentive for both to protect alligators from poachers. Typically landowners and hunters come to a financial arrangement where they both get a portion of the money raised from the sale of the skins and meat," explained Kinler.

Louisiana calls it the "Alligator Marsh to Market" program, and it's an effective conservation tool. It protects alligator populations and preserves critical wetlands habitats while providing about $54 million in economic benefits to the state each year. Kinler says that about 2.5 million acres are enrolled in the program.

Here's how it works: Wetland areas provide critical environmental benefits, like storm surge protection from hurricanes, wintering grounds for ducks, geese, and other species, and homes for alligators. Yet in Louisiana—as in most states—more than half the wetland areas are privately owned. While Louisiana swampland provides widespread benefits to the surrounding environment, for individual landowners the swamps are about as valuable as Arizona's desert. There is no financial incentive for landowners to preserve the swamps on their property—except for the Alligator Marsh to Market program.

Many wetland owners make a few bucks by leasing hunting rights to duck and deer hunters and fishermen. Activities like these are not big money makers, however. The going rate in southern Louisiana is about ten to twelve dollars an acre to lease hunting rights. Leasing hunting rights is very common in the South and Midwest. It is an economic incentive that keeps many farmers in business and encourages landowners to maintain a good habitat balance to support healthy populations of wildlife for people to hunt—basically, because of leasing, farmers leave hedgerows, woodlots, and wetlands intact. But ten dollars an acre won't pay the mortgage. This is where the Alligator Marsh to Market program comes in. It works on lands that aren't being farmed, lands that are only earning a little cash from sportsmen. It gives landowners an incentive to keep their marshlands wet and natural, rather than draining the land for crops, cattle grazing, or development.

There are around 3.5 million acres of coastal wetlands in Louisiana that qualify as alligator habitat, according to Kinler. Nearly 75 percent of that habitat is privately owned, and with a few small exceptions, virtually every piece of land that qualifies is enrolled in the alligator program.

The Marsh to Market idea was conceived in 1972. Previously, alligator hunting in Louisiana was a virtual free-for-all. As a result, alligator numbers had fallen so much that hunting was banned in 1963. Biologists spent several years studying the life cycles of alligators, which led to a management and harvesting plan that eventually became the Marsh to Market program.

One problem the program almost eliminated was poaching. "When a landowner sees an alligator that could be harvested as an economic asset," says Kinler, "you can believe that if he sees someone poaching on his property, it's going to be reported." Florida should heed this example of hunter-driven conservation.

Harvested wild alligators are tagged, enabling tanners around the world to show that the hides were legally acquired. "The program has garnered a tremendous amount of respect from virtually every conservation organization, and is held up as an example of a conservation success," says Kinler.

Alligator eggs are harvested from the nesting sites of wild alligators throughout the state during midsummer months. The eggs are sold to alligator farmers, who incubate them and grow the young alligators in tanks. After about two years, when the alligators reach about three to four feet in length, they are sold for their skins and meat; as a result, about 75 percent of all wild alligator hides, along with about 85 percent of all farmed hides used by tanners around the world come from Louisiana. Officials credit the Marsh to Market program with helping to stabilize wild alligator numbers. To complete the cycle, about 17 percent of the alligators hatched in captivity are released back into the wild as one- or two-year-olds, or a total of 35,000 to 40,000 alligators a year, which is about as many as are shot by hunters every year.[15]

"It's a win-win situation for everyone," says Kinler. "The farmers have a constant source of eggs, and landowners get a substantial economic value for maintaining critical habitat, and alligators rarely grow big enough to endanger people."

The state determines how many alligators can be killed after biologists do nest counts during the summer. Hunters bring the alligators to central processing sheds, and then the meat and skins are prepared for market.

According to a recent economic impact report on the Marsh to Market Program, sixty-four alligator farms were operating in Louisiana, raising nearly half a million alligators. Alligators are priced by the foot. Over the last decade, a farm-raised alligator averaged four feet in length and sold for about $77. Wild alligators averaged slightly more than seven feet and brought about $19.50 per foot in 2004. As a result, hunting alligators in Louisiana is an act of conservation. When someone buys an alligator product they're supporting the preservation of critical habitat that benefits not just alligators, but also the entire wetland ecosystem. In Louisiana's swamps, capitalism and conservation have struck up a mutually beneficial relationship—and it was hunting that brought them together. The people of Louisiana, who live free of alligator attacks, also benefit from this marriage.

Maybe Florida's wildlife biologists should take a field trip to Louisiana before they have another deadly week like they did in May 2006. In early 2007 the FWC did propose some positive solutions, however.[16] After a survey found that 58 percent of the public wanted more done to control alligators, the FWC proposed lengthening hunting seasons, liberalizing bag limits, and increasing hunters' access to public lands. So perhaps the FWC will let hunters save human lives while generating revenue for wetland protection, after all.

Gator Attacks by the Numbers

Alligators attacked seventy-eight people during the 1980s, 159 people between 1990 and 1999, and ninety-seven between 2000 and 2005. By comparison, there were only five recorded alligator attacks between 1830 and 1969. As of July 2006, twenty people had been killed (eleven since 2001) and over four hundred have been attacked in Florida since 1948.

"Historic Alligator Bites on Humans in Florida," Florida Fish and Wildlife Conservation Commission.

Chapter 3

WHY BEAR ATTACKS
ARE INCREASING

When anti-hunting environmentalists get what they want, people get killed. Here's a case in point: the grizzly that in June 2005 killed Isabelle Dube, a professional mountain bike racer, grew up in a politically correct, no-grizzly-hunting area in and around Alberta's Banff National Park. The bear noted that people ran away like teenagers in a horror movie whenever it showed itself and so came to the conclusion that humans are just a bunch of wimps; as a result, the bear decided it was at the top of the food chain. So, like the grizzly that ate intrepid environmentalist Timothy Treadwell in Alaska's Katmai National Park in 2003, this four-year-old bear started to think of humans as prey.

Oh, there were warning signs. In May 2005, the grizzly approached a woman on a hiking trail near Canmore, located about forty miles west of Calgary. She escaped unscathed. And the bear began frequenting a golf course, causing golfers to fear the back nine. In response, wildlife biologists darted the grizzly with a tranquilizer and moved it about a dozen miles away to Banff National Park.[1]

Now, according to Dave Ealey, a spokesman for Alberta Sustainable Resource Development, the bear was relocated not because of aggressive behavior, but simply to discourage it from approaching people. It's not clear how waking up in a national park is supposed to teach a bear

Guess what?

- To bears with no fear of humans, gunshots sound like dinner bells. They know that a deer or elk is waiting and hunters won't do anything to stop them from taking it.

- Hunting reduces human-bear conflicts, keeping people and pets safer.

- You're more likely to be attacked by a bear in an area where hunting is forbidden, such as a national park.

anything other than, "Whoa, I must've eaten some bad moose last night!" What we do know is the grizzly walked right back home from Banff. Wildlife officials knew the bear was back. Its radio collar gave its precise location, yet they did nothing. The biologists decided that a grizzly that approaches people isn't aggressive, and so hadn't thought it necessary to warn the public.

So a few weeks later, in early June 2005, when Dube and two friends went jogging on a hiking trail, they had no way of knowing that a grizzly that had lost its fear of people frequented the area. When the women jogged around a bend and saw the bear coming up the trail, they moved away slowly. But the grizzly kept coming. Dube panicked and climbed a tree. The other two women backed out of the area; however, before they were out of earshot, they heard Dube screaming desperate, bloodcurdling things.

About an hour later, one of the women made it back with a warden who shot and killed the grizzly, but it was too late for Isabelle Dube.

The appalling part of this tragedy is that Dube's death was avoidable. After all, if grizzly hunting had been allowed in the area, certainly any bear brazen enough to approach people would have been shot quickly. You can almost hear a hunter gushing, "Yeah, the bear hunt was too easy. This bear just came right for me. Offered an easy shot." Even if hunting wasn't possible or palatable to Canada's virulent anti-hunting movement, shouldn't the biologists have, at the very least, used negative conditioning (such as shooting the bear with rubber bullets) to reinstill a fear of humans into the potential man-eater? Such tactics are hardly unprecedented.

However, instead of learning from their mistake, Canada's wildlife officials' next response was total appeasement. After the 2005 season they terminated the hunting season in the areas in Alberta where grizzly hunting was allowed. Alberta's provincial Ministry of Sustainable Resource Development explained that the grizzly population might be declining, so they needed to do studies to find out. One has to wonder how Dube would feel about that hypothesis, especially when you consider that the wildlife officials also reported that the number of citizen complaints about aggressive bears, livestock losses to grizzlies, and other problems associated with bears had continued to rise. In fact, while bear hunting was legal, the Canadian government reported annually that the grizzly population was growing at a rate of 2 to 3 percent per year.[2] So what changed? Not the scientific facts. What happened was that political pressure from anti-hunting environmental groups triumphed over realistic bear management. Despite Dube's death, the officials fell under the sway of environmentalism's pacifist view of predators; they refused to open their eyes and see wild animals—and our role in nature—for what they are. It should also be noted that they wouldn't have unabashedly closed the grizzly season right after Dube's death if the press were interested in printing the truth, not just anti-hunting political correctness.

If you find this outrageous, you should know it's not a unique situation; in fact, grizzly and black bear attacks on humans are at all-time highs in North America partly because bears are growing bold in areas where hunting is deemed politically incorrect.[3]

Bear attacks are at a historic high

According to research by Steve Herrero, an environmental science professor at the University of Calgary, there have been at least 131 verified human deaths from grizzly and black bears in North America during the twentieth century, with fifty-nine deaths—nearly half—occurring in the last two decades. By comparison, there were six fatal bear attacks in all of the 1940s and only one in the 1930s, says Herrero. But the most shocking thing found was that an increasing number of these attacks are occurring in areas where hunting is prohibited or isn't being used effectively.

For example, grizzly attacks have been rising for years in Wyoming, Idaho, and Montana because the un-hunted bears are losing their fear of humans. Violent deaths have resulted. But environmental groups, like Defenders of Wildlife and the Sierra Club don't care. They've been fighting the U.S. Fish and Wildlife Service's efforts to take the bears off the endangered species list for years. The bears have been officially eligible for removal since 2002. But because doing so would enable states to allow hunting as a way to reduce conflicts, the environmentalists oppose removal. Common sense might lead a discerning mind to conclude that environmentalists would favor hunting because an increasing number of bears are being killed in self-defense, which is unnecessarily throwing blood on the grizzly's already gory reputation and turning the public against the bears. But environmental groups aren't practical or scientific when it comes to grizzlies. They'd rather people were killed than bears.

There is scientific proof for this assertion. Grizzlies in the Yellowstone ecosystem (where grizzly hunting hasn't been allowed for decades) have developed a surprising learned response: gunshots sound like a dinner bell to them. It seems counterintuitive, but some bears have learned that there are gutpiles at the end of rifle reports, and if they get there fast enough, maybe an entire elk or deer can be taken from a hunter. A collaborative study by the Wildlife Conservation Society, the National Park Service, the U.S. Forest Service, and the Montana Department of Fish, Wildlife and Parks in 2004 found that in September hundreds of grizzlies leave the protective boundaries of Yellowstone National Park to feed on gutpiles left by hunters field-dressing their kills. These bears are sometimes attracted to gunshots, said the study. These bears don't remember being hunted; as a result, indicated the study, attacks are on the rise.[4]

To insert some practical wildlife management into this mad situation, in March 2007 the U.S. Fish and Wildlife Service (USFWS) released its "Final Conservation Strategy for the Grizzly Bear in the Greater Yellowstone Area." The move was designed to allow the USFWS to finally take the grizzly in the Yellowstone area off the endangered species list and to allow states to manage bear populations with hunting. All three states have submitted bear management plans, which would utilize hunting to control bear populations and to reduce human-bear conflicts.

For example, Dave Moody, the trophy game coordinator for the Wyoming Game and Fish Department, says, "We've concluded that a grizzly hunting season could help us reduce human-bear conflicts. We'd like to issue tags for problem areas so that hunters can harvest a scientifically set number of grizzlies, because when you utilize hunters, you raise money for conservation, you don't spend needed funds unnecessarily, and you help to instill a fear of man into the bears."[5]

Many state biologists agree with Moody; in fact, in their proposed Grizzly Bear Management Plan (a plan that will be enacted if the grizzly is removed from the endangered species list), the Idaho Department of Fish and Game states:

> The success of grizzly bear recovery in the Yellowstone Ecosystem justifies a management paradigm shift from one of preservation to one of conservation. The basis of conservation is sustainable use, which for wildlife resources includes regulated hunting. Recognition of the grizzly bear as a game animal will ensure that the proper resources for population and mortality monitoring will be allocated. This will benefit the long-term viability of the bear, as it has for Idaho's other hunted, large mammal species. Classification of the grizzly bear as a game animal can also be expected to improve the

Myth Debunked

Most attacking bears, the myth goes, are mothers with cubs. In truth, bears that are alone are involved in attacks eight times more often than females with cubs.

Tom S. Smith and Stephen Herrero, "A century of bear-human conflict in Alaska: analyses and implications," a study by the U.S. Geological Survey, September 2003.

level of acceptance of the bear by the public living within grizzly bear range and to increase the number of stakeholders favoring grizzly bear conservation. Hunters have been long-term supporters of conservation, and the presence of legal hunters in the field may minimize the poaching of bears by those opposed to their recovery. Additionally, hunting may act as a form of reverse habituation, thus decreasing the likelihood of human/bear conflicts. The removal of individual bears will open up home ranges for subadults, also minimizing conflicts with bears that might otherwise disperse to human-use areas. Thus, hunting tends to reduce the number of management actions needed. Management actions that involve capturing bears are expensive to conduct and, to the extent that hunter harvest can substitute for this, costs will be reduced.[6]

The U.S. Fish and Wildlife Service listed the grizzly bear as a threatened species in the lower forty-eight states in 1975. In 2005, there were more than an estimated 1,100 grizzlies in five separate populations in Montana, Idaho, Wyoming, and Washington State.[7] The USFWS published those numbers in 2005, but they are hardly exact figures. Bears are reclusive and hard to count, but there is also a lot of politics involved here. The Endangered Species Act allows the USFWS to remove a species from the official endangered list when its numbers rise to a certain target level. According to the USFWS, the bears have met the specified criteria every year since 2002, yet environmental groups continued to oppose their removal from the list.

In the final report of the USFWS, despite what anti-hunting groups say, the government biologists determined there is "little relationship between hunter numbers and human-caused grizzly mortality." In other words: the presence of more elk hunters and deer hunters is not the real cause of more bears being shot. They found that the reason hunters have killed more bears in recent years is that "bears have learned to seek hunter-killed game." As a result, USFWS data indicate that because these bears are losing their fear of people, they're becoming more dangerous.

Two hunters met such a bear on a warm Montana afternoon in early September 2001. The air was clear and the aspens turning gold. The two men were exhausted, but satisfied. They'd already packed out half of the elk they'd killed. They were climbing the steep slopes over a Western panorama to retrieve the rest of the meat when they heard the warning *woof* of a grizzly. The bear was eating their elk. They stopped, goose bumps rising. Then she came. A grizzly can run as fast as thirty-five miles per hour and charges like a pit bull: head held low and mouth partly open, big gums bouncing, slobbering; body stiff, rigid; legs reaching, clawing the earth away in a sprinter's short bounds.

The hunters ran. A stupid, all-out run on tired legs down a vertical slope. Somewhere behind the female grizzly stopped.

The hunters left the wilderness and reported the incident to a Montana Fish, Wildlife and Parks office. Some official wrote the incident down and thought nothing more of it. These things happen.

This event was repeated several times more in September and October north of Missoula, Montana. But such incidents are relatively common these days. State biologists and game wardens didn't do anything about the sow. This large grizzly with two cubs had learned the same neat trick that many bears had: a gunshot means fresh meat. But the state didn't warn the public or try to negatively condition the bear by scaring it with loud noises or shooting it with rubber bullets, as some wildlife professionals do when grizzlies boldly enter towns.

So when Tim Hilston left his home in Great Falls, Montana, before daylight on October 30, 2001, to go elk hunting, he didn't know about the sow. Sure, he knew he was taking a calculated risk. Hilston was aware that grizzlies inhabited the Blackfoot-Clearwater Wildlife Management Area, located about thirty-eight miles northeast of Missoula, but he didn't know a grizzly was around that was becoming particularly aggressive with hunters.

The grizzly didn't know hunters could do it harm. Fear of man is not an immutable characteristic in wildlife. Animals can lose their fear of humans. People can approach moose, elk, and bears in Yellowstone National Park and snap a photo, but they can't do that just outside park boundaries, where the wildlife (except for grizzlies and wolves) is hunted. Such is the situation Tim Hilston walked into. When Hilston didn't return that evening, a search party was organized. The next day, Hilston's body was discovered not far from a partially buried elk carcass. Investigators theorize that Hilston was field-dressing an elk he'd killed when a grizzly approached him. Tracks suggest he began backing away. Because his gun lay unloaded, Hilston was defenseless when the bear came to kill him.

Biologists later trapped and killed an adult female and two yearling cubs at the kill site. This is where the story takes a strange turn; as a result of the attack on her late husband, Mary Ann Hilston filed a lawsuit against both the U.S. Fish and Wildlife Service and the Montana Department of Fish, Wildlife and Parks (FWP). Mrs. Hilston's suit[8] contended that both agencies were aware that an aggressive sow grizzly with cubs had earlier claimed another hunter's elk carcass in the same area, and neither did anything to warn unsuspecting hunters of the possible danger. Rangers said the bear had been seen on several gutpiles and carcasses and learned to associate the sound of a gunshot with food, according to the suit. In addition, the suit claimed that the FWP's practice of planting livestock carcasses in order to draw bears away from ranch lands created an increased risk of conflict between bears and humans, because it taught the bears to associate humans with food—what biologists call a "learned response."

In May 2007, the Montana Supreme Court ruled against Hilston. Her chances of winning the suit were always slim. Courts have dismissed negligence cases involving bear attacks before because of a rule that protects government employees from liability for performing discretionary functions and duties. But liability has been imposed when officials failed to follow mandatory policies. Hilston's attorney, Floyd D. Corder, believed park rangers at the Clearwater Wildlife Management Area violated their own policy by not warning hunters that a "nuisance bear" had been reported. The U.S. Fish and Wildlife Service and the state of Montana share responsibility for the refuge. "If they had followed their own regulations, this would not have happened," Corder said. "At the minimum, they should have told Timothy Hilston, 'You should not hunt by yourself.'"

Perhaps Hilston's widow should take to court the environmental groups that have blocked removing the grizzly from the endangered species list. Certainly people accept a known risk when they enter the forest, but by not using hunting to keep the bears wild and their fear of humans intact, are wildlife managers shirking their duty?

What environmentalists don't want you to know

To answer such questions, Tom Smith, a biologist with the U.S. Geological Survey, and Steve Herrero constructed a database of Alaskan bear-human encounters that spans the twentieth century.[9] They wanted to find out why bear attacks are more common now than in any time in recorded history. According to their calculations, grizzlies are twenty-two times more likely to attack a human than black bears are. When they summed up the number of attacks in five-year intervals, they found that grizzly attacks on humans in Alaska have gone up from fewer than ten per half-decade in the early twentieth century to more than a hundred between

2000 and 2005, meaning that there are ten times more grizzly bear attacks today than there were in 1900.

Smith and Herrero concluded the biggest reason for this increase is that there are nearly ten times as many humans in Alaska today as there were in 1900, which increases surprise encounters and habituates some bears to people. Some grizzlies, like the one that ate Isabelle Dube, are losing their fear of people. At the same time, bear populations, which used to be considered vermin and were shot on sight in many parts of Alaska, are now thought to be at historic highs, though no reliable record of bear populations was available until late in the twentieth century. So there are more people and bears out there running into each other, but there's a lot more to it than that.

According to their records, between 1900 and 2005 Alaskan grizzlies killed fifty-two people and injured hundreds more. Smith explained, "Many bear-human conflicts are occurring in Alaska's parks and refuges where hunting isn't allowed, which is resulting in area closures, property damage, human injury, and loss of life. And to be fair, human activity in bear country has also resulted in injury and death to bears. We are currently doing studies to determine how to prevent attacks and bear-human conflicts in the areas where hunting can't be used, such as in Glacier Bay National Park."

Smith's research shows that the way people behave has a lot to do with whether they are attacked. Only 19 percent of the people attacked were hunting, which doesn't support the oft-repeated point that because hunters are creeping about they're more likely to startle a grizzly and be attacked. In fact, in hunted areas bears are very sensitive to human intrusion. Bob Rob, a freelance outdoor writer and outfitter who lived for several decades in Alaska, explains that as a hunter, "you don't just stalk around looking for a grizzly. If you do that they'll either see you first or they'll pick up your scent. When that happens the bears will move miles away to avoid you. What you do is set up on a ridge and spend days looking through your binoculars. It's the only way...that is, unless you're in a national park and just want to have a look at a bear. In the parks the bears aren't that cautious about people; as a result, they're more dangerous."

Because of his research, Herrero feels hunting is needed to keep bears fearful of humans. Where hunting is outlawed, such as in national parks, Herrero argues that aversive conditioning, such as shooting bears with rubber bullets, needs to be used. Good bear management, says Herrero, needs to "encourage shyness as the characteristic behavior of bears in the presence of humans." He argues in his book, *Bear Attacks: Their Causes and Avoidance*,[10] that the European brown bear is a member of the same species as the American grizzly yet attacks people much less often. He feels this is because hunters have been weeding aggressive bears out of the European gene pool for millennia. He argues that hunters need to be allowed to do the same with North America's bears.

According to Smith and Herrero's research, 65 percent of the people who were attacked were hiking, and 16 percent were working. Most of the bears that attacked were alone—single bears are involved in conflicts eight times more often than females with cubs. Also, about 10 percent of the grizzlies that attacked were predatory (meaning they ate someone). Smith sees this as evidence that Alaska's grizzlies are making judgment calls, not just attacking out of the rage that earned them the scientific name *Ursus arctos horribilis* (the horrible northern bear).

About 33 percent of the bears attacked when they were startled. So one-third of the attacks began when someone did surprise a bear. This is often thought to be the leading factor that results in attacks. And it is a major factor, but get this: your chances of being attacked are twice as high if you camp alone in Glacier Bay National Park (where hunting isn't allowed) as they are if you camp in a hunted area, according to Herrero. He found that 85 percent of bear-human incidents in the park occur at night, while outside the parks, a majority of bear-human encounters occur in daylight. This leaves little doubt that many of the park bears have lost their fear of people and see humans as a source for food.

Indeed, a sharp decline in bear-human conflicts occurred at Glacier National Park in the early 1990s as a direct result of a policy that required campers to store all food in bear-resistant food containers. The bears had lost their fear of people and were increasingly associating humans with food. By denying human food to bears, problems were reduced, though they rose again over subsequent years as un-hunted bears found other ways to get food from campers.

According to Herrero, most bear incidents at campsites (68 percent) last longer than an hour. These bears are circling tents, popping their jaws, and just seeing how much they can get away with. After a while, if park officials don't shoot the bear (which they sometimes do) these bears might cross a line, and a two-hundred-pound man is no match for a thousand-pound grizzly.

A general conclusion drawn from these studies is that attacks are increasing because conflicts are rising in un-hunted areas in national parks and because there are more people in the woods then ever before. In areas of Alaska that allow hunting, your chances are much lower of having a conflict with a bear, especially one in camp. Smith says, "The numbers in our database indicate that hunting has some effect on keeping bears wary of people, but to date there is no study conclusively proving that point. It's just too hard to perform a controlled study to show how hunting affects bears—how do you measure caution or fear?"

"What hunting bears definitely does," said Smith, "is take the big males out of the population. When you do that the bear population goes up. This happens because big males kill cubs. They kill cubs because if a female is suddenly bereft of her cubs, then she'll come into heat, which gives the big male an opportunity to breed her. We think the biological reason for this behavior is that this is a way for the strongest males to make sure their genes get into the gene pool, but that might just be rationalizing something that is distasteful to us. Regardless, by killing the big males, hunters are killing the most dangerous bears. So in this way hunters are reducing attacks."[11]

Black bear attacks are increasing, too

Black bears are also attacking more people than ever, and the attacks are often the result of anti-hunting political correctness. Typically, black bears kill two people in North America each year. Black bear attacks on people happen a lot more often than killings, but Steve Herrero says there is no reliable way to count black bear attacks. Many attacks go unreported and many others are difficult to verify; however, "there is definitely an upward trend in bear-inflicted injuries," says Herrero. "Attacks really began taking off two decades ago."

According to the North American Bear Center (NABC), as of June 2006, there had been fifty-seven documented killings of humans by black bears in North America since 1906. The NABC's count appeared in dozens of regional and national stories after a black bear killed a woman and her two children in Tennessee in April 2006, where it was often referred to as the "official number," though the source was often left out.

The problem with journalists citing "official numbers" with regard to the number of humans killed by bears, however, is that there is no comprehensive record of humans attacked or killed by bears in North America. Some states keep records, but no one department is assigned to officially track such tragedies. Wildlife Services, a segment of the U.S. Department of Agriculture, keeps records of attacks on livestock, but not on humans. Often bear attacks or other animal attacks can't be conclusively proven. If a person has disappeared it is impossible to verify the cause of death, and even if a body is found it can be difficult to assign blame because scavengers (bears will eat meat they find dead) can make it impossible for even a trained forensic expert to ascertain the cause of death. This leaves journalists with numbers from official public sources that aren't comprehensive or even trustworthy.

As a result, journalists quote organizations like the NABC. NABC's statistics were compiled by a single privately funded biologist who looked at recently published books and articles and called state game departments (while admittedly making "judgment calls" as he went). Quoting these figues without giving the group's background is like reporting that "officially Martians abducted twenty-two people in 2004," without saying that the figure came from the People for Peace with Mars, who all wear tin-foil hats so their minds won't be read by secret agents flying about the countryside in black helicopters.

The NABC has a shoestring budget and a staff smaller than most gas stations, but it is a widely respected, science-based organization that is helping to educate people about black bears. The problem with the NABC is that it oversells a bear-friendly image to combat headline hype, which undermines its credibility. Lynn L. Rogers, the NABC's founder and resident biologist, says his mission is "to make people understand that black bears are not dangerous."[12]

He added up the "official" number of humans killed and explained, "The figures I gathered on the number of people killed by bears could be understated. There is just no scientific way to count these incidents. I only included the reports I really felt were legitimate. When I couldn't verify a killing with multiple sources I left it out. As for attacks, you can't count them. How do you decide what counts as an attack? When a paw swipes someone, is that an

A Fact the Media Won't Tell You

Bears are more likely to attack you in a national park. According to a recent study on Alaskan bear attacks, you are about twice as likely to be attacked by a grizzly when you're camping in national parks, where hunting is not allowed.

Herrero and Smith, "A century of bear-human conflict in Alaska: analyses and implications."

attack? I've been swiped and bitten many times. It's not a big deal. Each time I only had a few stitches."

To which I just had to ask, "How did you get swiped and bitten many times?" Rogers chuckled. He's a character, a Jane Goodall of black bears. He explained that he often spends his days hanging out with wild black bears in northern Minnesota. He has earned their trust, he says. He follows them around all day, often sitting within feet of them. He said, "I used to think black bears were very dangerous, but my thinking evolved in much the same way people have changed their attitudes about gorillas. I now interpret aggressive displays by black bears in terms of their fear rather than mine. Black bears' most common aggressive displays are merely rituals they perform when they are nervous. When I see any bluster, I feel safe. It means the bear wants to talk about the problem it has with me. I have never had one come after me and hurt me. The only times I have been bitten is when I initiated the contact."

So okay, Rogers is a little different. But get this: though Rogers doesn't hunt, and has a guarded stance when it comes to black bears, he supports hunting. He even fought to have black bears upgraded from "vermin" to "big game" in Minnesota, so that hunting seasons could be set and the bears managed, not destroyed on sight. This way the bears would retain their fear of man and money generated from hunting could be used for habitat preservation and population studies, says Rogers. Though Rogers loves bears, and fears his wild "friends" will be shot, he believes in hunting them for the sake of bears and people. He even explained why his bears don't get shot: "The wild bears I've become friends with have learned to avoid people. They're very cautious. Hunting probably had something to do with their fear of people. When they hear a human voice, they move away from it. Even when I'm hanging out with them! The average bear killed by hunters is just two years old, which are actually the bears most likely to attack humans, because they are young and naïve and hungry and often pushed into new areas by older bears."

Despite the fact that records of attacks are not trustworthy, most biologists agree that black bears are attacking people more often than ever before. To find out why black bear attacks are increasing, let's go into the field.

The front lines of bear control

Ian McMurchy spent a lifetime on the front lines of bear management. He's a retired animal damage control specialist for the Saskatchewan Department of Ministries and has a lifetime of experience dealing with problem bears. When asked what makes a bear a killer, McMurchy grimaced and let his grandfather voice find its conviction:

> I've hunted down a few bears that had lost their fear of people and had become dangerous, but one was a real monster. It was a hit and run bear. She was smart. She'd chase people away from campsites, snapping her jaws and really threatening. Then one evening she attacked some campers. It was lucky she didn't kill one. We were at the scene in minutes.
>
> It was right at last light. I took point and moved in. When I was within maybe forty yards, the big bear came at me in a blur, low to the ground, hissing pure fury. No jaw-popping warnings. No growling. Black bears make an unforgettable sound when they're really furious; like a hiss roaring from bottom of their black chests.
>
> All I could see was a large black shape hurtling down the trail right at me. Meanwhile, somewhere behind, my partners yelled, "HERE SHE COMES!" as they sensibly ran for the truck.
>
> So there I was in an idiotic spat of bravery in the middle of a hiking trail with my shotgun aimed at a charging black ball of muscle topped with teeth. Somehow my knees held and

when that sow got to about one stride away, I pointed the shotgun barrel just under her chin and pulled the trigger. The shotgun jumped against my shoulder. Then there was silence. Dead silence. Everything was dark and still. I shucked another slug into the chamber and heard the guys shouting, "Ian, you okay? What's going on?"

After my knees quit trembling, I slowly backed away. We returned to the site with flashlights and found the bear. The impact of the slug had knocked her off the trail. She died on impact. I was damn lucky.

Now, I know what you're picturing, so I'll ask you to redraw the image. We weren't in some wild place in the deep, dark recesses of the forest. I was in a popular Saskatchewan campground facing down the camp bear on a trail dozens of people used every day. People created that monster. They fed her and thought of her as a large dog. Some wanted us to immobilize and relocate the bear. We knew if we did, we'd merely be moving the problem. We had to take her out.

Then McMurchy spelled out his hardest-earned conviction:

There are two types of bears to really fear; one is pure wild, but the other, the real monster of the two, is created by us. First of all, there are the bears that have never seen a person before. Such bears don't know what to make of you. Most such bears run away, but a very small percentage decide to find out if you're food. These bears will come for you. They might begin to stalk you. Some may just move closer as they stop frequently to really look at you and wonder, "Can I eat this ugly thing?" A few will circle you and wait up the trail to ambush you. But mostly these wild bears aren't really dangerous.[13]

There are many examples of such encounters; for example, in July 2006, a wild bear that had likely never seen a person before decided to eat a human, reported CBC News. While portaging between lakes near Wawa, Ontario, Tom Tilley was ambushed by a bear. Tilley was on a twelve-day canoe trip with his dog, Sam. Four days into the trip, he heard his dog growl and noticed a bear closing in on him. He said he did what he'd been taught to do when a bear is close; he started waving his arms and slowly backing away. The bear moved off the trail but a few seconds later reappeared, cutting off Tilley's escape route.

"That's when I knew I had a serious problem. I was lunch," said Tilley. Sam jumped between the bear and Tilley. The bear jumped on the dog. While the bear was distracted Tilley pulled his six-inch knife and jumped on the bear's back. He stabbed the two-hundred-pound bear repeatedly, killing it quickly. Tilley's hand was bitten and Sam had puncture wounds, but both made it out of the woods in good shape. Tilley had recently purchased the knife that saved his life after reading the story of Jacqueline Perry, a young Cambridge, Ontario, doctor who was killed by a bear in September 2005. Perry's husband attempted to fend off the animal with a Swiss Army knife, the only weapon he had.

"When I read the report about her death, it really hit home to me that these things are possible," Tilley said. "I owe her husband a real debt of gratitude because if I hadn't heard her story and got that knife, I wouldn't be telling this story."[14]

According to Steve Herrero's research, eighteen of twenty black bear killings of people he investigated were the result of predation. The bears had decided to eat someone. The time of day could be verified in fifteen of these twenty attacks and, of those fifteen killings, fourteen occurred during daylight. The killer bears were predatory. Some were in wild, desolate places like the one that attacked Tilley, but most were in areas where humans frequented.

According to Ian McMurchy, the un-hunted bears that decide we're no threat are statistically the most dangerous. "Their transition starts innocently at first," explained McMurchy. "The bear eats your garbage, maybe your bird food. Then maybe it eats a pet. All that happens at night. When startled, such a bear runs off. That's all just the beginning. When that bear stops running from you or starts to show up in daylight and ignores people as it turns over garbage cans, then you've created a monster. Next, that bear might break into a home. And inside a home it's deadly dangerous. Even if it doesn't want to eat you, a person might accidentally corner it, which would instigate an attack. There was a woman killed in New Mexico a few years ago that way. The woman was ninety-three and didn't have a chance. But really, it doesn't need to break in to be dangerous. Bears that lose their fear of people might sooner or later decide to attack a person, especially a child.

"Sooner or later such monsters created by us have a bad day," remarked McMurchy. "Sounds funny, but it's true. One day such a bear will either be famished or it'll just have been beat up by a bigger bear and be ticked off and in the mood to assert its dominance over something or someone. This is the mistake Timothy Treadwell made. I'd say it's why he was killed and eaten by those Alaskan grizzlies. Sooner or later one of those bears was going to be in the mood to try him. He was in a national park where there is no hunting. He never gave them any reason to fear, or respect, him!"[15]

I shivered as I recalled that such an incident occurred in my neck of the woods in 2002. A black bear in New York's Catskill Mountains came onto a porch and took Ester Schwimmer, a five-month-old girl, in its jaws. Her father chased the bear and it dropped the infant. But it was too late. Ester was dead. People were used to seeing that bear in their garbage.[16]

McMurchy says, "That's why you have to kill bears that lose their fear of people, and it's why you should never let it happen. You can't move such bears. They have an uncanny sense of direction. Most just walk right back. Even if you move them a thousand miles, all you're really doing is moving a problem. This is why hunting is good. It lets bears know we're dangerous. It's nature's way. It's the most compassionate thing we can do."

Such a man-made monster attacked a family on April 13, 2006. This "camp bear" decided a child just might appease its appetite in the 640,000-acre Cherokee National Forest, located in Tennessee's Appalachian Mountains. The attack took place near a swimming hole in a camping area on Chilhowee Mountain, according to Dan Hicks, spokesman for the Tennessee Wildlife Resources Agency. Susan Cenkus and her two children, Luke, a two-year-old boy, and Elora, a six-year-old girl, didn't see the 350-pound bear stalk them, nor did they see it come in for the kill.[17]

Witnesses say the bear first picked up the two-year-old in its mouth. The bear wrapped its jaws around Luke's head and tried to run away with him. The boy's mother instinctively attacked the bear, hands swinging. The bear dropped the infant and went for her. The bear then picked up Susan Cenkus in its mouth and began to carry her off as she screamed bloody terror. She would have been a goner if not for several people who rallied, charged, threw sticks and rocks, and managed to drive the bear off, leaving Susan seriously injured and Luke in critical condition.

During the melee, Elora ran away to hide. Her wounded mother asked for her while lying in a pool of her own blood. People ran about calling out "Elora" all over the forest.

Elora was found dead an hour later with the bear hovering over her body not far from camp. A park ranger fired one shot at the bear before it bolted off. Elora had been stalked, killed, and partially eaten.[18] Park officials later caught and killed a bear that DNA tests proved was the killer.

Black bear killings of people are uncommon. Before that bear attacked the Cenkus family, the last killing of a human by a bear in Tennessee occurred in May 2000, when Glenda Ann Bradley was killed by a black bear near Gatlinburg as she walked on a trail in Smoky Mountains

National Park. The two attacks in Tennessee have something in common: both occurred in areas that don't allow hunting. Both bears had become habituated to people. They'd lost their fear and began to associate people with food, which is why "don't feed the bears" policies have been in effect so long that Disney was doing cartoons on them in the 1950s.

More un-hunted bears than ever

Another reason attacks are becoming more common is that bear populations are rising in or near urban areas all over America. These bears are sometimes becoming habituated to people and are often living in areas where there is no hunting; a recipe—as we saw with McMurchy's experiences—that increases the likelihood of violent encounters. For example, one of many such incidents occurred in 2003 in Colorado's Rocky Mountain National Park.

Patrick Finan and Tim Schuett were sleeping in their tent when a bear bit Finan through the tent's mesh lining. Finan woke up screaming and turned to see a bear trying to eat him. When people came to see what was going on, the bear ran off. This was another camp bear that was habituated to people. There is no hunting in the park, and so it had no reason to fear humans. It was just another uncounted black bear attack.[19]

There are at least 750,000 black bears in North America today, according to the International Association of Fish and Wildlife Agencies (IAFWA), a nonprofit organization that represents state and federal game and fish departments. That is a widely published number, but most biologists and state game departments have been reporting that the number of bears has been steadily increasing for decades, so much so that even Florida now has a nuisance bear problem. The state received 2,105 bear-nuisance complaints in 2005.

Tom Shupe, a biologist with the Florida Fish and Wildlife Commission who deals with human-bear conflicts, says it's only a matter of time before a bear kills someone in Florida, and when it happens it will be a human's fault. The un-hunted bears are breaking into homes more often than ever because people are feeding them and treating them as pets; as a result, they're losing their fear of people, says Shupe.[20]

Indeed, states from Texas to Tennessee also have growing black bear populations, and growing problems. Even New Jersey has a growing black bear population and associated conflicts. Bears have now been spotted slumming in downtown Newark; in fact, there were so many complaints about problem bears that the state started using hunting to reduce human-bear problems. This has sparked a lot of controversy, lawsuits, and political upheaval in the state. Hunting was stopped in New Jersey in 1971 because the bear population was too low. The bear population took off in the 1980s and in the 1990s became a problem. In New Jersey the number of bear-nuisance complaints skyrocketed from 285 in 1995 to 1,208 in 2003.

In 1997, the New Jersey Division of Wildlife determined the "cultural carrying capacity" of bears had been reached. State wildlife biologists determined they needed to manage the population with hunting. In 2000, the New Jersey Council amended the game code to include a three-segment black bear hunting season. The state wanted to reduce the bear population to 350 bears in order to reduce associated bear-human conflicts, including property damage and some violent encounters.

The New Jersey Division of Wildlife declared, "Hunting is a safe, legal, responsible use of the wildlife resource and the primary means of controlling black bears in twenty-seven states. Hunting is a legitimate and effective means to control the increasing population of bears, thereby reducing associated problems (vehicle collisions, home entries, livestock kills, pet kills, and property damage) in a cost-effective manner. Hunting is, therefore, considered one element of an integrated approach to manage bear populations."

New Jersey's first black bear hunt in thirty-five years took place in December 2003. That year, two bears attacked people, fifty-three bears

A Fact the Media Won't Tell You

Hunting increases bear cubs' chance of survival. A study by the University of Alberta found that cubs have a 25 percent better chance of survival in an area where black bear hunting is allowed than in a region where it is forbidden. "We compared a hunted population and an un-hunted population," said Sophie Czetwertynski, a Ph.D. candidate at the University of Alberta. "In the hunted population, we had much higher cub survival and higher productivity of females." The reason is that big male bears—the ones hunters seek—prey on cubs.

Bob Weber, "Bear Hunting Boon for Cubs, Study Indicates," *Canadian Press*, July 28, 2006.

broke into homes, nineteen bears were aggressive with people, and residents filed 1,308 complaints about problem bears.[21] During the December 2003 season, hunters killed 328 bears. Now get this: after the hunt in 2003, the number of nuisance complaints fell by almost 50 percent to 756 in 2004, and the number of aggressive bear encounters fell from nineteen to seven. People were safer because of hunting.

Despite the success, lawsuits from the Humane Society of the United States and other anti-hunting organizations combined with a nervous governor stymied the 2004 season. Subsequently, nuisance complaints and aggressive bear encounters rose to 1,104 in 2005, and twenty-one bears were aggressive with people—three times the number in 2004. These numbers leave little doubt that hunting has a direct cause-and-effect relationship with bear problems.

New Jersey managed to hold a bear season again in 2005. During the six-day season hunters killed 298 bears, nineteen of which had been captured in homes or in other human conflicts and tagged as nuisance bears.

While hunters were out in the New Jersey hills looking for bears, I interviewed hunters and activists at a New Jersey bear check station in Wawayanda State Park.

When I asked biologists what they were chuckling about as they examined a three-hundred-pound bear that had been killed by a hunter, one explained, "Oh, this bear is a criminal. She's wanted for a series of break-ins in Highland Lakes. It was only a matter of time before she attacked someone. We're glad she was killed."

Indeed, in August 2003, an eighteen-year-old woman was attacked by a black bear on a trail in Wawayanda State Park, the very park where I stood with twenty-six activists, eighty-two print and television reporters (I counted), and thirty-three law enforcement personnel at the bear check station. The woman who was attacked said the bear came up behind her, chased her down, and tackled her. She threw a hard elbow at its snout and luckily caught it right in the nose, stunning it and giving her time to escape. Biologists later said that the bear was likely young and had recently split from its mother. The bear didn't know that humans could be dangerous. Luckily, it was a juvenile, and so it didn't really know how to kill either.[22]

"The bear was in predatory mode," said Jack Kaskey, a state Department of Environmental Protection spokesman. "The bear was out to eat her. She had to fight for her life."

She escaped with only a set of four-inch welts on her midsection from the encounter, but the bear was never caught. That bear had lost its fear of people, and I hoped a hunter had killed it. The dozens of "Wounded Bear Rescue" activists on hand didn't share my point of view, however. By the end of the six-day season, a bunch of the activists were arrested for harassing and threatening hunters, who turned out to be undercover officers. It was a sting. The hunters killed the number of bears the biologists had hoped for, and the people of New Jersey were a little safer for another year.

According to Patrick C. Carr, a supervising wildlife biologist for the New Jersey Fish and Wildlife Bureau, black bears certainly are not wanton killers of humans, but results show that hunting does reduce human-bear conflicts. Certainly hunters can't prevent every attack. If there were one bear left on the planet, it's possible that bear could attack someone, says Carr. But humans can live alongside bears while keeping them wild; they can reduce the chances of bears attacking people by not feeding them and by continuing to hunt them. Despite this, New Jersey's newly elected governor, Jon Corzine, overruled the biologists and cancelled the 2006 bear season.[23]

Chapter 4

PREDATORS AREN'T PUBLIC PETS

On August 8, 2006, the Reuters news service posted an article titled "Killing Pumas Doesn't Lessen Attacks on Man." That same day a headline in *USA Today* proclaimed "Cougar Hunting Doesn't Lower Fatal Attacks." The articles were citing a study from the Mountain Lion Foundation, a nonprofit environmental organization based in San Francisco. The *USA Today* article began:

> No evidence proves sport hunting reduces fatal encounters between people and mountain lions, says a study out today that adds fuel to a debate over the trophy killings of big-game animals.
>
> The study comes as mountain lion attacks on humans, while still rare, are increasing, and reported sightings more common, especially where suburbs and second homes have spread into lion habitat.
>
> The study by the Sacramento-based Mountain Lion Foundation compared lion-people incidents in ten states that permit hunting with data from California, which banned cougar hunting in 1972. Nine states—Idaho, Montana, Utah, Colorado, Arizona, Oregon, Washington, Nevada, and New Mexico—had higher attack rates than California. Wyoming's was lower.[1]

Guess what?

- Wolves really do kill people—sometimes in our own backyards.

- Oregon has banned cougar hunting with hounds, but taxpayers are forced to pay specialists to get rid of cougars that attack and kill people.

- In 1994 in California, more money was raised for a cougar cub that was orphaned than was raised for the two human children orphaned by that cougar.

Neither this article nor the Reuters story bothered to point out that the Mountain Lion Foundation is officially opposed to hunting, which means it has a motivation to undercut justifications for hunting mountain lions—what journalists call a "biased source." Even worse, neither of the journalists (or their editors) critically evaluated the claims made by the study. The study begins with the premise that if hunting reduces mountain lion attacks on people, then shouldn't California, which banned mountain lion hunting decades ago, have more attacks than states that allow mountain lion hunting? The study then determines that California doesn't have more attacks than states that have hunting seasons, so therefore hunting doesn't prevent attacks.

That conclusion seems logical until you do some reporting. If the journalists had called the California Department of Fish and Game, they would have found that one hundred to two hundred mountain lions are killed each year (out of a population of four thousand to six thousand) by California landowners who attain state permits that allow them to kill dangerous mountain lions. Isn't this hunting? The reporters might also have found that California authorities kill dozens of mountain lions in urban areas and near schoolyards every year. This is no small oversight: Californians are killing more mountain lions today than they did when hunting was legal in the state.[2]

Then there's a statistical problem: the Mountain Lion Foundation didn't compare apples to apples. They measured the number of attacks by comparing California's total human population against lightly populated states like Wyoming and Montana. They then compared the number of attacks per 10,000 square miles of "mountain lion habitat" and adjusted for populations, not for the number of people hiking, hunting, or otherwise using the "mountain lion habitat." Instead of comparing the number of people who are potentially exposed to cougars (such as by comparing counties with similar urban/rural areas and populations), they compared people in areas that have no mountain lions (such as downtown Los Angeles) with areas that do. This statistical ballot stuffing leaves no doubt that the so-called study is bunk. The journalists, however, weren't interested in getting to the politically incorrect truth.

There is no reliable record of attacks

So let's take a realistic look at California's non-management strategy. Proposition 117, a voter initiative passed in 1990, ended the mountain lions' classification as "game mammals" and banned all cougar hunting. (The state had halted the season in 1972.) Since then, complaints about cougars have skyrocketed. While only four cougar attacks were reported in California from 1890 to 1990, that number has been exceeded since 1992. As of January 2007, California had verified a total of sixteen attacks on humans by mountain lions since 1890; eleven of those attacks had taken place since the ban on cougar hunting.[3]

But you can't believe those numbers, and there is no national record that's trustworthy. Many attacks, even killings, slip through the administrative cracks; in fact, a review of

Myth Debunked

Coyotes are not native to the East Coast. When Europeans first settled North America, wolves were found along the East Coast, but not coyotes. At that time coyotes were found only west of the Mississippi River. It wasn't until after the wolves were exterminated that coyotes moved in.

government sources, nonprofit databases, publications—*Cougar* by Harold P. Danz and *Cougar Attacks* by Kathy Etling—and state and federal records turns up discrepancies, attacks listed in one source but not another. There are many reasons for this. States often don't share reports, and some are better about keeping records than others. Incidents that don't lead to attacks are often not recorded. Organizations that maintain databases often have political agendas. The USDA's Wildlife Services keeps records of livestock loss but not attacks on humans. In fact, according to Doug Updike, the California Department of Fish and Game's senior wildlife biologist, "An attack doesn't become official until it meets very strict criteria."[4] Perhaps someone should tell that to the parents of Jaryd Atadero.

Authorities now think Jaryd, a three-year-old boy who vanished on a hike in 1999 near Fort Collins, Colorado, was carried off by a mountain lion. He was on a hiking trip that day and had been running ahead to hide so he could jump out and say, "Boo."[5] "Everything that we're finding is consistent with the theory that a mountain lion killed Atadero," said Larimer County sheriff Jim Alderden, according to the Associated Press. In 2003, Jaryd's clothing was found several hundred feet above the trail where he disappeared. But still, this attack isn't listed anywhere as an "official" attack.[6]

A more recent attack took place in a no-hunting area near Boulder, Colorado, in April 2006. Seven-year-old Shir Feldman was holding his father's hand as they hiked up a trail when a cougar jumped on the boy. The mountain lion grabbed Shir by the jaw, but the boy's family counter-attacked. They pelted the animal with sticks and rocks, and the cougar quickly dropped the boy and ran away.[7] The seven-year-old suffered a broken jaw and other injuries. He's lucky his family was with him when the cat attacked. Because there wasn't a fatality, this attack wouldn't be recorded anywhere "official," just like the one on Jaryd Atadero.

As a result of such attacks, in December 2006 Colorado wildlife commissioner Rick Enstrom told the *Denver Post*, "When [people] really understand the lion population and the prey base up there, it's a statistical slam dunk that something bad is about to happen. It's not going to be on my neck." Enstrom officially asked Colorado counties, especially Boulder County, where a lot of un-hunted cougars are causing trouble, to allow mountain lion hunting in open-space properties. But Boulder County officials, who are known for their anti-hunting environmentalism, brushed off the idea as preposterous. They're determined to live in peace with cougars even if the cougars won't sign the peace accord.

California cougars are overpopulated

Cougars hunt by night and hide by day, which makes them awfully hard to count. So as a result, even though the California Fish and Game Department says there are between four thousand and six thousand cougars in the state, it can't back up those numbers—nor can any other state with cougar populations. Game managers in much of the West make estimates based on harvest reports. In California, there's no such indicator.

Though it's unclear what the cougar population might be, it's clear that California is saturated with cougars, says Lieutenant Bob Turner, a warden with the California Game and Fish Department for thirty years.[8] The result, scientists agree, is that when kittens reach eighteen months and their mothers turn them loose, the young females look for nearby territories, but growing up is tougher for the young males—they have to run for their lives because any dominant male will kill them on sight. So they move far—often right into suburbia. In California, these young un-hunted cats have no real fear of people. Pets disappear, and now and then a cougar attacks a human.

Such an attack occurred in Orange County, California, on January 8, 2004. At about 1:25 p.m., a three-year-old male cougar weighing 122 pounds was sizing up Mark Jeffrey Reynolds, a thirty-five-year-old man who stood five feet, seven inches tall and weighed 137 pounds. Authorities speculate that Reynolds had stopped on a well-used trail in Whiting Ranch Wilderness Park in southern Orange County to fix the chain on his bike when the cougar pounced on his back and killed him, probably instantly. The cat dragged Reynolds a hundred yards into the brush.

The horror wasn't over.

About three hours later, Anne Hjelle was bicycling on the same trail when the same cougar jumped off a four-foot rise and knocked her off her bike. Her riding companion, Debi Nicholls, grabbed Hjelle's legs and screamed as the lion dragged both of them thirty feet down the slope. The screams brought Nils Magnuson and Mike Castellano of Long Beach to the scene. They called 911 and fought off the mountain lion by throwing bowling-ball-sized rocks at it. Helicopters zoomed in. That's when Reynolds was found—passengers in one of Hjelle's rescue choppers spotted his partially eaten remains. Authorities killed the cat, and Hjelle recovered from her injuries.[9]

Despite such conflicts, California game managers have to wait for a cougar to threaten a human before a tag can be issued. An average of one hundred to two hundred "problem" cougars are killed each year in California, which is about twice the number killed annually by hunters before cougar hunting ended in 1972. In fact, cougar hunting is so politically incorrect in California that some anti-hunting groups, such as the Mountain Lion Foundation, argue that hunters can't control cougar populations. This is hard to accept when you realize that over-hunting nearly wiped out cougars in the last century. In fact, Utah, Wyoming, Idaho, and other Western states already use hunting to balance cougar populations against human safety.

Most Western states are segmented into management units. Wildlife biologists establish an annual quota for each unit, and when the number of kills is reached, the hunting season ends in that unit. In this way, state game managers keep cougar populations healthy—not overpopulated, hungry, and dangerous as they are in California, parts of Colorado, and in other areas in the West. Hunting works because hunters target the big toms—the same animals that make the immature cougars flee to suburbia. And if they weren't hunted, then they're likely not afraid of people, because no hunter has ever treed them—something that often happens in hunted areas as hunters use dogs to tree cougars and then check to make sure the animal is a mature male before shooting. A homeless young tom with no fear of people is a dangerous animal.

The combination has become so dangerous in Oregon, a state that has also restricted cougar hunting, that in 2006 the Oregon Department of Fish and Wildlife proposed a government program to control the state's cougar population. Because Oregonians have twice passed voter initiatives prohibiting the use of hounds in hunting cougars, hunters have not been able to control cougar populations and thereby reduce cougar-human conflicts. Since the ban on hunters using hounds was passed in 1994, cougar attacks, livestock depredation, and other human-cougar incidents have gone up dramatically. As a result, the state proposed establishing a minimum cougar population of 3,000—in 2006, there were an estimated 5,100 in Oregon. Though sportsmen may not use hounds, existing state law does allow federal and state employees to use hounds and snares to deal with cougars that are causing human, pet, or livestock conflicts. The problem became so desperate that the Oregon House voted 40–19 in May 2007 to approve a measure authorizing the Oregon Department of Fish and Wildlife to use paid "agents" to hunt cougars with hounds in areas where cougars are becoming dangerous. State authorities were forced to find a way around the restrictions in order to use hunting to manage the problem.

However, despite the obvious and substantiated need for cougar management, some people feel that when cougars attack humans it's our fault for taking their habitat. For example, just after a cougar killed a person in California in 2004, California resident Karin Malinowski told the Associated Press, "I hate to see people die like that . . . but I feel really bad for the mountain lion that was killed. We're encroaching on their territory. What are they supposed to do?"

One has to wonder how much land is enough to ease that kind of guilty conscience. According to the National Wilderness Institute, 39.8 percent of the United States (and 52.1 percent of California) has already

A Fact the Media Won't Tell You

Californians kill more cougars now than before hunting was banned. Californians annually use permits to kill one hundred to two hundred cougars, which is more than hunters were killing when hunting was allowed.

been cordoned off for the wild. Also, the same voter initiative that banned cougar hunting in California set up a trust fund of $30 million a year for thirty years for state purchases of "cougar habitat," and cougar populations are healthy and stable across the West, Mexico, and much of South America.

So should we let the Californians throw themselves to the lions? The problem with this is that attacks breed hysteria, and it's the lack of basic management that leads to more attacks. This vicious cycle creates bloody headlines that hurts the cougars' chances of being accepted farther east, which, by the way, is something you should be aware of.

Cougars are moving east

Even if you live on the East Coast, this management debate will soon concern you. Cougars are fast becoming a national wildlife management issue. When guided by sensible regulations, hunting has helped cougars, like many species, become a wildlife success story. So much so, in fact, that the big cats are headed for the East Coast. As a result, the West's increase of problems near urban areas could foretell what might happen in the rest of the country if hunting is not used to manage wildlife populations.

Though cougars are now thought of as Rocky Mountain animals, before free-for-all hunting and federal government bounties wiped them out, the big, deer-eating cats lived in all of the lower forty-eight states. Now they're coming back. And why not? Many urban areas east of the Mississippi are overpopulated with the cougar's favorite dinner: deer.

In 2004, a cougar turned up in downtown Omaha. How it got there is anybody's guess. Weeks later, a cougar was killed by a car in Indiana. Must have been an escaped pet, authorities said. A train hit a cougar in Illinois that same year. It had a stomach full of deer meat, suggesting it wasn't an escaped pet. That November, an Iowa farmer shot a cougar prowling around his soybeans. Unlike most pets, it had all its claws and teeth. That week a deer hunter in Arkansas found a picture of a cougar on his trail camera. Then, just ten miles from Minneapolis, another trail camera photographed a cougar eating a deer. Meanwhile, a DNA analysis of scat samples found in Michigan determined they were from a cougar. These are just a few examples from one year.

Reports like these led to the formation of the Eastern Cougar Network (ECN) in 2002. The ECN maintains a database of cougars that turn up where cougars are not expected. ECN members have been compared to UFO believers, but they have some reputable people on their scientific advisory panel and conclusive evidence to back up claims.

There have been cougar sightings in every eastern state. "The cougar is the Bigfoot of the East," says Mark Dowling, cofounder of the ECN.[10] "However, we don't trust sightings. We've had calls from Canada, Europe, and every state in the U.S. from people reporting that they've seen a cougar. Some have even sent us photos of large house cats and golden retrievers. As a result, we only take hard evidence seriously—road kills, DNA evidence."

The thing is, there's a lot of hard evidence for the ECN to take seriously. From east Texas north, and east through Arkansas, Kansas, Missouri, Iowa, Indiana, and Minnesota, tangible proof of cougars has been found where cougars were run out more than a century ago. Let's start in Kansas, where until 2003 cougars hadn't been officially documented since 1904. The Kansas Biological Survey tested scat samples found on the Kansas University campus. The DNA analysis was conclusive.

"There's no doubt the scat samples are cougar," says Mark Jakubauskas, research assistant professor with the Kansas Biological Survey.[11]

Just north in Nebraska, John Hobbs, state director of Wildlife Services (the segment of the U.S. Department of Agriculture that responds to wildlife problems) said, "A few years ago there was a debate over whether we even had cougars in the state. The debate is finished. Cougars have moved through the river valleys right across the state."[12]

This could explain how a farmer in Ireton, Iowa, happened to shoot and kill a cougar in 2004, and how a Grand Forks County deputy sheriff happened to videotape a cougar near the Iowa-Minnesota border. And how Rich Staffon, Minnesota Department of Natural Resources wildlife manager for the Duluth-Cloquet area, came to say, "We're fairly confident there is a wild population [of cougars] out there."[13]

But farther east, in Michigan, the debate has gotten really contentious over whether the cats are state residents. In February 1997, just south of Mesick, Christi Hillaker caught a cougar on videotape as it walked through her yard. Since then, the number of sightings has soared and two people say they have snapped photos of cougars in the state. Meanwhile, Mike Zuidema, a retired state forester, earned the nickname "Crazy Mike" from his coworkers after he claimed to have seen a cougar. Zuidema has since interviewed seven hundred people who say they've spotted cougars in Michigan. He's even convinced the Michigan Wildlife Conservancy (MWC) that he's on to something.

The MWC now says it has seven scat samples that DNA analysis has proven to be from cougars living in both the Upper Peninsula and lower Michigan; the conservancy thinks it's a population that staved off extirpation thanks to efforts by sportsmen's clubs to preserve land and restore deer populations. Others, including the Michigan Department of Natural Resources and the ECN, have been skeptical. However, Brad Swanson, assistant professor of biology at Central Michigan University (where the scat was analyzed), says, "The DNA tests were conclusive. Seven of the scat samples are from cougars."[14]

If populations of cougars are sprouting and growing east of the Mississippi, states will be forced to choose between a rational model of control that includes hunting—for our sake and the cougars'—or they can choose the politically correct model, like California. As a parting aside, it's worth noting that after a female cougar killed Barbara Schoener in California in 1994, more money was raised for the cub the cougar left behind than was contributed to the memorial fund to help Schoener's two children.[15] Something is terribly out of balance with a society when an animal that isn't even endangered has more value to the public than a human. There might be wild places in the East large enough for cougars, but no place is large enough for that kind of thinking.

Without hunting even coyotes attack

The innocuous little coyote is next on the list of animals we're programming as predators. Weighing in at just thirty-five to forty pounds in the West, and growing somewhat larger in the eastern U.S., the coyote now lives from coast to coast; in fact, unless you live in a high-rise, coyotes are likely nearby (a few have been caught in Manhattan's Central Park). Coyotes are not indigenous to the East Coast—there were none east of the Mississippi when Columbus landed. Their progression from sea to shining sea during the last century is something of a wildlife riddle, but we know that coyotes are now in Canada and Mexico and all forty-eight states between.

Over the last decade newspaper headlines have screamed: "Coyote Attacks Toddler"; "Father Saves Girl, 4, from Coyote"; "Coyotes, Humans in Territory Clash." Wildlife agencies from California to Maine have dealt with reports of parents pulling coyotes off their children and pets.

Stunned skiers have found themselves in close-quarters battle with coyotes, using ski poles to fend them off.

They're known as stock killers and even deer slayers, but man eaters? According to a recent study, there have been fifty-three verified coyote attacks on people in California alone since the mid-1990s. Massachusetts residents have been shocked by several bloody attacks on children, as were residents in New Jersey, New Hampshire, Vermont, Wyoming, and New Mexico. And attacks aren't just happening out in the wilderness, where trailblazers realize the risk. With increasing frequency, most coyote attacks are taking place in suburbia.

"Tame" coyotes attack people

A skirmish typical of the clashes that have terrorized Californians occurred about five miles from Disneyland, in Fullerton, California, in 1995. "The coyote had been there for hours, [lying in some hedges] just feet from ten children playing in a sandbox—one of which was my daughter Jennifer," says Debbie Dimmick.[16] "We had just moved to town and knew nothing about coyotes. Jennifer was enjoying a romp with her new playmates, and I was keeping an eye on her from across the street.

"It was there, watching. You could see where it had lain in wait. You could even see [in the grass] where it had crawled closer."

At 6:30, it was time to come in for dinner. Jennifer walked close to the hedge as she headed indoors. The lurking coyote sprang, knocking the three-year-old to the ground.

"First, it goes for her throat, but she kicks and punches, so it bites her legs and chest," said her mother. "A neighborhood boy [stood] there in horror. But I couldn't see it. I just heard a blood-curdling scream—no, worse, it was just awful."

Sprinting across the street with a neighbor, Dimmick found her daughter "dripping with blood." One bite came close to severing her femoral artery. "She'd be dead," says Dimmick, "if the bite had been any closer. Her face is scarred for life, but she's alive." In fact, just days after the attack, Jennifer went house-to-house with her father, David, passing out flyers to warn the neighbors.

Attacks in California range from chase scenes (a coyote pursued three kids out of a playground at the University of California–Riverside, caught the slowest of them, a seven-year-old, and bit him) to domestic scenes (a twenty-four-year-old woman in San Diego was attacked in her backyard while on her cellular phone) to scenes straight out of horror flicks (a coyote sank its teeth into the face of a five-year-old girl while she was asleep in a sleeping bag next to her parents in the Reds Meadow Campground in Madera County).

There have been recent suburban attacks in Arizona as well—two just outside Phoenix and one in a playground in Rancho Vistoso, a Tucson

A Fact the Media Won't Tell You

Wolves kill dogs on sight. In August 2005 a federal judge ordered the Bush administration to step up efforts to restore the gray wolf to Maine, New Hampshire, Vermont, and New York. The ruling was in response to a lawsuit filed by environmental groups, including the National Wildlife Federation. Any urbanite who supports this measure should know that according to Ed Bangs, the U.S. Fish and Wildlife Service's gray wolf recovery coordinator, wolves seek out and kill domestic dogs for territorial and predatory reasons. The only way to prevent the wolves from killing pets would be with hunting, but the groups that sued to reintroduce wolves in New York and New England are anti-hunting.

"Feds told to bring gray wolf back to Northeast," Associated Press, November 19, 2005.

suburb. The latter was particularly vicious. A coyote "quietly attacked a twenty-two-month-old toddler" and threatened several other children, reported the *Arizona Daily Star*. The headline on the story quoted a witness's words: "the coyote was going for their throats."

In New Mexico, one of the worst instances occurred in August 1995, when a coyote grabbed a sixteen-month-old boy from a yard and tried to drag him off. The child's mother came to the rescue.

Don't wipe the sweat off your brows yet, East Coasters. In 1992, two hunters were attacked in separate incidents in Vermont, and a Massachusetts woman was bitten on the leg in 1994. But perhaps the most unnerving attack happened in 1998 on Cape Cod.[17] A coyote pounced on three-year-old Daniel Neal on July 30 in the town of Sandwich while he was playing in his backyard. His mother heard screaming and charged outside to see a coyote mauling her son. Later, she told police she beat the coyote over the head with her bare hands and finally "pried it off" her son, but to her horror the animal wouldn't leave. The coyote was so determined to get a meal that it was still there when police arrived. An officer shot the animal.

It's common for a coyote to stick around after an attack, says Glyn Riley, a federal coyote trapper with the USDA's Wildlife Services who specializes in trapping problem coyotes in Texas. A coyote's attack strategy is simple: it picks a target and locks on like a heat-seeking missile. It's relentless. If its target is big, it'll go for the throat and choke it to death. If it's small, the coyote may try to run off with it still alive in its mouth. If it's helpless and large (like a cow in labor), it'll just eat it alive. But in each case it'll stay locked on—one eye on its meal, the other looking for an opportunity.[18]

"It's genetic," says Professor Rex O. Baker of California State Polytechnic University in Pomona, who investigated attack scenes for various wildlife agencies and is considered the nation's leading authority on coyote attacks. "Coyotes have different modes, and when they're in 'attack mode,' they stay tuned-in to their prey, often staying at the scene. They may even return time and time again, just looking for an opportunity."[19]

Such tenacity can be attested to by a family from Newport Beach, California, a fashionable bedroom community south of Los Angeles. "A father was working on his backyard deck when he spotted a coyote stalking his two-year-old son," says Baker. "Bolting across the lawn, he snatched up his son before the coyote got him, but the coyote stayed right there until another man hit it over the head with a big piece of lumber. Still, that coyote came back every day at the same time for four days looking for the child ... until we trapped him."

People too often treat coyotes like they're boisterous pets, says Baker. "They have Walt Disney mentalities. They see wildlife and they just want to cuddle them, and that's the impetus for the attacks."

The textbook term for the coyote's recent shift in diet is "behavioral imprint change," and according to Baker, it works like this: people feed coyotes by leaving their garbage cans open or their dog's food dish out or even by leaving the dog itself out. After a while the coyotes begin to associate humans with food. This association is a national problem; in fact, attacks on pets are so common that most states publish guides on coyote awareness. Many state game departments won't even respond to attacks on Rover or Muffy; they instead refer the resident to a private animal damage control specialist.

Baker and Professor Robert M. Timm of the University of California–Hopland laid out the progression from urban phantom to urban fiend in a coauthored paper titled *Management of Conflicts Between Urban Coyotes and Humans in Southern California.*[20] In it they trace the seemingly mundane path leading to predictable violence. It starts with a few sightings, some knocked-over garbage cans or pet dishes that mysteriously empty at night. Next, pets start disappearing. But things don't get really serious until daytime activity escalates. When coyotes trot across the street at high noon, oblivious to people, it's time to be on the watch; soon they'll attack pets in front of their owners. This is actually becoming common, and not just in L.A., but also in Chicago, on the East Coast, and many places in between. When this happens, if people don't do something quick to reinstall coyotes' fear of people, a person (probably a child) will be attacked.

One such behavioral progression cited by Timm and Baker that went unchecked culminated in Los Angeles in 1994 and 1995. "Reports of coyotes chasing cats in front of people became common" in Griffith Park, and soon after, "coyotes began begging for food." This shows that they began associating people with food. Then they began "chasing people away from their picnic lunches." And after all the signs went unchecked, a coyote tried to run off with a small child, and several men were attacked while sleeping in the park.

Hunting stopped the attacks

Across the country coyotes are controlled and kept wild on a community level. A municipality may call in private companies or a U.S. Wildlife Services trapper. In their paper, Baker and Timm cite example after example of coyotes that simmered down after a few of their comrades lost their skins.

Baker went into L.A.'s Griffith Park to investigate the problems there and found piles of cat bones and containers from stolen lunches among coyote feces. He lobbied for immediate action, and because of the severity of the situation, a special team of animal pest management sharpshooters was brought in for three nights. Eight coyotes were killed, and though coyotes were still in the area, no more attacks were reported.

The University of California–Riverside also got serious. The school contracted a private company called Pest Management Services, Inc., and in the years since, the canines have behaved themselves.

Hunters can alleviate the problem in large parks and farms and woodlots around suburbia, but in tight quarters trappers are the safest and most effective solution. The public, however, tends to equate traps with the rack and thumbscrew. They're outdated and cruel, goes the argument. When people hear the word *trap*, they envision animals chewing their legs off in mad attempts to get free.

In reality, the modern leghold trap can be discriminating. It can be set to snap shut only on animals that are over a certain weight, and can be rigged with a pin that breaks if an animal is too heavy or too strong. These traps can also be padded to prevent injuries, says John Steuber, assistant director for wildlife services in California.

But even as coyote attacks proliferate, the public has voted to banish the traps in Arizona, Massachusetts, Colorado, and California. Massachusetts voters said no to traps in 1996, but after several coyote attacks and surging problems with out-of-control beaver populations the public is beginning to change its mind. Rob Deblinger, Massachusetts's assistant wildlife director, continually complained that his office is "handcuffed" by the trapping ban.

Arizona voters passed an initiative in 1994 banning the use of leghold traps, poisons, and snares on public land. But there are exceptions: traps can be used on private lands for the protection of human health, safety, and for research. Because of this wording, wildlife officials have been able to deal with dangerous coyotes, says Steve Fairaizl, the Arizona director for wildlife services.

Like voters in Massachusetts, Colorado voters said no to traps in 1996, leaving wildlife officials and the Colorado Department of Health in a dilemma. But as attacks on humans increase and newspapers report evidence of coyote "gangs" preying on pets, local agencies will be under increasing pressure to control the beasts.

Despite having the worst coyote problems in the country, California voters approved a 1998 ballot initiative that completely banned traps and poisons on all lands in the state. As a result, Gary Simmons, the California state director for wildlife services, found himself caught between frustration and rage: "As public servants we'll abide by the rules and do our best, but problems will increase. How dramatically? I don't know. I just don't know!"

Professor Baker, equally frustrated by the ban on common-sense wildlife management in California, said, "Communities will now have very little recourse when problems arise. Red foxes [which are not even indigenous to California] will threaten the already endangered clapper rail and other waterfowl, because wildlife biologists will no longer be able to keep them out of the bird's nesting areas. I just hope people wake up: just as carpenters need hammers, wildlife officials need traps and hunters."

Wolves need to be hunted, too

An environmental crisis has been brewing in Idaho, Montana, and Wyoming because of out-of-control wolf numbers, yet a realistic solution has been slow in coming because of PC pressure from anti-hunting and environmental groups. Back in 1974, when the gray wolf was officially listed as endangered under the newly created Endangered Species Act, it would have been inconceivable to think that in just a few decades about five thousand wolves would be hunting in the lower forty-eight states— and even more outlandish to think that no one would be allowed to effectively manage wolf populations. After all, up until that time state and federal programs had funded the wolf's extermination.

Leap forward to today and you find a very different situation. Hunting outfitters are going out of business because of plummeting elk herds, ranchers are losing livestock, and biologists are scrambling to determine the actual impacts on the ecosystem. In fact, Jim Zumbo, an outdoor writer and hunter who lives in Wyoming, noted, "Wolves seem to cause profound personality changes in otherwise laid-back, shy, gentle people."[21] From the beginning, environmentalists, ranchers, and hunters have been in a loud, litigious dispute over wolf reintroduction and management.

The wolves themselves have fueled the uproar by quickly increasing beyond all expectation. According to the U.S. Fish and Wildlife Service's 2005 annual wolf report, in late 2006 there were 134 packs and 1,020 wolves in the northern Rockies. Idaho has an estimated 512 wolves divided among 59 packs, while Montana had 256 wolves in 46 packs. Wyoming's 252 wolves were in 26 packs, 13 of which lived inside Yellowstone National Park.[22] Biologists thought it would take decades for wolves to grow to those robust numbers. And those conservative population estimates are in constant dispute; people have been reporting wolves in many parts of Montana where wolves aren't "officially" located, and some wolves have been spotted as far south as Colorado.

As wolf numbers have increased, so have conflicts with humans and the need for management. In 2005, officials in the northern Rockies killed 103 wolves, mainly due to livestock predation. In 2004, the anti-hunting group Defenders of Wildlife paid Western ranchers $133,662 in compensation for wolf-killed livestock, up from $5,701 in 1994. The environmental group volunteered to pay ranchers for livestock loss in order to dissuade ranchers from "shooting, shoveling, and shutting up." However, ranchers constantly complain that Defenders of Wildlife has unrealistic criteria for proving livestock was killed by wolves—they argue they are losing many more cattle and sheep than they can prove irrefutably according to the anti-hunting group's criteria.

While ranchers and environmentalists grapple over livestock losses, the wolves have been eating a lot of elk. In 2005, officials in Yellowstone National Park radio-tracked wolves during two thirty-day periods to assess kill sites. Of the 316 kills examined, 77 percent were elk. South of the park, where winter wolf kills have been monitored, of the 231 ungulate kills examined, 97 percent were elk. This predation is devastating herds. For example, by 2006 the northern Yellowstone elk herd, which numbered about 9,500 animals in 2006, had shrunk by 50 percent since the mid-1990s, mostly because of wolf predation. Many other elk populations in Wyoming, Montana, and Idaho have seen similar declines.

Outside Yellowstone in the Gallatin Range in Montana, the Department of Fish, Wildlife and Parks has reduced hunting opportunities for elk by about 90 percent, due to wolf predation on elk calves. In a region where big-game hunting is vital to the economy and culture, the wolves have been putting hunting outfitters out of business. "More elk calves would certainly survive if sportsmen could be used to reduce the number of

Myth Debunked

Healthy wolves do kill people. On November 8, 2005, Kenton Carnegie, a twenty-two-year-old University of Waterloo geological engineering student, was working at a co-op job with a survey company at Points North Landing, in northern Saskatchewan, when he decided to take an afternoon walk. When he failed to return after dark, his colleagues went looking for him. They found his body about a quarter-mile away, partially eaten and surrounded by wolf tracks. Prints in the bloody snow told a violent tale. Wolves hunted Carnegie and then chased him down. Carnegie tried to elude the animals before breaking into a terrified sprint for safety. He struggled to his feet at least twice before he was yanked to the ground and killed. Royal Canadian Mounted Police spokeswoman Heather Russell said, "There is nothing to lead us to believe that death was caused by anything other than injuries consistent with canine bites. There were wolves near the body and wolf tracks all around, and there's a history of wolves in the area."

"The death of Kenton Carnegie," CBC News Online, March 7, 2006.

predators," says Tom Lemke, a wildlife biologist with Montana Fish, Wildlife and Parks. "Just as we do in the rest of the state."[23]

This doesn't have to happen; wolves in Idaho, Montana, and Wyoming have actually met the criteria for recovery since 2002, according to the Endangered Species Act, which calls for thirty or more breeding pairs and at least three hundred wolves. So why haven't wolves been delisted? Officially the hold-up was Wyoming's state management plan. Before the feds will transfer management, they must be convinced that each state has adequate plans to sustain wolves. In 2003, Montana, Idaho, and Wyoming all submitted plans for review. The former two were accepted, but Wyoming's was rejected, mainly due to a state law that defines wolves as "predators," meaning wolves can be killed anytime by anyone when they are outside protected areas like Yellowstone.

The *unofficial* reason why wolves have yet to be delisted is because it is politically incorrect to do so. The mainstream media, the Sierra Club, Defenders of Wildlife, and other animal activist and environmental groups are going to court to prevent wolves from being managed with hunting. It seems that environmental groups have trouble grasping the purpose of the Endangered Species Act: to recover animal populations so they no longer need protection. For these groups, the act is just another way for the government to tell hunters what they can and can't do.

What does the future hold?

In early 2007, the U.S. Fish and Wildlife Service announced that it planned to delist wolves in Montana and Idaho from the Endangered Species Act. If this happens (lawsuits are already being filed by anti-hunting groups), states will be able to use hunting to kill wolves that cause conflicts with humans or that have detrimental impacts on wildlife populations. In fact, the announcement of the wolf's possible delisting caused such a positive stir with state game managers that the Idaho Fish and Game Department promptly announced that wolf hunting tags would cost $26.50 apiece for residents. "Officials are working on a wolf hunting and species management plan under the guidelines of the Idaho Wolf Conservation and Management Plan that would reduce wolf numbers in areas of conflict and try to stabilize numbers across the rest of the state," boasted an Idaho Fish and Game Department press release.

In response, environmental groups howled that wolves still need federal protection. They feel that a "natural balance" will be established as wolves control elk and deer populations. In truth, greens will get their "natural balance" only if they eliminate all humans from the continent. If wolves' only food sources were elk and deer, nature would serve as a nice regulator: when they depleted the elk and deer populations, wolves would start starving, which would keep wolf populations in check. But where humans live even remotely nearby with their pets and livestock, wolves who have almost wiped out the elk and deer turn their taste buds instead to Fido and Bessie. This isn't conjecture. We see it with other animals too; bear and cougar problems increase in urban areas whenever a drought, fire, or other circumstances diminishes the predator's wild food supply. Wolves (while already killing a good deal of livestock) are still stretching their legs in the West and Upper Midwest. But as their populations reach saturation—and they have no more wild areas to move to—human-wolf conflicts will magnify unless humans develop a management strategy.

Idaho, Montana, and Wyoming have foreseen this dilemma and so proposed to eventually regulate wolf populations with hunting seasons. Hunting, incidentally, is a wildlife management tool in which Ed Bangs, the U.S. Fish and Wildlife Service's gray wolf recovery coordinator, sees merit. He says, "The service strongly supports the hunting of wolves as a management tool. Hunting is the perfect way to keep the wolf from becoming a domestic dog."[24]

Bangs doesn't want the wolf to become "a domestic dog" because when wolves lose their fear of humans they become dangerous. In November 2005 Kenton Carnegie, a twenty-two-year-old college student, was chased down and eaten by a pack of wolves in Saskatchewan. And in July 2006 Becky Wanamaker, a teacher from Anchorage, Alaska, was chased down and attacked by a wolf. She managed to escape by running into an outhouse after being bitten on the back of one of her legs, according to reports in the *Fairbanks Daily News-Miner.*[25]

Attacks by wild, healthy wolves on humans are unusual but are not as unprecedented as today's PC media purports, according to Mark McNay, an Alaska Department of Fish and Game biologist. He spent two years researching wolf attacks in North America and unearthed thirteen substantiated wolf attacks on humans in the past thirty years. Eleven of those attacks involved wolves that had lost their fear of humans. These human-hunting wolves were not rabid. They just decided that humans weren't scary; in fact, the wolves that killed and ate Carnegie had been feeding in a nearby dump and were not being hunted.[26]

Chapter 5

NATURE'S DEADLIEST ANIMAL

Predator attacks command headlines, but when you mention hunting, the first animal that comes to mind is the whitetail deer. And if you mention the whitetail deer to a highway patrol officer, the first thing he'll think of is carnage.

So let's start with the grim facts: Bambi kills 150 to 200 people every year in the United States. In 2002, deer-auto collisions sent 26,647 people to hospital emergency rooms. In a typical year, deer kill ten times more people than sharks, bears, alligators, and cougars combined. While government safety data reports that there are 275,000 collisions with deer each year, the Insurance Information Institute, a New York-based group that looks into various insurance-related issues, says that most accidents go unreported. It estimates that there are 1.5 million deer-vehicle collisions each year, each costing the insurance industry approximately $2,000 per claim, or $1.1 billion annually.[1]

Hunters created the problem?

A commonly repeated fallacy—mostly by wildlife-ignorant journalists—is that during deer season hunters chase frightened deer across roads where motorists smack into them. The weakness in this argument is that, according to numerous studies, deer-vehicle accidents peak an hour after

Guess what?

- Deer kill ten times more people each year than sharks, cougars, bears, and alligators combined, and more people than all commercial airline, train, and bus accidents combined.

- No alternative methods of reducing the number of deer-vehicle collisions are as effective as hunting.

A Fact the Media Won't Tell You

When hunting is banned, deer-auto collisions go up. Most deer-auto collisions occur in suburbia, not out in the sticks. Why? Hunters have trouble gaining access to land in heavily populated areas; as a result, deer populations in urban areas, such as in Northern Virginia and in northern New Jersey, are often fifty to sixty deer per square mile, while deer densities in rural areas are typically below fifteen deer per square mile.

sunset. Hunters can't legally hunt an hour after sunset, so if people are chasing deer into roadways, they're poachers.

Hunters hate poachers. Poachers are game thieves. There are very few poachers left who kill deer because they're hungry. Most states have toll-free "poacher hotlines" set up so people can report these thieves. Now guess who calls these numbers? Yeah, hunters! Hunters take poaching personally. If you were to expose someone in a hunting club as a poker cheat, a cross-dresser, or a card-carrying member of PETA, the guys would look at him a little different. But if you proved someone was a poacher, that guy would just about be run out of town.

More deer are hit in the fall—your chances are four times higher of hitting a deer in November than in June—because throughout most of their range deer breed in November. As any hunter will tell you, when deer breed, the bucks move more. Hunters crave this period. Every hunting magazine tells hunters how to best hunt the whitetail "rut." Every deer biologist and hunting writer knows this is the best time to kill a buck, because they are on their feet actively looking for does in estrus (coming into heat). Also, in November it's dusk around five o'clock when most people are commuting, and deer are crepuscular, meaning they're most active at dawn and dusk.[2]

Hunters, however, *are* to blame for the current number of deer-auto collisions on our roadways. Really, they are! From 1900 to the present, hunters, through money generated from surtaxes on hunting equipment and from hunting license fees, have brought whitetail deer populations back. Once market hunting for deer was abolished and regulated hunting seasons went into effect in every state, wildlife biologists with state game departments (which, on average, get 75 percent of their funds from hunters)[3] and private hunter-conservation organizations transplanted deer from Minnesota, Wisconsin, and from other wild areas where they'd held on, and put them in every backyard from Canada to the Gulf of Mexico. Hunters and the state game departments then decided that shooting does was off-limits, because does were the sources of more deer. The herds needed to grow, they said. And grow they did.

The transplanted deer grew into a national problem. In 2001, hunters killed 7.4 million whitetail deer and drivers killed 1.8 million, out of a nationwide deer population of over 30 million. In contrast, when Henry Ford was first turning out the Model T, only about 500,000 whitetails were found in the entire U.S., according to the U.S. Biological Survey. In 2003 there were 201 fatal crashes, a 27 percent increase from 2002. In a typical year, deer-vehicle collisions kill more people in the U.S. than do all commercial airline, train, and bus accidents combined.

So next time you see a deer in your headlights, blame the sportsmen of the last century. By the way, the same goes for turkey, elk, moose, black bears, and many other wildlife species. Hunters, and their money, brought them back to bother us all. Here's the irony: now that hunters have brought game populations to historic highs (many wildlife biologists believe there are more deer in the U.S. today than when Columbus landed in 1492 because of the habitat changes we've made), some people don't want hunters to manage the herds. But we are.

In 2004, for the first time since 1900, the nationwide whitetail deer population actually fell, according research done by the Quality Deer Management Association, a hunter-conservation group that promotes balancing deer populations with habitat needs. Why? Hunters are practicing modern game management.

Here's how it works: For most of the twentieth century, hunters were told not to shoot does. So hunters shot only bucks. In many cases, such as in eastern Pennsylvania, hunters annually killed 80 percent of the bucks while letting all the does live and breed. (The upside for the bucks: if you evade the hunters, your dating options are pretty plush.) This practice began to change in the late 1970s as wildlife biologists started to rethink how to manage deer. Many herds had reached saturation and were actually beginning to destroy habitats.

As a result, wildlife managers started issuing doe tags. Some sportsmen resisted. Hadn't they been told for generations that does are the seeds for next year's deer? Some sportsmen are still not sure if reducing deer populations is a good thing. For example, in 2005 dozens of hunters with the Unified Sportsmen of Pennsylvania publicly burned their doe tags. Questioning game departments is a healthy sign of a democracy in action; after all, the public manages deer populations for the greater good. But most hunters agree with the shift in policy. The trend has been to reduce deer populations to keep them in line with what the available habitat can sustain. In fact, the nationwide whitetail population has actually begun to fall. Today, hunters nationwide are shooting more does than bucks. Hunters appreciate this game management philosophy because when herds are kept in line with habitat, bucks grow bigger. Drivers also like this approach because it puts fewer deer on the highways.

So deer-auto collisions won't get any worse and should start to fall— assuming hunting is allowed to continue reducing and managing herds. Get this: according to a study done by the Association of Fish and Wildlife Agencies, if hunting were stopped now, next year there'd be an additional 50,000 human injuries as a result of a 218 percent increase in vehicle-deer collisions. Also, auto repair costs would surge from $1.1 billion to $3.8 billion.[4] And these costs are already handed down to consumers; part of the calculation companies like Geico, State Farm, and

Progressive make when they give insurance quotes is your likelihood of hitting a deer.

Non-lethal alternatives don't work

Letting hunters continue to thin herds wherever possible is the most rational and cost-effective way to reduce vehicle-deer collisions. But it's not the only method. High-tech and low-tech answers are being invented, but they work only in specific circumstances, if at all. Here are a few things that have been tried:

➻ Fencing off highways on both sides has been shown to reduce collisions by 96 percent, but comes with a price tag of $250,000 per mile, according to Department of Transportation reports. This makes fencing a realistic option on major highways—about 5 percent of the road miles in the U.S.—but not everywhere.

➻ Some locations have installed "predator scent boxes" filled with wolf urine every fifth of a mile to scare deer away from roadways. "So, what do you do for a living?" "Oh, I'm a wolf-urine specialist. I refill highway-urine canisters!" As entertaining as that career choice sounds, the measure cut collisions by only 36 percent, according to a study done by the Department of Transportation. You're still left with one issue: how do you get the wolf urine? They trap wolves, cage them, and collect their urine in funnels positioned under kennels—animal rights folks are not so keen about this.

➻ In some parts of the country "wildlife underpasses" are being installed. The costs are staggering—one such project in Florida ran $3 million for a single underpass. But in the right places they work. In an antelope-migration corridor in Wyoming, a wildlife underpass reduced vehicle-antelope collisions by 64 percent, according to a Wyoming Game and Fish Department study. This is why the 2006 transportation bill passed by Congress included funding for wildlife underpasses.[5]

➤➤ Highway lighting and higher-visibility warning signs have not been shown to be effective. Studies on vegetation manipulation along roadways found that trimming the hedges doesn't decrease deer-auto collisions. At night drivers can't see more than a few yards off the road regardless of trees and shrubs.

➤➤ Studies on wildlife reflectors have produced conflicting results. Wildlife reflectors redirect light from vehicle headlights to the side of the highway, thereby creating a wall of light that theoretically stops deer from entering the roadway until after the vehicle has passed. In theory, wildlife reflectors create a "barrier" to wildlife only when vehicles are present at night. Two types of wildlife reflectors have been tested: a stainless steel mirror and the Swareflex reflector (a red plastic lens developed by the Austrian company Swarovski & Co.). The hypothesis is that deer are afraid of red light, because it has been suggested that a predator's eyes appear red to deer. The reflectors cost about $10,000 per mile. They don't work at dawn or dusk, or during heavy precipitation, and independent studies have not found a measurable decrease in deer-vehicle collisions with them installed. But, with their promises of creating "an optical warning fence," they sure sound fun.[6]

➻ Infrared deer-sensing devices have been invented. When a deer trips a motion sensor, warning signs at deer crossing areas light up. Though fun to talk about in a sci-fi sort of way, they are currently not being produced because no one wants to spend the millions necessary. And besides, a raccoon, dog, or even a hard wind shaking tree branches can set them off. These cost about $1,200 per unit.[7]

➻ Speed reduction does decrease vehicle-deer collisions; indeed, rural highways in Texas, Montana, and other states have posted daytime and nighttime speed limits. But try getting deep cuts in speed past the voters. The most amusing motorist speed reduction study was done in 1975. Scientists placed deer carcasses on highway shoulders close to deer-crossing signs. They found that vehicle speed was reduced by an average of 7.85 miles per hour.[8]

➻ Then there are ultrasonic devices. Wildlife warning whistles mounted on vehicles are supposed to warn animals of approaching doom. These ultrasonic devices operate at frequencies of sixteen to twenty kilohertz. Studies have found several of these acoustic devices to be ineffective, including the Sav-A-Life deer whistle marketed in the U.S. and Canada. In fact, most independent studies trashed the whole hypothesis on scientific grounds.

➻ Salting for deicing attracts deer to highways because of an increased salt content in vegetation—deer like salty snacks too. One Canadian study even found that the salt could intoxicate wildlife. According to the Canada Safety Council, a temporary, debilitating intoxication due to salt ingestion is a major factor in deer-vehicle accidents—drunken deer on the roadways can't lead to good things. Some studies recommend using non-salt deicers to reduce accidents, such as calcium magnesium acetate instead of sodium chloride. The problem with them is pollution. Although PETA might not mind this idea, leaving the roads icy so as not to lure the deer won't exactly reduce accidents.[9]

➤ Chemical repellants have been used in Europe to reduce deer-vehicle collisions. Repellents are sprayed along roadways in Germany to create "ungulate-avoidance fences." But this method has not been tested adequately. It seems that people aren't exactly thrilled when the state government sprays their neighborhoods with something that smells like bear dung or wolf pee.

A Fact the Media Won't Tell You

Lyme disease isn't the only worry from overpopulated wildlife. Diseases that originate with wildlife and then mutate to infect humans are a growing health threat. Scientists have documented thirty-eight illnesses that made the leap from animals to people during the past twenty-five years, according to Mark Woolhouse of the University of Edinburgh in Scotland.

Andrew Bridges, "Animal diseases pose threat to humans," Associated Press, February 21, 2006.

There are a lot of other well-intentioned ideas, such as low-glare vehicle headlights designed to reduce the tendency of deer freezing in the headlights (these are currently being used in Europe). However, low-glare headlights are illegal in the U.S. because people using them can't see where they're going (highlighting another difference in values between Europe and America). Infrared detection systems have been developed by General Motors that are currently being offered in some models (these help people see further than their headlights).

But though some of these solutions work well in localized areas and scenarios, they are not comprehensive solutions. The most effective solution in most of the country is hunting. The only places where hunting isn't working to reduce deer-auto collisions are the places where deer hunting is prohibited or overly restricted. For example, some herds in urban areas—such as in Northern Virginia and northern New Jersey—have reached more than one hundred deer per square mile; in contrast, rural areas typically have hunter-controlled deer populations between ten and twenty deer per square mile.

Why sharpshooters are necessary

For a case study in the obstacles hunters face in controlling deer populations (and therefore deer-auto collisions) look at the situation in Princeton, New Jersey, a few years back. This town's dramatic fight over how to control its burgeoning whitetail herd is a telling example of what is increasingly happening in urban areas from Boston to Chicago to Atlanta, where urbanites have lost touch with reality and therefore want someone to come and quietly take care of the problem.

In 2000, more than three hundred deer had been hit by automobiles in the seventeen-square-mile Princeton Township during a one-year period, and Princeton's mayor, Phyllis Marchand, was up in arms. Something had to be done. "Someone is going to die in a deer-related car wreck soon," screamed Marchand at a city council meeting.[10] The herd's population had climbed to one hundred deer per square mile, prompting some residents to refer to them as "rats of the night." One deer had jumped through a barbershop's plate-glass window; another had smashed through a windshield, landing bloody and kicking in a child's lap. And all this while some residents were dumping piles of corn out for the deer, naming them like pets, and gathering to form the Mercer County Deer Alliance, a group whose sole mission was to protect the deer.

Yes, a fight was brewing.

"The problem," said Marchand, "was that every solution was distasteful." Like many other urban mayors, Marchand found herself between what she saw as "fringe groups"—environmentalists and hunters. One side said, "You can't kill them. That's inhumane. Trap and transfer is the way or immunocontraception"—ideas she quickly dismissed because they are expensive, impractical, and often kill deer from stress. She then turned her ear to the other side and heard, "No problem, open the season and we'll come and shoot them." That, too, was out of the question, according to the Princeton Township Council. Hunters were not the sort the council wanted around. Besides, they said, "This is suburbia, we can't have bullets flying all around. Someone would get hurt."

"Both groups are outsiders," said Marchand. "Though there is some hunting done on private grounds in the township, there are not that many hunters in Princeton. And even most of the environmentalists who were getting vocal were from out of town. They just came to protest."

Yet something had to be done. "With 349 reported [deer-auto] collisions in the township in one year it was only a matter of time before someone got killed. And that wasn't our only concern. A few people had contracted Lyme disease [which is transmitted by deer ticks], and we'd heard that some towns were being sued for not acting when they knew there was a problem."

Then she found an easy way out.

Marchand heard about a deer sharpshooter with a perfect safety record who had quietly and professionally helped out many other mayors in such a fix. But then the city attorney told her of a glitch. State law regulates hunting, and it forbids the special hunt that a sharpshooter would need. Marchand simply retorted, "Then we'll change the state laws."

A year (and a lot of lobbying and testifying before committees) later, she did just that. The New Jersey state legislature gave the state's game commission the authority to issue special-hunt permits to municipalities. Marchand was then the first to apply for and receive a permit for the city of Princeton.

As soon as she had the permit in hand, Marchand called Anthony J. DeNicola, the president of White Buffalo, a nonprofit company in Connecticut that specializes in sharpshooting whitetails. She beseeched him to make it to Princeton in the next few months. "We're overrun," she said. "There will be protesters, but you'll have the complete cooperation of our police department." DeNicola said he'd fit them in.[11]

The date for the fight was set.

Enter DeNicola, a man whose intensity and mastery of his field overwhelms everyone who meets him. His resume includes a master's degree from the Yale School of Forestry and a PhD from Purdue. He lectures at Yale and has run sharpshooting programs in a dozen states. He has had protesters spit in his face while calling him "murderer" and "Bambi killer." He's been sued five times for doing his job—though he has never lost. And, from the other end of the spectrum, he gets at least two resumés a week from hunters who want to join his team.

What most people are never prepared for, however, is DeNicola's ability to go from a sharpshooter who can kill three hundred deer in two weeks to a scientist who is at the forefront of his field and knows it. His square jaw, high-and-tight hair cut, and thoroughly type-A personality give him the look and feel of a U.S. Marine Corps drill sergeant. But close your eyes and listen, and you'll hear the professor with the PhD.

While I spoke with DeNicola in his office, he answered the phone and found himself being berated by a member of the Humane Society of the United States (HSUS), the largest anti-hunting group in the U.S. By my count, it took him three minutes to shift the discussion from argumentative to instructive. He ended the conversation by recommending some of his recently published research papers, and the HSUS man respectfully said, "Thank you."

When asked if he was worried about the controversy raging in Princeton before his arrival, DeNicola shook his head and said, "The animal rights activists are repressed by me, because when I'm present, they can't muddle the facts. And I know the plaid-shirt-wearing rural crowd just as well—I am a passionate bowhunter. But they're out of touch. Hunters don't know how to speak to the urban lot."

So now he was headed for a conflict fought over an animal high on the cute scale that had become high on the nuisance scale, in a town more known for its Ivy League liberalism than its troubles with the local wildlife.

On January 24, DeNicola sent one of the five members of his team to Princeton to begin the prep work. He arrived later to visit landowners and oversee the operation. But as DeNicola knocked on the doors of residents Mayor Marchand thought were supportive of the project, the opposition was getting sour: the Mercer County Deer Alliance had tried to stop the sharpshoot in court the previous month, but had lost. The town council passed an ordinance making it illegal to feed the deer, and a game warden was now flying a helicopter (usually reserved for spotting marijuana gardens), searching for residents who were still feeding deer.

DeNicola's mission was to find safe shooting sites—areas with a secure backdrop that could preferably be hunted from above (from tree stands or even back porches). In this way, any shot that might pass through or miss an animal would safely hit the ground. DeNicola and his team members were also scouting public parks, taking note of when and where people walked their dogs, jogged and hung out, because DeNicola's White Buffalo team does everything possible to work around people's schedules.

After picking stand locations, DeNicola's team started putting out piles of corn to attract deer. They also started communicating with the Princeton police department, aligning their schedule with local meat processors, and arranging a way for the meat to be donated to a "Hunters for the Hungry" program (DeNicola always donates all meat harvested, which, says Marchand, swayed most of his opponents). This is all standard procedure for DeNicola's team. They do four or five major projects every winter, as well as half a dozen smaller shoots. Last year, during the four months of winter, each member of the team averaged 117 working hours per week.

Then the opposition began to get desperate.

Herb Greenberg, a local resident who opposed the shoot, offered $1,000 to all landowners who rescinded permission for the sharpshooters to shoot on their property (of the twenty-four residences working in cooperation with DeNicola, none accepted the offer). The Mercer County Deer Alliance was planning candlelight vigils and demonstrations. And despite fines, some people were still feeding deer in an effort to draw them away from DeNicola's baits.

A Fact the Media Won't Tell You

The U.S. isn't the only country that has trouble managing its wildlife because it's not politically correct to do so. According to an article by Reuters, in 2006 Italy's Piedmont Hunters Association went on strike because its deer cull had been portrayed "as an illegal massacre of young deer, artfully called Bambi, with the only objective of making hunters look like savages and cruel individuals." Italian hunters were supposed to cull as many as 50,000 deer to reduce crop damage and auto-deer collisions in 2006. Meanwhile, in October 2006 Japanese newspaper *Asahi* reported that the number of hunters is decreasing in Hokkaido (Japan's northern island), which is creating an environmental catastrophe because of escalating damage to crops and timber by a growing population of shika deer. In the 1970s there were about 20,000 hunters on the island but in 2006 there were only 9,463. In 2006 there were about 180,000 shika deer on the island and hunters were killing about 50,000 per year.

On the afternoon of February 15, DeNicola quietly gathered his team in Princeton. Making his last preparations, he chose his firearms. (He says he chooses from eleven different "weapons systems" that vary from dart guns to .30-caliber rifles). He prefers to use a light-caliber .223 equipped with a suppressor (silencer), but in some situations even lighter cartridges, such as a .22 rimfire, are necessary—safety is his first concern. In this case, the .223 was the right choice.

Though he prefers to work on private property, where trespass can be controlled, in Princeton he found he had to work to a bit on public grounds—he would save them for last.

That's when the ruckus started.

On February 17, the day the shoot was to begin, 150 protesters marched through town brandishing signs with slogans like "Hired Guns out of Princeton" and "Princeton Slaughters Wildlife."

While the protesters clamored in the streets, the shoot began with the quiet "thwack" of a suppressed .223 rifle. And so it went from February 17–26, when 203 deer had been culled from the herd of 1,600 (the plan was to continue the project over a few years until the herd had been cut to less that 400). DeNicola's team was fast approaching that season's goal of 300 with little trouble because the opposition couldn't pin them down.

On the night of February 26, one hour before the Princeton Township Committee was to hold its weekly meeting, one hundred protesters held a candlelight vigil and then flooded the meeting. Herb Greenberg appealed for a two-month moratorium for more research (because shoots must take place in winter, the moratorium would have meant a delay of one year). But Mayor Marchand would have none of it. The shoot would continue.

Even while protesters were making speeches and lighting candles, DeNicola and two of his team members were looking through infrared scopes and culling deer. Head shots are used because they mean instant death (deer shot in the heart or lung can run fifty yards or more, which would spook other deer). The dominant animals are taken first. This leaves the subordinate deer unsure without a leader. Also, if a large group of deer comes in to the bait, DeNicola doesn't shoot, because he can't get them all, and he doesn't want to educate any of them. (DeNicola claims he kills 90 percent of the deer that come to his baits.)

Trouble started the next night when a board with eight-inch nails pounded through it punctured one of the tires on DeNicola's truck. The board had been hidden under the leaves on a park road—a road that joggers use regularly. Then he knew something was awry: many of the deer in the park stopped coming to his bait. DeNicola went on a scouting mission to find out why the deer weren't coming to his bait. It didn't take him long to find a pile of corn that had been dumped on the park grounds to draw the deer away from his ambush site. Looking at the lay of the land, DeNicola found that it was a safe place to shoot, and so he set up his tree stand on the site. Later that night he shot twelve deer over the pile and finished his project with a total of 322 whitetails killed.

His work complete, DeNicola returned to his hotel, where he found a man waiting for him—seventy-year-old Princeton resident S. Leonard DiDonato.[12] DeNicola, who had been physically threatened by opponents of his service before, was ready for anything. They stood eyeing one another, then DiDonato held out his hand and introduced himself. DeNicola relaxed. DiDonato was a hunter. He'd fought the town twenty years before when Princeton passed an ordinance stopping hunting in the township. Now he wanted to meet the man who'd come to clean up the mess the town had made by banning hunting.

DiDonato sought out DeNicola for a reason: he was writing a report for his hunting club titled "Anti-Hunters Create Wildlife Tragedy." In the report's twenty-two pages he detailed the progression from when the township stopped hunting to its current situation. He told DeNicola about a nearby park called Baldpate Mountain, an area that the state recently opened to hunting to control the deer population. He explained that hunters had reduced the deer population there and that they had paid for the privilege—that the state didn't have to pay $90,000 for them to remove those deer.

DeNicola sighed. He'd heard this before. He was in Princeton because the residents didn't want to deal with reality. They wanted him to quietly—at night with a silenced firearm—kill the deer. They didn't want men like DiDonato bowhunting behind their homes. They didn't want to see deer on car tops or hunters coming and going.

The next day Mayor Marchand called the shoot "very successful." But DeNicola had already left town. He'd gone directly to New Jersey's Delaware Township, where another member of his team had been scouting the land and putting out piles of corn. Protests were planned.

But it wasn't over in Princeton. DeNicola would be back the next year and the next. Deer management can never stop, because deer never stop breeding. Deer need to be hunted, whether at night with a silenced rifle or in daylight by bowhunters.

Part II

HUNTING AS CONSERVATION

Chapter 6

HUNTING'S REFORMATION

A century and a half before Lewis and Clark reached the Pacific, the first hunting season in North America was established in 1646 in Portsmouth, Rhode Island, when the town decreed: "There shall be noe shootinge of deere from the first of May till the first of November; and if any shall shoot a deere within that time he shall forfeit five pounds."[1]

The ruling was something of a precedent. By the mid-1700s most of the colonies had established deer-hunting seasons or restricted the export of deerskins. Most colonies set seasons but not bag limits, and a few outlawed only certain hunting methods—for example, Maryland outlawed only hunting by firelight. Inadequate hunting restrictions, the need for meat, the money that could be earned from hides, and a lack of enforcement (for example, Connecticut, like other colonies, enacted a deer season in 1698 but didn't hire a game warden until 1866) combined to annihilate wildlife populations in North America, so much so that in 1705 the Rhode Island General Assembly noted that "great quantities of deer hath been destroyed...out of season, either for skin or flesh, without profit, and may prove much to the damage [not only] of this colony for the future...[but] to the whole country, if not prevented." The slaughter of America's wild game wouldn't be prevented.

Guess what?

- Hunter-founded conservation groups are primarily responsible for bringing back American wildlife that was nearly extinct in the last century.

- President Theodore Roosevelt, a passionate hunter, created five national parks, four big-game refuges, fifty-one national bird reservations, and the National Forest Service.

A naïve beginning

Records show that North Carolina shipped an average of 50,250 deerskins overseas per year between 1698 and 1715. It was the same all over the colonies. The records of the British Customs Service in Savannah, Georgia, show that between 1755 and 1773, about 2.6 million pounds of deerskins (from about 600,000 whitetails) were shipped overseas, mostly to English tanneries.[2] The slaughter of the continent's deer herds happened so quickly that in the early nineteenth century Daniel Boone lamented to John James Audubon that in the Green River region of Kentucky about thirty years earlier (in the 1780s), "you would not have walked out in any direction for more than a mile without shooting a buck."

Despite such early realizations, few people thought deer could be exterminated from much of the country; after all, the frontier went west into the unknown as far as the colonists could speculate. People needed meat and saw little reason why the endless forest couldn't keep providing; for example, in 1879, Maxwell House, a restaurant in Nashville, Tennessee, listed "Legs of Young Rabbits," "Domestic Duck, with Jelly," and "Kentucky 'Coon" on its menu, and no patron thought the selections daring. Wild game was listed on restaurant menus across the country until federal regulations in the early twentieth century halted market hunting.

While populations of woodland bison, elk, and whitetail deer were being eradicated along an expanding frontier, bounties were placed on wolves, cougars, and bears in early colonial America. The Massachusetts Bay Colony established the first wolf bounty in 1630 and other colonies were quick to follow. In 1644 any Massachusetts Native American could get three quarts of wine or a bushel of corn for one dead wolf.

These bounties continued for centuries until two of the most widely distributed large carnivores in the world, wolves and cougars, were nearly eradicated from the U.S. By 1840 wolves had been exterminated from the eastern United States, much of the Midwest, and could no longer be found in the southern portion of Michigan's Lower Peninsula; by 1910 they had completely disappeared from the Lower Peninsula. And by 1960, when the Michigan-paid bounty on wolves was repealed, they had nearly vanished from the Upper Peninsula.[3]

Further west, in Montana, one of the last places in the lower forty-eight states to have wild wolf populations before their reintroduction in 1995, a territorial bounty on wolves and cougars was enacted in 1883. That law

Myth Debunked

Humans are a natural part of the ecosystem. Why does the mainstream media laud Native Americans for having a symbiotic connection with nature, while so often portraying today's hunters as slayers of nature? After all, Native Americans have affected the ecosystems in North America for more than ten thousand years. Iroquois used controlled burns to clear vegetation because they knew wildlife numbers would increase when the cleared land sprouted new growth. The Cheyenne hunted their bison by means of "buffalo jumps"; they would drive whole herds of buffalo off blind cliffs. Various tribes farmed land all over North America, digging bear traps, setting snares, and otherwise affecting wildlife habitat and populations. In fact many tribes, including the Iroquois, market hunted deer without limits and sold the skins to the colonists—a practice that greatly depleted the deer herds before pioneers hunted those forests. New Jersey even passed a law in 1679 that prohibited the export of deer killed by Native Americans.

In contrast, today's wildlife biologists determine bag limits and set seasons based on specific needs of individual wildlife populations and ecosystems in order to manage, or micromanage, wildlife populations and habitat. So humans have had fundamental influences on wildlife and habitat in North America for more than ten thousand years and today are managing wildlife more scientifically than ever before, yet many people approve of Native Americans hunting, but not today's sportsmen.

was repealed in 1887, but a new bounty program was reinstated in 1891. By 1930, wolves were eradicated from Montana, and few cougars remained. The number of payments for wolves declined from a high of 4,116 in 1903 to zero by 1928. The number of cougar pelts in Montana declined from 177 in 1908 to two in 1930. In 1913, Wyoming took it to another level: the state passed a law stipulating that any person freeing a wolf from a trap would be fined $300.[4]

Bounties on wolves continued in some states until Congress passed the Endangered Species Act in 1973. At that time wolves no longer howled in most of the continental U.S., cougars were hunting only in the West's most remote areas, black bears inhabited only a minuscule percentage of their former range, and the grizzly had been killed out of California, Colorado, and all but a few areas in the West.

In just a few heroic, naïve centuries Americans accomplished what it took Europeans millennia to achieve: they felled a continent's forests, dammed its rivers, market hunted its bountiful bison, whitetail deer, and elk to scarcity, used punt guns to blast down its vast flocks of waterfowl, and thereby slaughtered North America's wildlife from sea to shining sea.

The overharvest of America's wild game happened in the blink of a historian's eye. Lewis and Clark sailed up the Missouri from near Saint Louis in 1804 to explore the wild lands and find a water route to the Pacific. Just thirty years later, in 1834, the American Fur Company would go bankrupt because of changing fashions and because the beaver would be nearly trapped out of the West. And all along, despite the wasteland

---

A Fact the Media Won't Tell You

Americans eat a lot of wild game. Americans consume more than 750 million pounds of wild game annually, an amount of meat that is equal to about two million slaughtered cattle.

"The hunter in conservation," a booklet compiled by the Council for Wildlife Conservation and Education, Inc.

in their wake, Americans gloriously reckoned that the subjugation of their continent's nature was their Manifest Destiny.

The resurrection of America's wildlife

Then, in the aftermath of centuries of unrestrained hunting, Americans stopped and gasped. By 1908 the American bison, which had swarmed over the Great Plains in unfathomable numbers, had been reduced in the U.S. to twenty-two overlooked animals in Yellowstone National Park. Relentless market hunting had driven whitetail deer populations down to 350,000 to 500,000 nationwide by 1900 (in 2007, there are more than thirty million). Moose in the eastern U.S. were just holding on in remote areas in northern New York and New England. Large predators, with the exception of a few black bears, had been exterminated from the eastern U.S. and were disappearing from the West. The Eastern bison was long gone and elk and antelope were just holding on.[5]

Then Congress passed the Lacey Act of 1900, prohibiting the interstate traffic of wild game taken in violation of state law; as a result, market hunting of deer and other big-game animals for commercial gain was finally stopped. However, it would take eighteen more years for market hunting of waterfowl to be halted.

Nineteenth-century waterfowl hunting was disastrously wasteful. For example, in 1821, nearly a century before federal protection of waterfowl would be passed, John James Audubon, a hunter and wildlife artist whose name was commemorated with the founding of the Audubon Society in 1886, described a shoot at Louisiana's Lake St. John:

The gunners had assembled early in the morning.... [S]tationed at equal distances they sat on the ground. When a flock approached every individual whistled in imitation of the plover's call-note, on which the birds descended.... Every gun went off in succession. . . . This sport continued all day and at sunset I calculated 48,000 plovers would have fallen that day. It may well be that this one day of annihilation permanently impaired the species.[6]

From the Saint Lawrence to Louisiana's marshes to every pothole in the Midwest, market hunters gunned down waterfowl with shocking success. Consider Atley Langford's hunting prowess. Langford was a market hunter on Chesapeake Bay. During the fall and winter his records show that he killed an average of two hundred ducks and/or geese per day—all his boat could carry. Indeed, he gunned down about ten thousand ducks and geese a year from 1900 to 1918. And he was just one market hunter. It is impossible to know how many such hunters there were because most areas didn't require licensing or any type of registration. Often, groups of boats would go out together and surround flocks. They preferred to shoot them on the water where their (often homemade) punt guns (small cannons) could spray resting flocks with lead shot.

Langford stopped only when the Federal Migratory Bird Treaty Act of 1918 was passed by Congress, making it unlawful to take, possess, buy, sell, purchase, or barter any migratory bird, including feathers, parts, nests, or eggs. The law ended market hunting of waterfowl. But the most remarkable thing is what happened next. After the federal law outlawed his occupation, Langford began working with wildlife authorities to catch the market hunters who refused to stop. Instead of slaughtering game, Langford began working to protect the critical areas waterfowl needed.[7]

It was the same all over the country. In the end, those who once wantonly killed game without limits were often the same individuals who worked to restore game populations. Many, it seems, simply needed to comprehend the consequences of their actions. Their love for the wildlife they hunted inspired them to change. President Theodore Roosevelt was one such hunter. He traveled to the West's hinterlands in search of fast-disappearing mountain lion and elk, but then during his presidency (1901–1909) became America's most famous conservationist by creating five national parks, four big-game refuges, fifty-one national bird reservations, and the National Forest Service.

J. A. McGuire, the founder and first editor of *Outdoor Life* magazine, a hunting magazine first published in Denver in 1898, had a similar story. McGuire printed grizzly hunting articles in the magazine's first issues and had a line drawing of a grizzly on the magazine's cover throughout 1899 and 1900. The bear was his favorite animal to hunt. But just a few years after his magazine's launch, he began to use the magazine to champion grizzly conservation. They were disappearing fast, he noted. Hunters had to do something about it, or no one would. In fact, his conviction that the grizzly needed to be managed with regulated hunting, not shot into extinction, drove him in September 1915 to write a bill that would be introduced in state assemblies all over the West, setting limits on the number of bears that could be killed.

Hunters were coming to the conclusion that America's wild resources were not inexhaustible. They were becoming protectors and managers of wildlife.

A Fact the Media Won't Tell You

Modern hunters in the U.S. have never caused a wildlife species to become extinct, endangered, or even threatened. In fact, every game species that is hunted in the U.S. has increased in number.

"The Hunter in Conservation," Council for Wildlife Conservation and Education.

The modern hunter-conservationist

Today's hunter-conservationist rose from the ashes of free-for-all hunting in the early twentieth century, a time when the nation's wildlife resources had been so completely destroyed that market hunting was already drying up on its own—there just wasn't much wildlife left to slaughter.

Congress passed the Pittman-Robertson Act in 1937, which taxed hunting-related sporting goods 10 percent on the manufacturer and 10 percent on the consumer. Money raised from this tax—and from the Dingell-Johnson Act, a similar tax on fishing equipment passed in 1950—passed through the U.S. Fish and Wildlife Service's Federal Aid Program to state fish and wildlife agencies to support conservation and education programs. The archery community entered the picture in 1972 with the passage of the Dingell-Goodling Bill, specifying an 11 percent excise tax on archery equipment.

With these funds and with revenue from hunting license fees, state wildlife departments began preserving land and devising ways to bring whitetail deer, wild turkey, and other wildlife populations back to every forest and field in America. In 1900 only a few states had established any kind of official conservation organization. Today, all fifty states have wildlife conservation agencies, financed primarily by hunters and anglers, for the protection and management of wildlife.

Thus *Outdoor Life* magazine may have been late to the game in 1947 when it devised and printed its "Conservation Pledge" for hunters, which reads, "I pledge to protect and conserve the natural resources of America. I promise to educate future generations so they may become caretakers of our water, air, land and wildlife." (It's an interesting footnote to this event

A Fact the Media Won't Tell You

Hunters feed the hungry. From 1997 to 2004 Farmers and Hunters Feeding the Hungry, which is just one of many such groups, processed 1,600 tons (nearly 12,800,000 servings) of venison and other big game for soup kitchens and food pantries across America.

that Rachel Carson, author of *Silent Spring*, the inspiration for Earth Day and the most venerated saint in the Church of Liberal Environmentalists, came in second in the contest to write *Outdoor Life's* Conservation Pledge.) The timing of the pledge's conception was apt, as a change of consciousness regarding the natural world had arrived. Conserving wild lands and the animals they shelter—a foreign idea for hunters in the nineteenth century—became a widespread concern in a matter of decades. For example, it became fashionable in the 1940s for duck hunters to buy more than one duck stamp, because the money went to conserving wetlands.

Hunters, now infused with concern for the wild, founded groups such as Ducks Unlimited, Delta Waterfowl, and other hunter-conservation organizations, and have since worked with the U.S. Fish and Wildlife Service to bring waterfowl back to numbers the U.S. hasn't seen since before market hunting. White geese (or snow geese) populations grew so much that the U.S. Fish and Wildlife Service had to declare a state of emergency in the late 1990s because the glut of white geese were beginning to ruin their arctic breeding grounds; as a result, hunting seasons were lengthened and some rules changed to allow hunters to kill more geese and to thereby reduce populations. Hunters have since done just that and the catastrophe has been averted.

All of America's wildlife benefited from this new conservation ethic. As recently as 1900, the total whitetail deer population of North America was an estimated 350,000 to 500,000, according to a study by the U.S. Biological Survey. At that time nearly every state in the nation had closed its deer-hunting season, and a good number of states need not have bothered. Massachusetts counted about two hundred, all on Cape Cod. New York claimed about seven thousand in the Adirondacks, and Pennsylvania had a small herd centered in Potter County. In Delaware and New Jersey, deer were considered to be extinct.[8]

Wildlife biologists spent the next half century trapping and transferring the remaining wild deer to areas that no longer had deer. For example, in 1939 Mississippi was left with fewer than five thousand deer statewide, but by the early 1950s, as a result of hunter-funded trap-and-transfer programs, there were about fifty thousand deer in the state. Today there are an estimated 1.5 million deer in Mississippi. The same progression took place all over the U.S., and as a result, by the early 1960s, every state allowed some form of regulated deer hunting. Currently, the white-tail deer population in the U.S. is estimated to be more than thirty million. Many of the highest concentrations are found in Midwestern farming states and along the East Coast, areas that were once completely devoid of deer. Today, in many urban areas where hunters often aren't allowed to control herds, expanding deer populations are causing hundreds of thousands of deer-auto collisions annually, an increasing number of Lyme disease infections (caused by deer-carried infected ticks), and extensive damage to farms and gardens.

In the 1920s the wild turkey was at the brink of extinction, with only about thirty thousand left across the country, says Dr. James Earl Kennamer, a National Wild Turkey Federation (NWTF) biologist. By 1813 turkeys had been wiped out of Connecticut, by 1880 Ohio didn't have any left, and by 1907 Iowa was without wild turkeys. The wild turkey has since been restored to healthy populations in every state but Alaska, where it is not native. Wildlife biologists tried releasing penned birds in the 1930s and 1940s, but the birds weren't wild enough to survive. After a lot of hunter-funded research, biologists perfected trap-and-transfer techniques. They then used rocket-propelled nets to capture wild turkeys in areas where the birds had held on, and released them in areas where they'd been killed out.

When the NWTF was founded in 1973, hunter-funded conservation had already increased the wild turkey's nationwide population to 1.3 million; since then, the number of wild turkeys has increased to more than 7 million birds nationwide. And the NWTF, a nonprofit conservation organization dedicated to conserving wild turkeys and preserving hunting traditions, has grown from 1,300 members in 1973 to 545,500 hunters today.

The story is the same with many other wildlife populations. In 1920, the total U.S. population of pronghorn antelope was about twelve thousand. Today there are more than one million. In 1900, there were about forty thousand elk left in the U.S., mostly concentrated in and around Yellowstone National Park (elk had once lived from the Atlantic to the Pacific). Today there are some 1.2 million Rocky Mountain elk in the U.S. Regulated hunting seasons and land protection saved the elk from extermination in the West, and today there are also growing elk herds in Arkansas, Michigan, Tennessee, and Pennsylvania. Since 1984, the Rocky Mountain Elk Foundation, a hunter-funded conservation group with more than 100,000 members, has permanently protected more than 1,000 square miles of critical elk habitat and improved another 3.5 million acres of elk country. The great majority of this land is now open to the public.

Now the wolf and the grizzly are making comebacks in Western states, and game department biologists are calling for open seasons so they can control these predator populations. Elk are overpopulated in Colorado, wild pigs are causing problems in California, Texas, and all over the South, alligators are growing to monster size in canals behind people's homes in Florida, black bears are showing up in downtown Newark, New Jersey, and whitetail deer are over-browsing eastern forests. All over the country wildlife populations are busting at the seams of suburbia.

Mainstream news outlets answer the daily conflicts between suburban homeowners and wildlife with the excuse "it's our fault, we're moving into their habitat." But the real, politically incorrect answer to these conflicts is that wildlife is moving into and reclaiming habitat it was killed out of a century or more ago; as a result, hunters are needed now more than ever to control wildlife populations.

Chapter 7

HUNTING IS BETTER THAN BIRTH CONTROL

There is an urban legend that turned out to be true about an old ambulance converted into a "mobile deer-spaying unit." The ambulance was wheeled around the wealthy, urban community of Highland Park, Illinois, by a team of "deer doctors" and animal rights activists searching for whitetail deer. When they found one, went the plan, they'd dart it with a tranquilizer, drag it into the ambulance, and spay or neuter the thing.

The effort was run by researchers from the University of Wisconsin–Madison and paid for by the good taxpayers in the city of Highland Park.[1] When the darting plan didn't work as planned, the team shifted tactics: they would bait deer with apples and other produce, trap them in nets, and use stretchers to tote them into the waiting ambulance, where the deer would promptly undergo surgery.

Hunting magazines and outdoor radio shows made fun of the effort with such glee that the ambulance became a symbol for foolhardy ways of controlling deer populations. And indeed, the ambulance admitted only a few patients before the mad effort was ditched. The cost per deer must have been outrageous.

Guess what?

- Deer birth control methods are prohibitively expensive, and still aren't proven to be very effective.

- Volunteer hunting groups have sprung up in several states to help control deer populations—for free.

Birth control for deer?

Unfortunately, non-lethal deer control isn't just a comical rogue effort; years have already been invested and budgets stretched well into six figures to try to control deer without shooting them.

The biggest effort to control a whitetail deer population with a birth control drug occurred on New York's Fire Island, where deer were eating themselves out of favor. A half-dozen scientists, along with dozens of volunteers, spent years trying to control Fire Island's runaway deer population with non-lethal control. But it was all going to be worth it, said the Humane Society of the United States (HSUS), because in the end the research would prove to the world that it doesn't take hunters to control deer populations.

HSUS is a national organization with a staff of about 250 and a claimed membership of around one million. It is the largest anti-hunting group in the U.S. and, despite its name, does not run animal shelters. It's an animal activist organization. Its literature describes lethal controls for deer as "irresponsible," making the group's agenda clear. But could this wealthy nonprofit organization find a way to control deer without hunters?

To achieve this goal, HSUS needed to prove it could control a wild, free-roaming deer population with immunocontraception (birth control). So its first step was to find a test area it could control. It settled on Fire Island, a thirty-two-mile-long and half-mile-wide barrier island near the south shore of Long Island, New York. It was a test model where most of the island's four thousand homeowners are affluent New Yorkers who use their island homes as weekend getaways. Fire Island's overpopulated deer herd was growing so large it was running out of food. The National Park Service, which owns one-third of the island, even let HSUS scientists use its parklands—HSUS couldn't have asked for more.

Next HSUS needed to prove that its sterilization drug could handle the job. The society used a drug called porcine zona pellucida (PZP), a natural protein derived from pigs that allows boar sperm to attach to a sow's ova. When injected into females of other mammal species, PZP elicits antibodies against that animal's sperm-recognition protein, thereby stopping sperm from entering the egg.

The Humane Society got control of the drug when Dr. J. F. Kirkpatrick, a scientist at ZooMontana's Science and Conservation Center in Billings, Montana (which is partially funded by HSUS), signed an investigational new animal drug document for PZP over to HSUS. This document, issued by the Food and Drug Administration, is important because without it, no person or organization can use the drug—unless, of course, HSUS signs on.

Dr. Kirkpatrick's employer, ZooMontana, was the only major producer of PZP. Its freezers were stuffed with pig ovaries from Iowa's slaughterhouses (yes, HSUS would sterilize deer with the help of slaughtered pigs). Its technicians began working year-round drawing PZP from sows' eggs. However, PZP is not perfect. It seemed like a miracle drug at first, because it will sterilize any mammal—human, goat, you name it—but its equal-opportunity nature makes it dangerous. You can't just leave it on baits for deer to ingest, because other animals might also eat the baits and ingest the drug. Scientists are not even sure whether humans would be affected if they were to consume the flesh of a PZP-treated deer. Because of this, Dr. J. Russell Mason, a biologist with the USDA's National Wildlife Research Center in Logan, Utah, argues, "What pharmaceutical company would make such a lawsuit-luring monster?"[2] This is the main reason PZP continues to be listed by the FDA as an "experimental" drug.

Still, Dr. Allen Rutburg, who was a professor at Tufts University and a member of HSUS's technical staff, said in 2000, "We do plan to gain FDA approval for the drug. One day we hope the drug will be used widely across the country instead of hunting."[3]

With this goal in mind, the researchers on Fire Island moved ahead to prove that PZP could be used to curb wild, free-roaming deer populations.

What they needed were numbers to support their hypothesis. The methodology, technological advances, and FDA approval would, they hoped, materialize along the way.

Excitement was high on Fire Island when Dr. Kirkpatrick arrived in 1993 to help start the study. He found himself rubbing shoulders with Calvin Klein, Geraldine Ferraro, and other rich and famous Fire Island homeowners who were footing much of the bill for the project. Several members of HSUS, along with employees from the Fire Island National Seashore, darted seventy-four deer. Darting the does, however, wasn't as easy as they had expected.

They started out using Pneu-Dart guns loaded to shoot darts filled with PZP. These guns (the manufacturers call them "projectors") have one problem: powered by air and not gunpowder, they have a trajectory like a rainbow. The $500-plus air guns weren't doing the trick, and so HSUS started exploring other options (the project sponsors always explained that part of the goal was to find and fix the problems before the project's end—which at the current pace might never arrive). Next, researchers tried blowguns, which are easier to use and much cheaper than dart guns. But their trajectory is even worse than that of the "projectors." On the other hand, they're a lot of fun to play with.

A Fact the Media Won't Tell You

Deer birth control is outrageously expensive. It costs $500 to $1,000 per deer, according the USDA's Animal and Plant Health Inspection Service.

"Birth control for deer: questions and answers," USDA.

Finally, they gave bio-bullets a try. The concept is simple: an air gun is used to send a bio-bullet (a time-release capsule filled with PZP) into the muscle in a deer's hindquarters. The capsule is absorbed into the deer's system over several months, slowly releasing the drug. This is a good idea because PZP-loaded darts don't always sterilize a deer. Sometimes a dart will sterilize a deer for several years and sometimes it won't—a fact that forced HSUS to dart deer twice a year.

The bio-bullet idea is brilliant, but the reality is a little bit disappointing. According to H. Brian Underwood, a research wildlife ecologist with the Biological Resources Division of the U.S. Geological Survey, no one is making bio-bullets right now.[4] It seems that there are too many problems with them. For example, finding the correct amount of air pressure is difficult: too much pressure and the bullet will kill the deer, too little and the bullet simply bounces off. This is doubly difficult because bio-bullets are so light they lose velocity quickly, and there's just no telling where a deer will show up, which makes it hard to choose the correct air pressure ahead of time. (The Humane Society did not give up on bio-bullets, however. It began trying a different approach: researchers stuck a small capsule on the tips of darts and then began shooting deer with them. This method has not yet proven successful.) The HSUS has found that as promising as baiting and darting deer sounds, it isn't practical. A digestible, orally administered drug would be less time-consuming. The Humane Society considered using RU-486 (the abortion pill now approved in the U.S.) to sterilize the deer, but public disapproval has kept HSUS from trying it.

According to Dr. Michael Holland, an Australian biologist who has worked with the USDA Predator Ecology Center in Logan, Utah, another option may be to isolate the gene in PZP that is sterilizing the animals and purify it.[5] DNA technology could conceivably be used to clone that gene, and it would then be theoretically possible to make a commercial vaccine that is species-specific. The vaccine could be put into baits or dropped from planes, much like rabies vaccines are scattered for coyotes. Dr. Holland says, "It would take millions of dollars and several years of work. And then you'd still have to start the long drug-approval process. But it could be done."

Things begin to get pretty sci-fi after that. For example, there are immunocontraceptives being developed in many countries for many species (humans included) that could one day be used on deer. Scientists are working on vaccines that inhibit brain reproductive hormones, pituitary hormones, and steroid reproductive hormones. But the award for the most innovative approach goes to Australia, where, according to Dr. Holland, scientists spliced a gene for a contraceptive antigen to a virus. The virus was then set loose. In the wild it passed from rabbit to rabbit, sterilizing them as it went. Now, of course, come the "what ifs?" such as, what if it mutates, and humans catch it? Dr. Rutburg said this scares HSUS too much to try.

Ecologist H. Brian Underwood said, "I've found out a few things they're [HSUS] not going to like. There are side effects to PZP. For example, in a treated herd the rut lasts seven months a year as does come into estrus [heat] again and again. But on the upside, PZP-treated does tend to be larger and healthier because they don't have fawns to feed. As for the bucks, the only problem is that the males may wear themselves down trying to breed the infertile does to the point that a tough winter will kill them."

The costs for the project have been as difficult to tally as the facts of this study, and so the per-deer cost of immunocontraception is unclear. But we do know that Anthony DeNicola, owner of White Buffalo, the most renowned deer control company in the country, charges between $500 and $1,000 per deer to treat urban deer herds with contraception such as SpayVac, a new drug that has not yet proven to be effective on a large, free-roaming herd. There are approximately thirty million whitetail deer in North America, according to the Quality Deer Management Association. Hunters in Pennsylvania alone kill about 500,000 deer per year. So, at a median $750 a pop, it would cost $375 million annually to do the job Pennsylvania's hunters are doing—and hunters *pay* to hunt deer. Figures like these leave no doubt that the quickest and most cost-efficient deer birth-control system wears orange.

However, when asked about Fire Island whitetail population numbers, Underwood gave it a positive spin: "There are five separate populations being darted on the island. Of these, one appears to be going down. Though this is a failure if you look at it as a population-reduction study, it has been a success from a research standpoint—we know much more now about PZP than we did." Similarly, Mariah Carey's acting career was a success—we know a lot more about bad movies and unskilled actresses than we did before.

Dr. Mason was more decisive. He said, "In eight years, with a controlled study and tons of volunteers working with a deer herd that was virtually all known on a first-name basis, they [HSUS] couldn't pull it off."

But while it is clear that HSUS does not yet have the technology to control a wild, free-roaming deer population, Dr. Kirkpatrick, who is a hunter, argued that we need to let them keep trying: "State-sponsored hunts in the suburbs can do more to fuel anti-hunting sentiment than all the rhetoric from anti-hunting groups combined; as a result, hunters should stay out of the urban deer struggle. The Humane Society will find a non-lethal solution."

Dr. Mason saw things differently. He said, "Hunters are the most effective management tool for controlling whitetail populations. Despite what HSUS says, right now deer contraception is up in the clouds somewhere."

DeNicola summed up the state of urban deer management with his typically authoritative candor: "HSUS is an agenda group; they'll do what it takes to accomplish their agenda. What HSUS is good at is dealing with the press and with suburbanites, which is exactly where hunters typically fail. But if hunters could get together behind a scientifically sound national organization that would hook communities up with responsible hunters, then I would be getting a lot less business sharpshooting whitetails."[6]

A cost-effective solution

I saw a group that might just fit DeNicola's description when I went to suburban Virginia and stood in the pre-dawn, viewing a scene that seemed wildly out of place. An army of bowhunters stood before sunrise on a construction site, with bulldozers and model homes silhouetted behind them. Hunters gather every fall in small towns across rural America, but this was suburbia.

Yet there they were, bathed in the headlights of a dozen pickups not thirty minutes from where George W. was probably still fast asleep, chatting in terse whispers over the background noise of barking dogs and bustling autos trying to beat the morning rush hour. One hunter, pulling a camo jumpsuit over a polo shirt, gushed, "Did you see all the deer by the road on the way in? The area's still loaded."

Another, busy swapping street shoes for hunting boots, answered, "Yeah, we have a lot of work to do."

Work? Yep. Maybe the finest bit of volunteer work there is, or so Eric Huppert, the leader of these troops, would tell you. He says it like he needs to pinch himself occasionally to make sure he's not dreaming. But assembled there were a dozen members of Suburban Whitetail Management of Northern Virginia, Inc. (SWMNV), a squad whose sole mission is to reduce urban populations of whitetail deer. They come at the behest of suburbanites with expensive shrubbery and $40,000 SUVs—homeowners who have gone to the trouble of obtaining special "kill permits" (issued in Northern Virginia with no questions asked) that allow the harvest of as many deer as they—or in this case, obliging bowhunters—can possibly kill.

Oh, they're rough and tough urban warriors, sure enough. There's Steve, an accountant who climbs into a tree stand one hundred-plus days a year; John, a retired U.S. Army colonel who spends his off time twenty feet up a tree and twenty-eight feet from a back porch; Daryl, an electrician who is watched out a back window by two children like he is some new form of reality hunting show; and Bogos, a rental car company employee who is so lethal "he could bag a deer in the Union Station parking garage," says Huppert.

Huppert's dream team has a secondary agenda to thinning deer, and he makes no secret of it. By linking responsible hunters with suburban homeowners, he puts hunters in a positive role, thereby battling the Bambi-killing, sport-hunting-for-the-thrill-of-killing image that anti-hunting groups spread. Which explains why this group of SWMNV members was giddier than a Cub Scout patrol. Not only were they doing what they love; they were doing it for a good cause.

"Imagine people thanking you for doing what they see as a selfless service every time you play a round of golf or fish a local lake," said Huppert, "and you'll know what it's like to be one of us."

Outfitted with handheld radios attached to headsets—like telemarketers gone commando—the hunters began to disperse into a forest that would rumble awake in a few hours as the heavy machinery lying idly about continued to clear 1,200 acres of land for 1,300 homes, a golf course, two schools, and a hospital. The developer sought help because he was afraid that by knocking down the forest he'd chase the area's thousand-plus deer onto nearby highways. And he had no time to spare. The houses, which started at around $600,000, were scheduled for completion within five years, and there were already more applicants than there were homes available.

A few years before, Eric Huppert watched as David Flagler, chief of animal control in Virginia's Fairfax County, was asked to present a solution to the surging deer population. A teacher had been killed when a deer, which had collided with another vehicle, was thrown over a highway divider and crashed through her windshield. The tragedy prompted a public outcry and forced politicians to stop pretending a problem didn't exist. After reviewing his options, Flagler stood in front of the county board and suggested that a crack team of bowhunters be used to cut down the deer population. "Are you serious?" the county's leadership asked. Hunting was not an option.

When Huppert spoke to Flagler, he listened as Flagler described the group of responsible bowhunters he wanted to call to arms. But soon, Flagler, disgusted, gave up on his plan and left the state. Then, one late, sleepless night, Huppert decided that he would create the group himself—county board be damned. He marveled at the idea: a group of bowhunters that would perform a free service and help landowners in three counties in Northern Virginia (Prince William, Loudoun, and Fairfax). Hunters would be in demand.

Huppert quickly decided on five central tenets:

1. The hunters in the group must be insured, so there would be no liability to landowners.

2. The hunters must be proficient marksmen.

3. The hunters must be ethical and accountable.

4. The group must be open to all who qualify.

5. The meat harvested should go to the poor.

Inconceivable is the only word to describe what Huppert did next: he put an ad in a newspaper that urged, "Bowhunters, Volunteer Now!" Soon he began to hear the phone ringing in his sleep and learned to hate the "you've got mail" voice on his computer. Now, just a few years later, the number of rules the one hundred card-carrying SWMNV members have to follow would impress an IRS agent. Each hunter must leave a decal on his vehicle's dash when he's hunting. All arrows must be marked with the member's ID number. Members must take off their camo and stow their bows when they leave the woods and must cover deer that are being transported. The group's bylaws are extensive in order to keep the group's profile low—not because they're doing anything wrong, but because they believe in showing respect for those who don't want to see what must be done.

"I don't know what I would do without them," said Tom Marable, the property superintendent who was in charge of the $50.5 million Loudoun project. "When one of these bulldozers drops a tree, a dozen deer start feeding on it right in front of the bulldozer, which makes it hard to continue work."

Marable planted thousands of dollars of ornamental flowers, but the deer had already eaten them. "They're starving. Look at that browse line," he said, pointing to the forest, which looked like an over-dedicated gardener with a souped-up hedge trimmer had clipped off all the growth below six feet.

"Sharpshooters wanted $400 per head. Multiply that by a thousand and you'll see why we didn't pay up," said Marable. "But these boys are doing it for free. Last year they took about a hundred and fifty deer off this property. This year I hope they'll—"

A red SUV skidded to a stop, breaking the conversation and throwing a cloud of dust over the hunters. An agitated real-estate agent was at the wheel angrily screaming into her cell phone: "There are hunters here! There's a bunch of guys in camo right on the site!" But then she eyed Marable, who was waving her off like an angry cop at a busy intersection. She dropped the phone and made a speedy retreat. A few of the hunters were left rubbing dust out of their eyes and shrugging their shoulders.

Marable bemoaned, "Some people just can't see the natural disaster right in front of their noses." The angry agent, like the protesters in Princeton, New Jersey, was just another person who benefited from hunting while holding it in disdain.

More and more people are starting to understand what's going on. All the bowhunters build relationships with the property owners they help. As a result, hunters are suddenly both amenable and accountable. If a homeowner has a problem, he or she can call one of the group's leaders.

The hunters' valuable service, in turn, gets related over fences in subdivisions everywhere they've gone. Sam Rotolo, who uses the group, joked, "That's my house, that's where my garden was before the deer ate it, and that's my Daryl," as he pointed to Daryl Whitt, the SWMNV member thinning out the deer on his property.

Huppert once took his group to a whole new level by boldly setting up a booth at a county fair. He then spent the day with several SWMNV members talking to hundreds of suburbanites. People came and went, and Huppert's pride was growing from the generally warm reception, until he found himself confronted by a woman who sneered, "You're murderers!"

Huppert kept his indignation in check and countered: "Let me explain. Deer are starving to death and people are being killed on the highways when they hit deer that are looking for food." The woman crossed her arms, but she was listening. "Deer contraception is not yet feasible." She still looked like she didn't give a damn, so he dropped the bomb, "And all of the deer we shoot go to feed the hungry."

That's when her arms unclenched and she said, "Really?"

"For most, though," said Huppert, "the problem has to hit them where it hurts, in the cabbage patch. For example, one of the landowners we help has a dozen bunny-hugger bumper stickers pasted on his car. When we first went to his residence to scout it out we saw the stickers and thought we had run smack into an activist. But he surprised us; he pranced out and said, 'I used to hate you guys. I'm a vegetarian. But the deer have eaten enough of my vegetables. I want you to kill them all.'"

Bogos, one of Huppert's hunters, is a native of Somalia. When asked how he learned to clean deer so well, he said, "In my homeland, you can't go to the supermarket. When you want to eat, you grab a goat." He lived up to his lethal reputation. In the early light, when the forest was still a blur of grays and browns, two deer came up from behind his stand and found some limbs Bogos had pruned off while climbing the tree. The famished deer stood there eating every precious leaf. Bogos waited, blinking his eyes until the sun gave sharper contrast to the red-brown deer against the brown-brown forest floor. Then, when one of the does stepped just far enough out, he put an arrow through her heart.

The doe's ribs could be counted in a glance and her stomach was flatter than a greyhound's—there wasn't much meat to donate to the hungry of Northern Virginia. Huppert looked at the deer and sighed. "This is why we're doing this." He made it sound like his group was on a lonely quest, but many similar organizations are forming across the country. In fact, two have already followed Huppert's lead: Suburban Whitetail Management of Northern Georgia and Suburban Whitetail Management of Maryland. And bowhunters are now being utilized in dozens of other urban areas, though these examples are still the exceptions to the rule.

As we drove down one of the capital's four-lane highways, Huppert had something to say but seemed to be searching for words. In the brief silence, I noticed that everywhere I looked another field that had once been a forest was now freshly leveled earth or a new subdivision with all the homes packed like eggs in a carton. And every few miles there was another deer lying by the roadside.

One of the road-killed deer prompted Huppert to summarize what was on his mind: "Picture the day when people can call 1-800-HUNTERS, and a stout-looking fellow—a plumber in camo—comes by to control their populations of deer, or bears, or geese. You see, interest is not our problem. Even the counties are starting to trust us enough to send troubled landowners our way. Within a decade we'll be one thousand strong," he said, sweeping his hand across the front of us. "There's a quiet army out there, restless and eager to mobilize to solve this whitetail overpopulation problem. And they'll fund conservation for the privilege. They won't charge hundreds of dollars per deer to use a non-lethal tactic that likely won't work. Urbanites need hunters! Let us help."

Chapter 8

WHY VEGETARIANS
OWE HUNTERS

Here's an uncomfortable detail for vegetarians who turn their noses up at omnivores: most states have special deer permits that farmers use to kill problem deer. Without these permits and regular hunting seasons, many farmers would be eaten out of business. It's a simple cause-and-effect relationship: when hunting is stopped, wildlife damage to crops increases dramatically. If this were to happen nationally, the cost of produce would skyrocket, which would make it difficult for the poor to afford to eat well-balanced meals. These aren't unsubstantiated viewpoints—wildlife studies prove how much farmers need hunters. The research just isn't politically correct enough for the mainstream media to print. So here's the truth about how hunters help vegetarians.

Guess what?

- Organic farmers need hunters more than traditional farmers.

- If hunting were ended nationally, the costs to taxpayers and consumers would be in the billions because of wildlife damage to crops.

Wildlife damage: The big numbers

Currently wildlife damage to U.S. agriculture is about $944 million per year, according to estimates by Wildlife Services, a division of the U.S. Department of Agriculture. An estimated $750 million of that is attributed to deer.[1] But that number is based only on those who have filed reports with Wildlife Services. No one knows just how bad the problem is nationally, because multiple agencies are involved and because most wildlife damage goes unreported. For example, deer damage to crops was estimated to be $75 million per year in Pennsylvania alone, according to Dennis Wolff, Pennsylvania's state agricultural secretary.[2]

With a healthy food supply—such as the crops that would be your groceries—un-hunted whitetail deer populations increase by 50 percent annually until they overpopulate and destroy their habitat, according to U.S. Department of Agriculture studies. At that rate of growth, it would take just three years before unchecked deer herds would send many small farmers to the unemployment line.

For example, because of reports of escalating deer-caused crop damage, in 1998 the New Jersey Department of Environmental Protection's (NJDEP) Division of Fish, Game and Wildlife initiated a comprehensive, yearlong study to determine the impacts of deer on agriculture in the Garden State.[3] (Yes, New Jersey has more than highways and smokestacks—there are thousands of farmers there, too.) The 2,142 farmers who participated in NJDEP's study said deer were responsible for 70 percent of their wildlife-caused crop losses; 39 percent of the farmers reported that crop losses were so intolerable they were thinking of taking extreme actions if the state didn't do more. They were frustrated because there were between $5 and $10 million in crop losses in New Jersey in 1997. In fact, it was so bad that 25 percent of responding farmers reported that they had to abandon a parcel of tillable ground because of excessive deer damage, and 36 percent of the farmers said they had ceased growing their preferred crops as a result of excessive deer damage. In total, responding New Jersey farmers expended an estimated 67,855 paid labor hours and spent $620,073 to control losses due to deer in 1997.

It's the same in other states. The New York State Department of Environmental Conservation finds that specialty crops such as zucchini, grapes, pears, and cucumbers, which comprise a significant portion of New York's agriculture industry, are particularly at risk for deer damage.

In 1997, New York's market value of specialty crops was $206.9 million for vegetables, $185.1 million for fruit, and $284.7 million for nursery and floriculture crops. In 2001, the state recorded 1,579 complaints of deer damage (an increase from 1,409 complaints in 2000) totaling more than $3.7 million in estimated losses to these specialty crops. This estimate is "very conservative," says the state, because "agricultural damage is often not reported by growers unless a crop depredation permit to kill nuisance wildlife is requested." During 2001, New York State issued 1,430 deer kill permits, resulting in 4,505 deer being taken on these small farms.[4]

In December 2006 the Ohio Farm Bureau Federation, which has 225,000 members (55,000 of whom are farmers), announced it would lobby to cut the state's deer herd in half, from 500,000 deer to 250,000, because of severe damage to crops. Keith Stimpert, the bureau's senior vice president of public policy, said the federation would push legislators to liberalize hunting seasons and crop depredation permits even further to achieve this goal. When Dave Risley, Ohio's wildlife division's executive administrator of wildlife management and research, heard about the proposal he commented, "I have met with farmers, and they sometimes have severe damage." However, Risely wasn't sure hunters could reduce the deer herd that substantially, because they already kill about 200,000 deer annually.[5] Not long after announcing its move, the Ohio Farm Bureau Federation withdrew its plan; it wasn't considered feasible.

Myth Debunked

Every cabbage, carrot, and apple we eat is raised by farmers who kill deer, rabbits, or rodents that would eat them out of business if left unchecked. So vegetarians shouldn't feel morally superior to hunters.

Even the upper Midwest has deer problems: Julie Langenberg, a wildlife veterinarian with the Wisconsin Natural Resources Department, told *BusinessWeek*, "We are absolutely dependent on hunters to help us manage our deer population."[6] Wisconsin has 1.5 million deer, which Langenberg said is about half a million too many. "Whole ecosystems are in trouble, both agricultural and forest lands," she said. Although Wisconsin hunters kill about 460,000 deer each year, the state still has to shell out $1.5 million annually for crop damage.

The West has similar problems. In south-central Washington State's Hanford Reach National Monument, hunters were barred from controlling the elk herd; as a result, in 2005 wildlife managers counted 770 elk, or 400 more than the area could support. Local farmers like Bud Hamilton complained that the ever-increasing herd of elk was devouring their crops. "They come out at night, eat my fields, and go back to the federal land in the morning," said Hamilton. In the five years after the un-hunted herd overpopulated the area, Washington State had to shell out more than $500,000 in crop damage payments just for this herd of elk. Hunters would have been happy to pay for the right to prevent the crop damage, but instead, taxpayers were forced to make up for it. As of this writing, Washington State was aggressively trying to implement a plan that would allow hunters to manage the elk on Hanford Reach.[7]

No-hunting areas hurt farmers

In New Jersey in 1997, farmers reported that approximately 20 percent of their rented farmlands were closed to all hunting because the lands weren't in their control or because housing developments were too close for hunters to safely kill deer with firearms. These farmers were able to control hunting activity only on half the land they rented or leased. "Those producers whose losses were least tolerable had less control over deer hunting on rented ground than did producers without a deer damage problem," determined the NJDEP.

Now get this: 43 percent of the New Jersey farmers said there was a hundred-acre or greater area of land that was serving as a deer refuge within one mile of the area of their most severe crop losses. And 50 percent of the respondents with "intolerable" losses indicated there was such a refuge within a mile of their most severely affected field. Most of these deer refuges were privately owned. The NJDEP determined that there was no doubt that people who didn't allow hunting were substantially hurting farmers, because deer would stay in the refuge during the day and move out to eat the nearby crops at night.

As a result of the study the NJDEP recommended that the state open as much public land to hunting as possible, including parks and "open space" properties. To stop the huge losses of crops the NJDEP decided hunting was the wisest and most cost-effective solution, because when hunting is stopped farmers have to give up farming.

There are populations of deer, elk, moose, bears, geese, and other wildlife all over the country that overpopulate "safe" areas and move out at night to cause damage. According to the West Virginia Division of Natural Resources, large acreages that are not hunted due to posting or other restrictions offer refuges to deer and may aggravate the problem on adjacent lands. New York State's Department of Environmental Conservation has a similar message: "New York's deer hunting seasons span about three months.

A Fact the Media Won't Tell You

If hunting were ended nationally, the costs to consumers would be in the billions. A study done by the Association of Fish and Wildlife Agencies determined that if hunting were ended, three years later American consumers would be paying an extra $511 annually for fruits and vegetables.

"Potential costs of losing hunting and trapping as wildlife management methods," a report by the International Association of Fish and Wildlife Agencies, May 25, 2005.

When taken advantage of, these seasons provide the means to manage deer populations. Successful management hinges on hunters being allowed adequate access so that they may take sufficient numbers of antlerless deer, most importantly adult does."

The small farmer takes it on the chin

Without hunters, the only farms that could stay profitable are the corporate agri-businesses that can afford deer-proof fences or that can handle the expense of losing a large percentage of their crops to deer and other wildlife. It's actually the small, family farmers—especially the organic farmers—who really need hunters. The Department of Agriculture's standards for the label *organic* doesn't mention hunting; it only explains that to raise and sell certified organic produce such farms cannot use pesticides or other chemical products that might deter insects, disease, deer, or bird damage.[8] If you won't use chemicals to dissuade geese, deer, and other wildlife from binging on your vegetables, you need to control the deer population. This means organic farms need hunting to reduce crop loss more than traditional farms do. So, all you vegetarians who eat only organic—have you thanked a hunter lately?

While ending hunting might not drive the big corporate farms out of business, it would force them to make some changes. Without hunting, the big farms would start to plow up hedgerows, cut timber and brushy fields, and otherwise alter their land to make the habitat undesirable for pheasants, deer, and rabbits. Right now many farms make money by leasing land to hunters and through state-funded hunter-access programs, such as Montana's Block Management Program, which uses hunter-generated funds to pay ranchers and farmers to allow hunters on their land. If hunting were outlawed it would no longer be in the farmer's economic interest to have any wildlife habitat. Instead wild animals would only be a liability, impelling farmers to plow under wildlife habitat. Once again, hunting puts the profit in wildlife conservation.

In fact, if hunting were ended nationally the costs to taxpayers and consumers (that is, *you*) would be in the billions, according to a study done by the Association of Fish and Wildlife Agencies (AFWA). Founded in 1902, AFWA is staffed with wildlife scientists, and its core functions are inter-agency coordination between state and federal wildlife departments and promoting wildlife-friendly legislation. A cost analysis by the AFWA found that if hunting were ended, in three years every American consumer would be paying an extra $511 annually in the produce section, the cost for rabies control would go up $1.45 billion, there would be $128 million in increased aircraft damage due to waterfowl and deer on the runways, and there would be a $3.03 billion increase in damages to crops and livestock.[9]

So when your vegetarian sister-in-law sneers at your venison entrée, let her know that whether they accept it or not, even vegetarians need hunters.

Part III

AMERICA'S REAL
ENVIRONMENTALISTS

Chapter 9

SOME ENVIRONMENTALISTS CARRY GUNS

Most Americans don't know their tax money is paying professional hunters to work in every state to solve human-wildlife conflicts. This public ignorance isn't the result of a PR failure by the government. Actually, the feds like it that way: in the late 1990s the U.S. Department of Agriculture quietly changed the name of its "Animal Damage Control" division to "Wildlife Services." The politically correct move was designed to give animal rights organizations less ammunition. The word *kill* was also expunged from the department's mission statement, which now reads in part: "The Wildlife Services program carries out the federal responsibility for helping to solve problems that occur when human activity and wildlife are in conflict with one another."

Despite its new and softer name, Wildlife Services is still staffed with about 750 professional hunters, people who hunt down animals that kill us, eat our livestock, or decide airport runways are good places to hang out. At New York's John F. Kennedy International Airport they control goose and gull populations so the birds won't get sucked into jet engines and cause horrific tragedies, in Texas they averted a major rabies outbreak by airdropping vaccines coyotes found delicious, in Iowa they help farmers find environmentally friendly ways to control crop-eating birds, and in Utah they often deal with mountain lions in the suburbs.

Guess what?

- Wildlife collisions with aircraft cost U.S. civil aviation more than $500 million annually.

- Livestock losses attributed to predators cost ranchers and producers more than $71 million annually.

They are federally paid hunters. We couldn't get along without them, though not everyone sees it that way. Critics have labeled this division of the U.S. Department of Agriculture "cowboy welfare" and argue that it benefits only a few ranchers out West. But then they board commercial airliners like the rest of us and don't even consider that Wildlife Services personnel are killing waterfowl on the runways with subsonic loads so the geese won't fly into a jet engine and take their plane down. The threat is serious. According to Wildlife Services research, wildlife collisions with aircraft cost U.S. civil aviation more than $500 million annually. In fact, nearly six thousand wildlife collisions with civil aircraft were reported in 2003 alone.[1]

Anyone who thinks hunting is not necessary to control wildlife populations should know that in September 1995, the U.S. Air Force lost twenty-four airmen and $190 million as a result of aircraft colliding with Canada geese. In 2000, the engine of a B-747 was destroyed in a fiery explosion after ingesting a western gull during takeoff from Los Angeles International Airport. Parts of the engine fell onto a public beach and the pilot was forced to dump eighty-three tons of jet fuel over the ocean before safely landing the aircraft, which was carrying 449 passengers. In September 2004, an MD-80 carrying 107 passengers ingested a double-crested cormorant in an engine after departing Chicago's O'Hare International Airport. The engine caught fire and numerous parts fell into a Chicago neighborhood. The pilot was able to return the aircraft to O'Hare on one engine for an emergency landing.

Wildlife Services works at approximately 565 airports around the U.S. to identify potential wildlife hazards and reduce the threat they pose to air passengers. In 2003, Wildlife Services trained 1,458 airport personnel at 151 airports across the country on how to reduce the odds of a duck taking down a 747.

Despite these life-saving deeds, in 1999 the U.S. House of Representatives voted 229–193 to cut the program by $10 million, but then reversed itself the next day (232–192) when some members found out what they had voted for. The program was established in 1931, and its name change to "Wildlife Services" was apt—the division had changed since the 1930s. Back in the day, the agency killed wildlife indiscriminately. Then known as Animal Damage Control personnel, they helped to wipe out wolves, mountain lions, and bears in many regions. Now they target specific problem animals. They no longer slaughter game indiscriminately—just as America's hunters now manage game, Wildlife Services doesn't exterminate deer or goose populations. Without these hunters we'd have no one to call when a bear dens under our porch, a coyote eats our poodle, a beaver dams a roadway, or a mountain lion chases us back into the house.

However, even with these professional hunters working all over the country to control predator populations, there are still losses. The U.S. Department of Agriculture's National Agricultural Statistics Service (NASS) documented a $19.9 million loss of sheep and goats to predators in 1999, while losses to cattle producers in 2000 exceeded $51.6 million. In 1999 cattle ranchers lost 69,350 head to predators. In 1994 coyotes, bears, and mountain lions killed 368,050 sheep. Overall, livestock losses attributed to predators cost ranchers and producers more than $71 million annually, according to the most recent surveys by NASS.

The above are very conservative numbers. Ranchers have to prove they lost livestock before they can be compensated. In other words, they have to find the bodies, which is pretty hard to do when mountain lions and bears habitually carry their kills to hidden places, where they bury the remains under brush and earth so scavenging birds can't find them.

To see firsthand what our federally paid hunters are up to, I asked Wildlife Service's public relations department if I could go out into the field with a cougar expert. After weeks of convincing them I was actually a journalist who understood the need for professional hunters and not some liberal mole, they set up an appointment with Mike Bodenchuk, the head of Utah's division of Wildlife Services.

Meet our last line of defense

Bodenchuk turned out to have the looks to match his macho part. He's a tall man with a graying mustache, an earned cowboy squint, and the round-rimmed hat to top it off. He shook my hand with an iron grip, chuckled, boasted that he'd show me what they do all right, and promised that when the trip was over I'd know why we need federal hunters even in the twenty-first century.

Bodenchuk decided to take me on a hunt in Utah's Book Cliffs for a particularly troublesome mountain lion. We'd be going into an area that pales for roughness only before the Grand Canyon, but I didn't know that at the time. We'd be riding mules as we tried to catch up to a cougar that was eating a reintroduced herd of bighorn sheep into extinction. Bodenchuk looked at me, squinted, and challenged, "I hope you can ride!" He dropped this loaded phrase in such a strapping way there was no doubt I'd be emasculated if I said anything but "Yup."

Before I left the Wildlife Services state headquarters building with Bodenchuk, however, I met an employee in a wheelchair who appeared to be the life of the office. He didn't seem like he'd been in the chair for long, either. His features looked like they were shaped by hard days on his feet. Indeed, he shared stories with me of daring rides on mules chasing stock-killing bears and cougars.

When we left the office I asked Bodenchuk how the man had been injured.

"Mule accident," he deadpanned.

"Oh, that's just wonderful," I replied, feeling like a journalist headed into a war zone, and wondering about my employer's workers' compensation package.

As we drove south to Utah's Book Cliffs, the raw taste of adrenaline in my mouth pushed me to ask what had gotten Bodenchuk into such a gritty, old-school occupation.

He squinted at Utah's red hills as he drove his pickup and sermonized, "I wouldn't live anywhere else, or do anything else. We worked hard to bring the wild animals back to Utah. Now we have to control our predators to keep them wild. People need us now more than ever. Once was, men like me exterminated predators. Now we manage them. These days, if we weren't around, those people in those sub-developments all around Salt Lake and across the country wouldn't have anyone to call when a mountain lion eats their Labrador and starts thinking about them next."

No doubt about it, he was a straight shooter all right.

Then he started to tell tales of bravado, and it was clear that his career could be serialized in an Old West dime novel. He chased one stock-killing

A Fact the Media Won't Tell You

Endangered species need hunters. Though environmental groups won't say this aloud, Wildlife Services predator management specialists protect endangered species by preserving island ecosystems in places like Hawaii, Puerto Rico, and California's San Clemente Island. Non-native, invasive predators can be devastating to island ecosystems where a lack of natural enemies and competition for resources allows these species to wipe out native wildlife. For example, in 2001, Alaska's Aleutian Canada goose was officially removed from the list of federally threatened species, due in part to Wildlife Services' efforts to prevent predation by the arctic fox. With Wildlife Services' help, the Aleutian Canada goose population grew from a few hundred in the late 1970s to more than twenty thousand today. In Florida alone, Wildlife Services protects fourteen threatened and endangered species, including five species of sea turtle.

female mountain lion on foot up a cliff, where he cornered it on a ledge under ancient Indian pictographs. He crawled into a mineshaft after another livestock-eating mountain lion and killed that cat in total darkness by shooting at the sound of its deep snarl. He killed two lions that were living under a porch, feasting on housecats. He'd killed a lot of mountain lions in residential neighborhoods around Salt Lake City. He'd never tracked down a man-eater, but he'd tackled quite a few cougars in urban Salt Lake City that were losing their fear of people and becoming monsters.

The landscape fit his persona. We drove south of Salt Lake City over and around hills red as Mars. It was June, and summer's dust was already hanging in low red clouds. The backdrop was all six-gun Western: buttes and saddles and coulees. It would be a perfect place to film a Clint Eastwood movie because, though Utah is mostly desert at low elevations, the landscape changes quickly with altitude. In an hour you can go from cactus desert to cottonwood gorges to aspen Rocky Mountain high country. We'd see all three on this adventure.

When I pushed to find out how Bodenchuk became a hunter on the federal payroll, he guffawed. "I'm about convinced there is such a thing as an adventure gene! Actually, back in the sixties they used to run this ad in all the hunting magazines. Look it up. It seduced me!"

I did. I found the ad in a 1963 issue of *Outdoor Life*. It read:

FREE FACTS on how to become a GOVERNMENT HUNTER. Don't be chained to a desk or store counter. Prepare now in spare time for exciting career in conservation. Many Forestry & Wildlife men hunt mountain lions, parachute from planes to help marooned animals or save injured campers. Plan to live outdoor life you love. Sleep under pines. Catch breakfast from icy streams. Feel and look like a million.

The hyperbole sounded good to him, though he now laughs about the ad's ludicrous tone. Sure, he said, it was all true, except that they left out the fights with stubborn mules, the frozen evenings lying in bedrolls at ten thousand feet, the getting up at 4 AM to find a cougar track, the endless hours of setting traps. Bodenchuk had picked a tough but satisfying career. And he isn't alone.

The front lines of wildlife management

As wildlife populations have increased in the last decade, so has a dramatic increase in beaver populations. Wildlife Services in Oklahoma has seen beaver damage triple since 1985. And in North Carolina, from 2001 to 2004, Wildlife Services received more than eight thousand requests for assistance with beaver damage problems. As a result, the agency has developed a new textural repellant that has had favorable results. In addition, Wildlife Services employs certified explosives experts who are frequently called on to remove beaver dams that stop up water flow, flooding forests and other wildlife habitat.

However, Wildlife Services employees don't just hunt down rogue predators and trap habitat-flooding beavers. Before beginning any type of damage management program, Wildlife Services checks to see if non-lethal management measures are being utilized. Its National Wildlife Research Center (NWRC) is at the forefront of research about coyote ecology and behavior, significantly adding to the effort to develop non-lethal tools. NWRC is the only federal research facility devoted exclusively to resolving conflicts between people and wildlife. In 2004, about $12 million, or 75 percent of Wildlife Services' total research funding, was spent on efforts relating to developing or improving non-lethal controls for birds, deer, coyotes, and other animals. But sometimes hunting is the best alternative.

So as we drove south across Utah and as the land rolled red under an intense Western sun, I asked Bodenchuk to tell me about the worst stock killer he'd ever encountered. I needed to put this endeavor into perspective; though I'd always hunted, I knew nothing about livestock-killing predators.

"The worst stock-killing incident in Utah state history took place on the Old Woman Plateau," he said regretfully. "Where mountain lions, one big tom in particular, drove several sheep herders out of business in the late 1990s. Most people think predators only kill what they need to eat, because that is what the Discovery Channel and other mainstream outlets tell us. Well, that isn't always the case. Sometimes animals kill for fun."

The worst livestock kill in Utah history

Bodenchuk told me the following tale, an account so daring and extreme that I did more research on my own. After a lot of interviews, here's what I found: On July 26, 1992, Billie Worthen, a woman with the gumption to spend summers in a high-country sheep wagon, watched the western sky fade to stars before unloading her rifle and leaving a herd of 876 sheep grazing in Spring Canyon, eight thousand feet above sea level in Utah's Fish Lake National Forest. She gave the guard dogs the night shift.

When the sun came back around the other side, Worthen left her sheep house and rode her mare up to the herd in the soft sunrise. She was within a few hundred yards of the sheep when her horse began to spook. She soon discovered what was making her horse edgy—the smell of blood.

Hours later, federal Wildlife Services hunters had to place rocks on the carcasses as they counted the bodies to be sure they didn't count the same animal twice. It was the worst single stock-killing incident in Utah state history: 102 sheep dead. The guard dogs had run away from the cougar.

Bending down to look at a track of the culprit, Kelly Joe Wright, a predator specialist with Wildlife Services, saw that the animal responsible for the carnage was a mountain lion. Bodenchuk also looked at the track and had little doubt that he and Wright would make short work of the cougar responsible for the bloodbath. Historically, few lions have lived long enough to earn a reputation, because once they put a target on their backs by killing livestock, they can be pretty easily hunted; when hounds or wolves get close, a mountain lion's natural defense mechanism is to climb a tree. But this cat was an exception; as a result, Bodenchuk's life was about to become intertwined with a lion's.

The tom's territory was basically all of the Old Woman Plateau. Roughly forty square miles, the plateau is jammed between I-70 on its western edge and a rim on its eastern edge, a thousand-foot plummet that zigzags north like a lightning bolt. From the interstate the plateau seems shoved together under clouds hung low over a wild Rocky Mountain panorama. Up close, canyons appear and ridges rise. Distances triple and then quadruple as two dimensions grow to three, until all around is the kind of country that caused mountain men to linger.

Bodenchuk found the lion's scratches at the borders of the plateau—leaves and dirt piled into a heap and urinated on to mark a territory. Male lions don't quite get along with each other, and this stock killer was the dominant male. If a dominant male catches a juvenile male in his territory, he kills him. If two big toms cross paths there could be a heck of a fight. After hunters, fights with other cougars are the chief cause of death for toms.

John Wintch, a rancher who resides in Manti, Utah, held the grazing permit for the Old Woman Plateau, as his father and grandfather had before him. He hired herders to live from April through September in little white wagons and guard his flocks from lions, coyotes, and bears.

A Fact the Media Won't Tell You

Ending trapping has environmental consequences. After animal rights activists convinced California's voters to end trapping in 1998, via a ballot initiative, reality bit back. The trapping ban put some endangered species in peril. Red foxes were annihilating the California clapper rail, a small shore bird that lives in the 21,500-acre San Francisco Bay National Wildlife Refuge. The Sierra Club, one of the measure's leading proponents, argued that there are more humane alternatives than the leghold traps, such as cage traps. Wildlife managers, however, said they couldn't save the California clapper rail without leghold traps because red foxes are difficult to catch in cage traps. Meanwhile, other communities that had relied on leghold traps to control aggressive coyotes were now defenseless. Because of these and other problems, the legislature had to pass many exceptions to this ban.

On April 10, 1993, eight and a half months after the 102 sheep were slaughtered on the same plateau, a herder found one of Wintch's sheep killed by a lion.

There's no mistaking a lion kill. Coyotes rip animals to pieces like sharks in a feeding frenzy. Black bears maul their prey to death. But lions kill by biting the back of a sheep's neck and twisting its head with a powerful forepaw to snap the spine.

After the killing of so many sheep, this was what Bodenchuk was waiting for. Today, Wildlife Services hunters slay only stock killers and predators that endanger humans or recovering wildlife populations; they no longer use cyanide and bounties to indiscriminately exterminate populations of meat eaters. To be sure he killed the cat responsible, Bodenchuk had been waiting for the cat to kill again.

Seeing the four-inch tracks around the attack site, Bodenchuk knew the big tom had drawn blood again. He loosed his hounds—Gomer, a bluetick, and Brutus, a redbone. The dogs' wails echoed up the canyon's walls, but the lion went up a cliff as though he knew the dogs couldn't leap like he could.

Three days later the tom killed again. "He was a hit-and-run lion," says Bodenchuk. "He was smart enough to eat from a kill just once."

When the dogs started bawling, the tom beelined for the precipice at Saleratus Creek. Stepping off his gray mare to see where the cat lost the hounds, Bodenchuk couldn't make out where he'd jumped to; the tom had just launched into space as if he had wings.

Wright and Bodenchuk had taken five lions off the Old Woman Plateau in 1993, but they never treed the king. Wintch lost a fifth of his sheep to predation that year. The tom was earning his reputation as a killer. The following four years were dark and bloody for Wintch's sheep and cattle: he lost an average of six hundred sheep a year from his herd of three thousand on the plateau.

After years of loss, Wintch had to make the toughest decision of his life. The lion wars were over. He wouldn't put sheep back up on the plateau. He says it was "like trying to hold on to a handful of sand—no matter how hard you try, it just slips through your fingers." When he was a boy there were twenty-nine herds of sheep in Saleratus Canyon; now there are none. Bodenchuk shrugged when I asked if the sheep business was doomed. "No," he said, "there is a balance being struck. Some places aren't meant to have sheep or other livestock. When over-hunting and eradication programs killed the predators from these hills, the sheep were safe. But in today's more wildlife-friendly times, we're learning to live with predators, not wipe them out. We need hunting to control livestock loss and human-predator conflicts, but there are places where livestock doesn't belong—such as that canyon."

I found myself thinking that Bodenchuk is a modern breed of game referee. He feels that predator populations should be managed, not destroyed wherever they're found, as was the way until only a few decades ago. He also doesn't put predators before people, as environmentalists so often do. It's his job to solve problems between people and predators so that they can coexist in the state of Utah. He's a cowboy sure enough, but he has a modern soft side.

Bodenchuk used regular hunting permits to chase that old tom for the next four years. He finally caught the cat at the lip of the Saleratus Canyon, the place where the big male cougar would always lose the dogs. In the red dust of a dying Utah evening Bodenchuk met the tom eye-to-eye as the cat stood in a small tree. The cougar was eight or maybe nine years old then—old age for a dominant male. It wouldn't be long before a younger tom killed him for his territory. Bodenchuk and the 150-pound mountain lion looked at each other for a long, lurid moment, then the tom jumped from the small pine just feet in front of Bodenchuk. The hunter fired his revolver and ended the reign of perhaps the most renowned stock killer in Utah history. It was a bittersweet moment for Bodenchuck, who loved the hunt and knew the importance of his job, but who also loved this awesome creature.

Reintroduced wildlife needs hunters

We pulled into Green River, Utah, our jump-off point into the Book Cliffs, where another cougar was causing trouble. A big tom was eating a threatened herd of bighorn sheep into local extinction. The herd had just been reintroduced by the state, and it needed a chance to grow before it could stand up to natural predation. This one cat could prevent the fledgling herd from making it in the Book Cliffs. Bodenchuk explained, "If we don't get this cougar, that herd of bighorns is doomed."

He continued, "This is just another example of why wildlife needs hunting. Let me give you a broader case. There are a few areas in this state that are off-limits to hunting. One is located right on the west side of Salt Lake. Most of the problem cougars I deal with come from there. In other units, sportsmen kill a select number of cats each year. Biologists set the annual quotas so that we can balance their populations with human concerns and with the needs of the ecosystems they inhabit. This keeps the mountain lions afraid of us, and it minimizes human-lion conflicts.

"Also, what you have to realize is that female mountain lions breed about every eighteen months. When they want to breed again they chase off their young. They may have one to three offspring. Now when these young mountain lions no longer have the female's protection they're in trouble. The female young will probably be fine, and will likely stay in the area they were raised in. But the male juvenile mountain lions have to move out in a hurry, because the resident male will kill them on sight. If the population isn't saturated, because hunters are thinning them out, then they can stay in the mountain range or area they were raised in.

"Now here's the thing, those young males have to go where there isn't a mature male. If all the areas around them are full, because they're not hunted, then they'll end up in suburbia. That's what happens on the lands owned by the Kennecott Copper Corporation. That area in the Oquirrh Mountains just west of Salt Lake is not hunted; it's currently an active copper mine. There is also a cougar-research project being conducted there. The area is saturated with mountain lions. All the mountain lions I have to deal with in Salt Lake come from that area. Those lions aren't hunted, and have little reason to fear people. Those young, desperate, bold mountain lions are dangerous."

Bodenchuk, Cory Vetere, and I spent four days on the backs of mules in Book Cliffs trying to catch up to that bighorn-eating tom. We found the tom's tracks and territorial scratches and even his kills—bighorns with their necks broken—but we never caught up to the cat. After four days in the saddle, jumping ledges and having the pride scared out of me as I rode along three-hundred-foot precipices following mountain lion trails, Bodenchuk and I headed back to Salt Lake. I'd attained a lot of respect for the tough lives these professional hunters lead.

When we came into an area with cell phone service, Bodenchuk checked his messages, gasped, and pushed the accelerator down. "I'll have to drop you off early at the airport. There's an aggressive mountain lion in Salt Lake. Another mountain lion has come out of that un-hunted population in Kennecott. I hope I can get there soon enough."

We zoomed north through sun-drenched red landscapes and Bodenchuk said, "Sorry, I'll have to drop you at the curb. The homeowner says the mountain lion showed its teeth. It was sitting in her backyard. I'm sure it's still around. It'll move after sunset, so I'll have to get my hounds and hightail it up there!"

"Where?"

"Oh, in one of the suburbs minutes from downtown Salt Lake. You just never know where one of them will show!"

He left me at the curb and raced off to protect an urban homeowner from the wild predators living all around. He had some hunting to do, for the good of us all. Weeks later, Vetere caught up with and killed the big tom in the Book Cliffs. "They're gonna make it," he boasted of the bighorn sheep, who now had one fewer predator.

A week after the Book Cliffs hunt, I interviewed David Stoner, a graduate research assistant from Utah State University who was heading up the research project on mountain lions Bodenchuk had mentioned. Stoner and I were standing with a dozen wildlife professionals in a suburban Salt Lake parking lot. Stoner was busily trying to find a signal from a young male mountain lion's tracking collar. The cat had left the research area and headed right into the housing developments in the valley, just as Bodenchuk had described. I asked Stoner why the cat was there.

Stoner explained as he fooled with his telemetry device. "This cougar is part of a study population. The objective of this study is to examine movement patterns and prey selection of cougars in and around the urban–wild land interface, We are interested in cougar use of small-scale habitat corridors that may serve as conduits for hunting forays outside their traditional habitat. Much of this land is being converted to subdivisions, and conflicts between wildlife and suburban residents are increasing, therefore we hope to document cougar spatial use patterns before this land is completely developed."

I scratched my head. "How's that?"

"Cougars need pathways, wildlife corridors from Kennecott on the west side of Salt Lake to the Wasatch Range on the east. We need to create these wild corridors so that cougars can move through the residential areas freely, so they don't have confrontations with people," he explained.

"But wouldn't those corridors pass through housing developments?"

He frowned. "Yes, but what can we do? If we don't do something these cats will end up in backyards."

"Won't the corridors be in backyards?"

"In a manner of speaking."

"If the population you're studying was hunted, could hunters reduce the population so that young cougars would have space where they were raised? Isn't that how the state managers cougars all over Utah?"

He shrugged and said, "We're trying to find ways to control human-cougar conflicts without hunting."

"Any luck?"

"We still have a lot of research to do."

He couldn't locate the cat. Weeks later, while flying in a small plane to locate collared cougars, he picked up its signal. The cougar was on the other side of Salt Lake. Somehow it had crossed several highways and went through miles of suburbs undetected.

Chapter 10

WHY SONGBIRDS LOVE DEER HUNTERS

T he Fund for Animals, an anti-hunting group, filed a lawsuit in Washington, D.C., federal district court in 2003, attempting to force the U.S. Fish and Wildlife Service to ban hunting on thirty-seven wildlife refuges. The Fund for Animals has since merged with the Humane Society of the United States (HSUS) to form the largest anti-hunting group in the world, and HSUS has continued to push the lawsuit through the courts. What HSUS had going for its lawsuit was that the areas are called "wildlife refuges," a misnomer that sounds like the areas should be wildlife sanctuaries free any human intrusion. What HSUS had going against its case was: scientific wildlife management, precedent, the fact that ending hunting would imperil wildlife species, and the fact that hunters paid for the portion of the refuge system that was purchased from private landowners.

Let's start with science. William Koch, refuge manager of the Great Swamp National Wildlife Refuge, said if deer hunting were terminated on the refuge the eight-thousand-acre property would be a barren, deforested landscape after only a few years. "Deer hunting is vital to the health of the area. Deer can have a very negative impact on habitat, which is not only habitat for deer but also for many other species," he explained. In fact, each refuge's management follows specific rules before they decide to use hunting as a wildlife management tool. There is a set process for opening

Guess what?

✖ Hunting saves trees and plants from overbrowsing by deer.

✖ Quality deer management programs allow hunters and biologists to keep deer populations to what the environment will support—which benefits other wildlife as well.

A Fact the Media Won't Tell You

Where hunting isn't allowed, national parks can't control their game populations. In 2006, Rocky Mountain National Park's un-hunted herd of elk was so overpopulated that it was destroying its habitat; as a result, the National Park Service (NPS) proposed killing seven hundred elk per year, hunting them at night with silenced rifles. Under the proposed NPS plan, some carcasses would be left in the woods for animals that eat carrion. The NPS estimated the project would cost $858,426. In 2006 each nonresident hunter in Colorado paid $496 for a bull elk tag and $251 for a cow elk tag, so if the NPS were to sell 350 tags for each at that rate, it would raise $261,450 from hunters instead of spending $858,426 in taxpayer dollars. In response, the state of Colorado offered to manage the herd for the NPS with hunting.

areas to hunting that might include an environmental assessment or an environmental impact statement. Each refuge has a stated purpose, and it has goals and objectives. Hunting can enter into its management strategy, as it does at Great Swamp, where deer hunting is a management tool used to preserve low-growing vegetation that many wildlife species need.

Koch explained, "Great Swamp's main purpose is to provide habitat for migrating waterfowl. Because of that, waterfowl hunting isn't allowed. This isn't a large refuge. If we put waterfowl hunters out there, these birds wouldn't have much resting and feeding—a few would be harvested by hunters, but the rest would be chased out. However, exotic, invasive species of plants tend to take over when deer are allowed to eliminate the natural understory of the forest. That's a very undesirable situation. It sets the stage for invasive plants to move in and take over. We need [deer] hunting on this refuge so there's a place for other wildlife."[1]

But Kristin Leppert, HSUS's campaign manager for hunting issues, doesn't care. She argued, "The U.S. Fish and Wildlife Service has strayed far from its own policy directing that 'wildlife comes first in the National Wildlife Refuge System,' and is rapidly converting these treasured natural places into playgrounds for sport and trophy hunters."[2]

Don't be surprised that HSUS doesn't care that ending deer hunting will hurt waterfowl and other bird populations. The Humane Society's calculation is simple: hunting is morally wrong and "fundamentally at odds with the values of a humane, just and caring society." According to HSUS, letting a forest die, and many other species with it, is more "humane, just and caring," than allowing people to hunt deer.

As for precedent, the National Wildlife Refuge System encompasses nearly one hundred million acres in 545 national wildlife refuges across the country. According to the U.S. Fish and Wildlife Service, "Priority uses of the National Wildlife Refuge System are *hunting*, fishing, photography, wildlife observation, environmental education, and interpretation." (Emphasis added.) Hunting has been part of the refuge system for over half a century.

Now onto sportsmen's dollars: since 1934 the sale of migratory bird hunting and conservation stamps (commonly known as duck stamps) has generated about $477 million for the refuge system. The stamps originally served as hunting licenses, but today they are a tool to raise money for conservation; ninety-eight cents out of every dollar go to the National Wildlife Refuge System. Another $197 million has been added to the Migratory Bird Conservation Fund as an "advance loan" from the U.S. Treasury. And about $153 million has come from import duties on firearms and ammunition and from refuge entrance fees. These funds have purchased about 2.7 million acres. An additional 1.4 million acres have been purchased using about $1 billion from the Land and Water Conservation Fund.[3]

Deer need to be hunted

Outside the U.S. refuge system, more officials are beginning to realize that they need hunters to control deer numbers for the sake of other wildlife. For example, in 2005, for the first time in its hundred-year history, the New Jersey Audubon Society asked the state to reduce the population of whitetail deer. The bird-watching group claimed that deer had become an ecological "stressor" for birds and other wildlife because the does and bucks ate away the natural landscape. Hunting, the Audubon Society argued, is a viable option to bring the deer population down to a manageable number in order to prevent deer from browsing away the songbirds' nesting cover.

"I can't look at myself in the mirror anymore," said Eric Stiles, vice president of conservation and stewardship for the New Jersey Audubon Society. "As stewards of the forest, we have to do something to stop this disaster."[4]

The report concluded that deer management methods such as fencing and birth control have very limited success. Deer were devouring the forests, and so the state needed to aggressively use hunting to reduce the deer population. The Audubon Society demanded state wildlife authorities revamp deer management strategies statewide, because hunting policies were geared toward keeping enough deer around for hunters rather than trying to reduce the state's population of nearly two hundred thousand deer. The deer population needed to be brought in line with the carrying capacity of the land.

Do hunters want more deer, period?

There is some truth to the criticism that state game agencies sometimes keep deer populations too high in order to please hunters. But this complaint is losing its validity. In New Jersey, during various seasons and in different regions, each hunter can legally harvest more than a dozen deer per year. In 2005–2006 they shot 59,653 deer—20,508 bucks and 39,145 does.[5] The fact that they kill nearly two does for every buck shows they aren't just "trophy hunting" but are trying to reduce the herd.

Depleting the concentration of bucks doesn't do much to slow or reverse population growth—each buck just fathers fawns with more does. As a doe can be pregnant only once a season, hunting the ladies is the key to controlling population, even if they don't make for good wall mounts. With this in mind, New Jersey uses its "Bank-A-Doe Program" to require hunters in some zones to shoot two does before they can shoot a buck. Even with these initiatives, however, a lack of access to private land is making it increasingly difficult for hunters to control the state's deer population.

While hunters are doing all they can within their confines, the state of New Jersey could also help out by allowing capitalism and hunting to meet. The state has a "recreational use statute," which basically immunizes a landowner from legal liability if he allows public access to his hiking trails, hunting woods, or fishing holes—as long as he doesn't charge for this access. If the state expanded this protection to include landowners who charged for access—or who were compensated by the state—then New Jersey's hunters would find much more land opening up to them as long as they were willing to pay. Otherwise, New Jersey could adopt programs like

Myth Debunked

Hunting is allowed in national parks. Though common opinion has it that hunting is forbidden in national parks, the truth is that 59 out of 390 properties administered by the National Park Service allow hunting. In total, 35 percent of the Park Service acreage uses hunting to manage game populations: 29,943,312 acres—of which 19,677,033 are in Alaska.

those in Kansas and Montana (see chapter 11) that grease the skids for both hunters and landowners to benefit from hunting.

The national deer population has risen from about 500,000 in 1900 to about thirty million today, largely because of hunters and state policies to build herds. Some state agencies were slow to switch from rules designed to augment deer herds to regulations that are proactive about reducing populations to carrying capacity.

Today, however, most states practice some type of quality deer management. Biologists aim to use hunters to keep deer herds small enough so that the habitat is not harmed. In this way they manage for the entire ecosystem, not just for deer. While it's not uncontroversial among hunters, most like this strategy. Although they'll see fewer deer, the methodology improves the health of the herd, which means hunters are more likely to see big, mature bucks.

Texas started a quality deer management movement in the late 1970s. Most of the South and Midwest followed in the 1980s and now practice some form of quality deer management. States now issue more tags for female deer than they do for male deer so they can reduce and control deer populations. The Northeast was last to implement herd-reduction policies.

Pennsylvania's reformation

One of the last states to embrace quality deer management was Pennsylvania. Over one million people hunt deer annually in Pennsylvania, where hunting is often viewed as a passage to manhood—a ritual and a family affair. Changing the deer-hunting regulations in Pennsylvania causes controversy. So in 2002, when I headed to Pennsylvania to meet the maverick who was trying to change the way Pennsylvanians hunt, I knew I was about to walk into a volatile situation.

On that cold day in January 2002, the most controversial man in Pennsylvania, Dr. Gary Alt, sat across from me, both of us slouched in chairs in a quiet conference room in Harrisburg. Downstairs, meanwhile, a thousand deer hunters were taking turns telling the Pennsylvania Game Commission (PGC) just what they thought of Alt, the state's deer-management specialist.

The year before, in order to push through a combined buck and doe season, Alt stood in front of assemblies of as many as ten thousand aggravated sportsmen like some besieged president trying to sell the masses his agenda. Alt had angry men (including the leaders of the sixty-thousand-member Unified Sportsmen of Pennsylvania) accuse him of trying to rid the state of deer. Alt spotted a few serious-looking guys who pushed back their coat jackets to display shoulder holsters. And some detractors had even sold T-shirts at his appearances bearing the slogan "Osama bin Alt." As a result, Alt had neatly hidden a bulletproof vest under his button-down shirt and was compelled to come into speaking engagements through side doors with fierce-looking bodyguards. Deer hunting is not taken lightly in the Keystone State.

Alt was going to tell Pennsylvania's one million deer hunters that they shouldn't be allowed to shoot young bucks—the bucks most likely to be found hanging from their camp poles in November—so that the entire ecosystem could be managed properly. He wanted to augment the good that deer hunters were already doing by allowing habitat to recover from deer overbrowsing. He wanted to take hunters to new heights from the good conservationists they were already, as most state wildlife biologists had already done. Pennsylvania was behind the times. He wanted to bring modern game management to the state. But not everyone wanted to change.

Short and stout and shiny on top, Alt looked more like *Seinfeld*'s George Costanza than a visionary smasher of the status quo. At best, his stature and ambition made you think "Napoleon complex"—he's been accused of it before—but the label didn't quite fit. Alt was not dictatorial; he was a politician in a PGC uniform who knew public opinion can swing either way.

So as hunters downstairs were expressing their opinions of Alt to the PGC, Alt calmly explained to me that he knew he had to sell these changes or he'd be out of a job. He wouldn't be the first one. Noted biologists like Aldo Leopold and Roger Latham ended their careers because of disputes over changes in deer-hunting regulations. In fact, it was only a sense of self-preservation that kept Alt from proposing a season or two with no buck hunting at all; biologists who had tried to protect Pennsylvania's bucks and back in 1928 and 1938 were fired in the ensuing public outcries. Alt says he didn't try passing a point restriction (a requirement that a buck have a certain number of antler points before it can be legally killed) three years before, because if he had, Pennsylvania's deer hunters "would have gutted me and hung me to bleed." Back then they just weren't ready; now he hoped they were, for the good of everything from songbirds to rabbits to deer themselves.

A Fact the Media Won't Tell You

Hunting saves trees. Hunting is currently permitted on more than 90 percent of the roughly seventy million acres of woodlands managed by the forest products industry. Why? Because hunting deer alleviates overbrowsing of the trees the timber industry is growing. The side benefit is that songbirds and other species gain as well.

Walking downstairs to find out, Alt flinched when he saw who was at the podium. A local high-school science teacher who'd confronted him on numerous occasions was all but screaming into the microphone, "Alt is going to destroy our great state's deer herd!" The teacher's speech was rancorous but short. The next speaker up, to Alt's delight, was a hunter holding a small four-point set of antlers. "This is what I've been shooting on my property for thirty years," he said. Nobody looked impressed. Then he raised a huge ten-point rack and made Alt's point: "This is what I shot this year after only two years of following Alt's advice!" Now the crowd was standing and applauding and the members of the commission were taking notes like a panel of impressed judges.

Alt was going on the road.

A month later I was at the Wallenpaupak High School auditorium in northeastern Pennsylvania. From the front-row spectators to the deputies standing at the rear doors, the room was packed with eight hundred ardent deer hunters. And Alt, who was halfway through his forty-city, ten-week tour—and looking every night of it—was about to tell those eight hundred sportsmen why they shouldn't shoot year-old bucks anymore in a county where typically 62 percent of the yearling bucks are harvested on opening day.

He stepped into the spotlight and the auditorium went church-quiet. Alt took a deep breath and joked, "My twelve-year-old son, after attending one of these meetings, said to me, 'Dad, your job sucks!'" Alt had learned that it's hard to hate a likable person; you may disagree with him, but you won't want to punch his lights out.

The joke brought chuckles and helped the audience empathize with him. Next he had to convince them that his plan was the right one. Alt maintained that scientific deer management has failed in the past because no one educated the public. With that in mind, Alt gave the audience a lesson in deer biology 101. He explained that much of the state had a browse line over the deer's heads; as a result, they're not getting the necessary nutrition. Songbirds, grouse, and even rabbits are disappearing as well. He described an environmental catastrophe that few recognized, and that even the environmental groups didn't see. He knew that hunters, for their own good, needed to publicly change their image from users of a resource to game managers. He knew that if hunters couldn't show what good they can do statewide, they'd continue to lose access, as they had already around much of Philadelphia. And when hunting is banned, the deer herd explodes, causing more traffic accidents, cases of Lyme disease, and massive damage to ecosystems.

Alt continued through his slide show, stopped and pointed to a picture of himself standing outside a fenced enclosure, and said, "We fenced off a one-acre parcel of public land four years ago. Now look at it; inside it looks like a jungle, while on the outside it's a desert. On the inside you'll find rabbits and grouse and other animals, on the outside there is only barren ground. This is what the state's 1.6 million deer are doing to our forests."

The considerably complex equation of deer management in modern America has a fairly simple solution, according to Alt: hunters can control the herd, repair the environment, and restore equilibrium—and they'll pay for the privilege of doing so. Alt had sold the message before. He turned Pennsylvania's bear program into an international success story. The BBC, National Geographic, and the Discovery Channel have all given positive coverage of his black bear program in the Keystone State, and this time he was getting them interested in deer management. More than that, he was going to make them understand that hunters are the right people to make the management plan work.

After two hours at the Wallenpaupack podium, Alt was covered with sweat and almost panting. Nobody had left during his lecture. He had poured his scientific heart out, keeping them riveted. As he opened the floor to questions, he was about to find out if they supported him. Three podiums were set up at the base of the stage, and as Alt turned to the one on the right, he winced. A disgruntled sportsman didn't even wait for his cue to scream, "I've been hunting in this state for fifty-five years, and I say you're dead wrong. You held up those big antlers to gain support, but I say you're going to decimate the herd. What you're really holding up is an empty hand."

Alt began to answer but was quickly cut off by a heckler: "Sit down, you selfish ——. Alt is right!"

Alt looked relieved, but the angry sportsman turned and answered the heckler by shouting, "I just wanna shoot my buck. I don't care about big antlers. And what's wrong with that?"

Suddenly, the bulk of the audience let Alt know whose side it was on. Voices from all over heaped reproach and derogatory remarks on Alt's critic. The audience wanted a healthy ecosystem. On this night, Alt's message had won over the crowd.

Today, Gary Alt is out of a job; he resigned in 2005. There were too many critics, some still red-hot angry that the state reduced the number of deer. Since 2000 the state had reduced its deer herd by as much as a third. Pennsylvania, which had the most deer-vehicle collisions in the country, had since lost that awful distinction, and its habitat was recovering. When all the shooting was over in 2002, hunters harvested a total of 517,529 deer—352,113 antlerless deer and 165,416 antlered deer. About 70,000 more antlerless deer were harvested than the previous year, accomplishing another part of the mission: to reduce the state's deer herd while preserving and improving the state's habitat.

A Fact the Media Won't Tell You

Hunting helps habitat and wildlife. As a management tool, hunting deer, elk, and other wildlife:

➤ Boosts plant diversity

➤ Prevents a browse line

➤ Wards off erosion

➤ Protects populations of songbirds and small-game animals

While the criticism was harsh and constant, state-sponsored polls have consistently found that a large majority of Pennsylvania's hunters supported Alt's deer management changes. Alt converted quite a few hunters. For example, consider Ed Grasavage's road to Damascus. When Alt took over the job of Pennsylvania's deer management specialist, Grasavage, who also lived in Pittston, Pennsylvania, decided to take matters into his own hands. With his sleeves rolled up, he stood outside the Kingston

High School auditorium one evening waiting for Alt to arrive. Alt was to give a speech detailing the proposed radical changes to the state's deer season. Grasavage was going to "punch Alt's lights out," as he put it.

When Alt wisely entered via the back door, Grasavage went into the auditorium in hopes of catching Alt as he was leaving after his talk. But by the time the meeting ended, his plan had disintegrated—Alt had convinced him that it's better not to shoot young bucks and to manage the herd for the entire ecosystem.

The conversion was complete. Grasavage became the president of Pennsylvania's chapter of the Quality Deer Management Association, a role that took him throughout the state to preach Gary Alt's good word.

Meanwhile, around the country most states are way ahead of Pennsylvania. Quality deer management practices are being used in most states. Hunters know that when they reduce deer populations, the habitat recovers and deer get bigger and healthier. It's a win-win. So state game departments from Texas to Vermont are using hunters to reduce deer populations to what the habitat will sustain. Wildlife biologists study the state of the habitat and then give out more doe permits in units where deer are overpopulated, lengthen seasons, and some actually require hunters to shoot does before they can shoot a buck. The result has been remarkable for habitat and wildlife.

All over the country today, deer hunters are augmenting songbird populations, which will continue as long as the American public realizes that anti-hunting groups like the Humane Society hurt wildlife; they don't help songbirds, deer, and rabbits when they end hunting seasons.

Chapter 11

HUNTING IS INCENTIVE-BASED ENVIRONMENTALISM

F ly west from the northeastern U.S. on a clear day, and you'll see cities break to suburbs that give way to farmlands bisected by the forested spines of the Appalachian Mountains that soon flatten to Midwestern corn, alfalfa, and soy all sliced into endless squares. Over the Mississippi and the Missouri rivers, urban areas appear again and break into suburbs and then to checkerboards of crop fields for a long ever-browning stretch, until the Rockies rise out of the Great Plains in relief-map proportions. All along the high, seemingly wild, tops of snow-capped mountains you'll see fire towers and logging roads and ski slopes.

Somewhere on such a flight you'll realize that people, in one way or another, manage nearly every acre, and therefore every ecosystem, in the U.S. This is where environmentalism's preservationist movement runs aground on reality. The preservationists—as opposed to conservationists—want to fence off wilderness and preserve it in a "natural" state. But their "natural" utopia doesn't exist—nature never has been static.

On a virgin continent, ecosystems have natural population control mechanisms: when predator populations increase too much for the available prey, the prey population (say deer) plummets and the predator populations (wolves, cougars) fall too. Next, because the predator population is down, the prey population comes back and the predator populations

Guess what?

✪ People won't buy or lease land to hike, bike, or picnic in, but they will spend money on land devoted to hunting.

✪ Hunting does more to preserve animal species on private land than the Endangered Species Act.

✪ A crucial bill to preserve wetlands in Missouri was ignored by environmental groups—but eventually passed with the help of the National Rifle Association.

eventually follow the prey numbers up. Then the cycle repeats. This can be a predictable cycle as long as nature doesn't throw a fire, drought, hard winter, or other such interruption into the mix. Today another variable has been added: our lawns and crop fields feed deer, elk, and fox in bounty and in drought. Deer, elk, moose, and hundreds of species of animals all over America spend their days in woodlots and public forests and then amble into farms and suburbia at night to eat. Cougars, coyotes, bears, and the rest of the predators also overflow into suburbia when they're overpopulated or simply famished to feed on deer and rabbits and even our pets. As a result, because we are augmenting wildlife populations, we also have to *control* their populations. We can't opt out by outlawing hunting and asking the wildlife nicely to stay in their forests, as the preservationists swear we can.

Across most of America, hunters are currently controlling wildlife populations for the greater good, so much so that hunting has made wildlife into a cash crop for farmers, ranchers, and rural economies, thereby influencing farmers to preserve wildlife habitat. Hunting is even a major factor in rural land prices. Though not written about outside of small-town newspapers, hunting has created incentive-based environmentalism that is working to preserve land and benefit wildlife all over America.

Hunting fuels rural land prices

Land prices are no longer set according only to what land can yield from farming, ranching, or development. Hunting has become an economic variable, so much so that even in traditionally agricultural-only areas—southern Illinois, northern Missouri, the "pheasant belt" in South and North Dakota—many properties are worth two or three times more than agricultural values. This is because hunters are buying and leasing farmland.

This capitalism is benefiting wildlife. Now that farmers see quail, deer, and turkey as cash crops, they're preserving wildlife habitat because it's in their economic interest to do so. Many no longer plow under hedgerows, burn brushy fields, or drain ponds, because without places for deer, pheasant, and ducks to live and breed, hunters won't come and lease their land. And get this: practices that enhance game animal populations also benefit non-game species, such as songbirds, raptors, amphibians, and everything else.

Hunting-fueled free enterprise is at work for wildlife. Competition for access to hunting land in many parts of the Midwest and South has gotten so intense that hunters almost have to lease hunting rights if they hope to keep hunting; in fact, some sportsmen have been priced out of their own backyards in whitetail deer hotspots in Illinois, Iowa, and Ohio.

The numbers are impressive. In 2001, according to U.S. Fish and Wildlife Service records, 982,000 hunters leased land in the U.S. The average tract size of land leased for hunting was 229 acres, and the nationwide average lease rate was just $2.77 per acre. A statewide survey conducted by Kansas State University in 2003 indicated that private land leased in 2001 and 2002 for deer hunting averaged $2.50 per acre in Kansas and ranged from $0.25 to $12 per acre across the rural Midwest and South.[1]

A Fact the Media Won't Tell You

Hunting clubs augment wildlife populations. Duck-hunting clubs flood rice fields for waterfowl, Southern plantations create quail habitat, and deer-hunting clubs plant "food plots" for deer. They do these things because they want more game for economic and for selfish reasons, but the result is more wildlife and more non-game species.

Those costs are outdated, says Mike DiSario, president of Outdoor Expeditions International and OEI Properties, a company that invests in hunting lands. According to DiSario, a white-hot real-estate market since 2000 has been driving up land assessments, taxes, and therefore hunting lease costs everywhere, making wildlife into an even bigger cash crop for landowners.[2]

Myth Debunked

Urban sprawl doesn't hinder wildlife populations. It seems like a logical assumption that when a house goes up, deer, rabbit, and coyote populations go down, but the opposite is often the case. Houses create more edge habitat—browse for deer and other wildlife. A mature forest doesn't produce much food for wildlife, except when mast-producing trees annually drop nuts or fruit. This is because in a mature forest, very little light makes it through the canopy to the forest floor, and grasses, forbs, and new saplings can't grow without sunlight. But when a house is built—especially if it's zoned for an acre or more—its lawn, flowers, and hedges are good rabbit and deer food. As a result, deer and other wildlife populations can actually go up when houses go up.

Hunters are buying land like never before—people don't buy land to hike in, but they do buy land to hunt. In the past few years a lot of players have jumped into the recreational real estate business. Mossy Oak, a company that designs hunting camouflage, jumped in early, and now there are dozens of companies that specialize in hunting-recreation land. Even Century 21 now has professional "game managers" on its payroll who help hunters find and purchase game-rich tracts. Its website warns: "Every year, we have less land to sell. Within five to ten years, there will be none. . . . Buy now!"

"We're looking at farms in the Midwest that two years ago were going for $600 per acre, but that are now costing $1,500 to $1,800 per acre," says DiSario. "Acreage prices are so high now that many banks won't mortgage properties, because they're selling for a lot more than assessment values. Meanwhile the land in our properties division is moving. Hunters are buying this land and then spending more money to improve and restore its habitat so that the hunting will improve."

Nationwide, rural land prices rose 11 percent in 2004 and then another 11 percent in 2005, which is the biggest jump since 1981, according to the U.S. Department of Agriculture. Another good barometer of the value of land is the costs incurred by American Farmland Trust, an organization that seeks to place land in conservation easements and to thereby protect farms from development. The group says average costs have gone up from $1,519 per acre in 1999 to $2,899 in 2004.

Even timber companies now see hunting as a huge revenue stream. "This has never happened before," says DiSario. "Timber companies are acknowledging that the wood isn't where the money is. The money is in the wildlife; as a result, timber lands, which historically were viewed as akin to public land, are being leased to hunters, and timber companies are changing some of their methods to enhance wildlife populations."

As if all that wasn't enough pressure on rural land, between 2000 and 2004, eighteen of the nation's twenty-five most populated cities had more people leave than move in.[3] The few exceptions are found in the South and Southwest. Manhattanites are heading south and west; Californians are moving to Las Vegas, Salt Lake City, and Phoenix; Chicago residents are looking for richer job markets; and in just about every major city, people are fleeing to the fringes of the suburbs. The New York metropolitan area lost more than 210,000 residents a year from 2000 to 2004.

As people flee urban centers for affordable housing, they cause urban sprawl, which makes hunting land even scarcer. In fact, according to the National Resources Inventory, about 2.2 million acres of land were developed between 1992 and 2002.

A hunter-financed solution

Because of complaints from hunters being priced out of their own back-yards, state governments are learning how to help rural economies with hunting; for example, twenty-one states now have some form of private land access program for sportsmen. As of May 2006, private land access programs had opened 26,799,824 acres to hunters. The biggest complaint from hunters in Kansas used to be that there was nowhere to hunt. More than 98 percent of Kansas's land is privately owned, and landowners had little incentive to allow hunters on their property. Then the state realized the beauty of the profit motive. Hunters pay for hunting licenses. If landowners got a cut of that money in exchange for allowing hunters on their property, suddenly more land would open up for hunting—and game populations would be controlled. Now, with one million acres opened to hunting thanks to sportsmen's dollars, hunters have places to go and farmers have incentives to preserve habitat.

Bill Smith, a senior wildlife biologist with the South Dakota Department of Game, Fish and Parks, summed up how his state's program created a sportsman's theme park of a state: "We created this open space by going to private landowners and negotiating with them one at a time. We've enrolled 900,000 acres for the 90,000 nonresident sportsmen who visit us each season, hunters who spend $122 million in South Dakota annually. Funding for the walk-in area program currently comes from a five-dollar surcharge on hunting licenses....Wildlife is benefiting from hunting in a big way."

Montana's block management program is another good example of how hunting is economically helping wildlife conservation. Montana's program opens private land to sportsmen. All a sportsman has to do is jot his name on the sheet positioned at an entrance to a property enrolled, and he is free to use the land. Because landowners get paid based on the number of people who use their property, they have a financial incentive to maintain healthy wildlife populations and to withhold their land from developers. In 2005 the average property enrolled in the Montana program earned $3,000 annually. "An enterprising rancher can make more by charging day fees," said Alan Charles, coordinator of landowner/sportsman relations for Montana, "but the landowners enrolled don't have to deal with hunters constantly begging permission. Every year more landowners want to enroll in the program than we can afford." In Montana a mandatory hunting access enhancement fee ($2 for residents, $10 for nonresidents) funds the state program. Thanks to maps printed by the state, about 180,000 hunters use these areas each year.

Think about this Montana program in contrast to a much more famous effort to protect wildlife habitats: the federal Endangered Species Act (ESA). The ESA drives down property values by severely limiting what landowners can do with their own land; Montana's hunting access program drives up property values. The ESA gives landowners an incentive to kill endangered species or destroy their habitat so as to avoid the costly and crippling intervention of the federal government (they call this "shoot, shovel, and shut up"). Montana's program gives landowners incentives to protect all species and habitat.

While the Montana program is administered by the state government, the basic business model at play shows that when profit motive and hunting combine, they can do much more for nature than well-intentioned federal bureaucrats ever can. If hunting were to end today in Montana and Kansas, these conservation land economies would crash, farmers would plow under wildlife habitat, and ducks and deer and so many other species would lose their most ardent defenders.

Hunters are wildlife's best defenders

To see a controversial example of hunters fighting for wildlife and smart land use, I hopped a plane to St. Louis to meet duck hunters standing in the path of urbanization in order to save a fast-disappearing ecosystem.

As the jet descended, I looked out in mid-afternoon at the confluence of the Mississippi and the Missouri rivers north of St. Louis and knew there was something profound there. I was looking at a special, almost extinct ecosystem that developers and some politicians were trying to drain and pave. I was there to meet a new environmental group made up of an alliance of duck-hunting clubs.

Adolphus Busch, a direct heir to the Anheuser-Busch fortune, founded the Great Rivers Habitat Alliance in 1999 to save one of the last wetland areas along the Mississippi River. Busch started the group when he saw that development actually increased after the area was under water following a huge flood in 1993. He contacted several environmental groups for help, at first calling the traditional groups nationally known for fighting sprawl. As it turned out, St. Louis wasn't sexy enough for them. There were no endangered species involved. Their resources weren't ample enough to help, they said.

Disgusted, Busch turned to duck hunters for help, to the men and women who for two hundred years have been preserving the flood plain at the Confluence, a forty-mile-long, two- to ten-mile-wide triangle of incredibly fertile ground and wetland wedged between the Missouri and Mississippi rivers just north of St. Louis.

I didn't know then that in a few weeks Hurricane Katrina would land on the Gulf Coast and sink New Orleans, bringing to national condemnation the practice of urban sprawl in the flood plain of our nation's greatest river. But there was no doubt this place was special.

As I drove along in the flood plain between these two rivers to see what was being fought over, I was surprised to see so many duck clubs. Their signs lined the roadways—there were "Fowl Play" and "Blind Luck," "Duck Point" and "Poor Boy Duck Club," "Mallard Farms" and "Duckaway Farms," "Webfoot" and "Whistling Wings," and so many more. I wondered how they survived so close to a sprawling city. Then I noted the rich earth, bottomland planted with corn and sorghum and laden with wetland. The air, heavy and damp, smelled riverine. I knew there was no doubt this was waterfowl's paradise, that it was remarkable, even rare, riparian habitat.

Stopping in here and there along the way, I saw that some duck clubs, such as the swanky, highbrow Raccoon Ranch, were too audacious to be believed, but others, such as the Donald Duck Club, were Everyman's organizations. Then I saw the national wildlife refuges and the state-owned areas open to the public—the Great River National Wildlife Refuge, for one, which protects approximately 11,600 acres along 120 miles of the Mississippi River. And even though it was summer, it was clear this was the greatest waterfowl intersection in the United States—the very spot where migrating ducks and geese following these two vast river systems converge when late autumn cold gets them flying south and when spring thaws urge them north.

But my guide to this threatened region, Dan Burkemper, the communications director for the Great Rivers Habitat Alliance, wasn't boasting as we drove along—he was spinning a dark tale. "This all might be gone soon, and with it the ducks and geese. This could all be suburbs of St. Louis soon—downtown is ten miles that way," he said, hooking a thumb south. "If that happens, the waterfowl will only have the refuges left, and they'll be severely impacted by the levees that'll have to be built."

Myth Debunked

Hunting is not destroying Africa's wildlife. Janneman Brand, a professional hunter and outfitter who owns Kalahari Safaris in Namibia, says, "Before the economic influence of hunting, farmers shot all the wildlife out of much of Namibia because the kudu and springbok and other plains game animals were seen as competition for cattle. But now that farmers see an economic benefit to wildlife, kudu, springbok, and oryx are common in Namibia. Hunters are definitely Africa's greatest environmentalists."

We stopped in at the Dardenne Duck Club to get the scoop; the Dardenne was founded in 1811—yeah, less than a decade after Lewis and Clark paddled by on their way up the Missouri.

"Ducks can't land on Wal-Mart's roof," scoffed Tom Sherrill, farm manager of the Dardenne Duck Club, as he gave me a strong, one-pump handshake. He was all fired up. "Look, we have fifteen hundred acres here, most of it flooded wetland in the fall. We leave large portions flooded through the winter too, so ducks have somewhere to stop and feed on their way back north. We've been here doing this for two centuries. We care about this resource—about the wildlife—and we're not an exception. Sportsmen have been preserving this land for nearly as long as we've been a country, but now some want to levee it off and build. They want to destroy this unique ecosystem for what? More sub-developments? We've already done that up and down the Mississippi and there's darn little country like this left!"

His outrage was easy to understand when you consider that back to antiquity, fall flocks of ducks and geese have winged down the great flowing funnels of the Mississippi and Missouri, resting and feeding in an unending chain of wetlands. A century ago the oxbows and sloughs in the flood plains of these rivers were kept brimming by yearly floods. That was when Missouri had about five million acres of wetlands. Now much of those wetlands are gone, and only about sixty thousand acres remain in southeast Missouri, much of it right here between the rivers.

In fact, since early in the twentieth century, the United States has lost half its wetlands—all the strict government regulations don't keep the country from continuing to lose thousands of acres each year. But still millions of ducks and geese travel the Mississippi flyway each fall and spring. Each acre of wetland, be it new or old, public or private, is valuable. Waterfowl crowd into the Missouri wetlands that remain, some on public land but many on private property managed by people like Sherrill. About 75 percent of the wetlands remaining in the United States are owned privately, and there are thirty thousand acres of wetlands in private hands just north of St. Louis.

Hunters are ducks' best friends

To show me how much danger this critical wetland was in, on the way out from St. Louis we stopped in Chesterfield, along the banks of the Missouri River. Burkemper wanted to point out what is purported to be the largest strip mall in America, all built after the 1993 flood, within sight of a levee—a levee that broke in 1993. "See all that land now taken up by that Home Depot, that Wal-Mart, that Bentley dealership? It was under water a dozen years ago. And this development is pushing north, right into the flood plain and duck central," he said.

I asked Wayne Freeman, executive director of the Great Rivers Habitat Alliance, about that. I found the organization in the back end of an industrial park. They'd recently moved from a building that had a date with a wrecking ball and weren't sure how long they could stay at their current address. They were a charity case and so would move wherever they had to, just as long as the rent was nothing and they could string in a phone line to keep up the good fight. "Most people don't have a problem with the development in Chesterfield. But they will the next time the levee breaks and their taxes go to rebuilding billions of dollars' worth of real estate that is backed by federal flood insurance. Look, this is David and Goliath stuff. It's our little outfit and local sportsmen against the big developers and some of the politicians."

There is some truth to the man-against-the-machine stance of the organization, but it does have some influential benefactors. The alliance was founded after the 1993 flood, when local residents found that development of the flood plain had actually accelerated after the area was deluged. Adolphus Busch was the impetus for its formation; he lost his house to the flood and feels a large part of the area should be preserved as is. He'd like to form a large conservation area and preserve the habitat and the way of life on the flood plain. To describe what he's after, he liked to use a new-age term: "smart growth."

To see what he means by that loaded phrase, we went to see the section of ground the Great Rivers Habitat Alliance was founded to save.

We stopped on a levee on state route 370 looking at crop fields, hardwood forest, and wetland the city of St. Peters wanted to pave, and Burkemper explained, "This is only sixteen hundred acres, but if they get this they can get all the private land piecemeal. This could set a precedent. This isn't smart growth. There are other areas south and west of here where people can live free of flood insurance."

Some in the city of St. Peters didn't agree. In 1960 St. Peters had 404 residents. Up until then the town's greatest claim to fame was having the world's largest TNT plant, built during World War II and closed at the end of the war. St. Peters grew from a town of 486 in 1970 to a burgeoning suburb of 15,700 by 1980, when it won the distinction of being the fastest-growing city in Missouri. Annexations became commonplace, increasing the town's area from less than a square mile in 1970 to more than eleven square miles in 1979. In 2000, there were 51,381 people in town, and growth was finally slowing as the community ran out of room. To make room, the mayor and city council recently decided to look to the flood plain.

The controversy surrounding their move to develop the flood plain turned out to be more explosive than their TNT plant had ever been. The

A Fact the Media Won't Tell You

Hunters are eco-tourists. To regulate and enhance wildlife populations, many African countries are sharing hunting revenues with local villagers and wildlife officials. By creating an economic incentive for the locals to leave wildlife alone, poaching has been greatly diminished, game populations are being scientifically controlled, and hunters are pumping cash into poor rural areas.

local press covered the issue daily, public hearings were volatile, lawsuits were pending, the town of St. Peters spent millions, and a developer had been found. The town of St. Peters offered controversial tax increment financing (TIF) to developers. TIF is a creative form of corporate welfare that allows a corporation to use a portion of taxes in excess of its pre-developed value to finance costs of a project.

It's a win-win for a developer, but taxpayers are left with no extra revenue until the developer has recovered its investment. Often TIF is used in areas where public infrastructure is needed but developers have no economic incentive to build. In the case of St. Peters, there was plenty of economic incentive, but there were legal problems associated with building in a flood plain. For some reason, St. Peters decided to clear the legal hurdles for a developer.

Wayne Freeman summed up the fight over the town's expansion this way: "We've unearthed corruption at the highest levels of our local government. They want to grow at all costs, to increase their tax base and power. There are places that shouldn't be paved, such as wetlands, and yes, the flood plains of our nation's two greatest rivers. Some of the things they have done are criminal!

"There are things about this project that I really hope come out," he continued. "Because if they do, people will go to jail. In fact, I'd like to get sued for libel. That way all the truth would come out in the depositions. They'd hang themselves."

Freeman went on about local politics at its nastiest. Essentially, the Great Rivers Habitat Alliance tried to end the debate by offering a compromise: the organization would pay $12 million for the land (its board of directors is made up of successful men and women from the St. Louis area), and as a compromise two hundred acres would be developed. But the town took a $42 million bid from a private developer instead. Because the Alliance had offered to compromise by developing part of the land, its critics accused it of hypocrisy.

Busch had something to say about that. We sat in the barn on his 1,500-acre property located in the flood plain discussing the alleged hypocrisy: "We are not going to work with our hands tied behind our back and then lose everything. We're in this fight to win, to save as much of this land as possible. That's why we offered a compromise. This is a war of many battles. That sixteen hundred–acre property is a key battle to saving this waterfowl-rich paradise, but we have to be flexible."

I knew the Busch family had a long history of conservation. Adolphus's father, August A. Busch, even donated 6,987 acres in St. Charles County as a conservation area. So I took his passion as genuine. Then I knew he was being forthright when I saw his kitchen. Newspaper articles covering the issue plastered his walls—many sections yellowed by a highlighter. He has a home office dedicated to keeping abreast of the issue and a calendar loaded with events and interviews to get the word out. No doubt about it, saving this land is his life. Busch also had the local citizenry behind him. In a poll paid for by the Alliance, only 40 percent of residents of St. Peters were in favor of the development, and only 32 percent of the residents in the whole county were for it.

But as I talked with Busch, I knew the Army Corps of Engineers was poised to give a permit to the town of St. Peters to build a levee around that piece of contested bottomland. The Corps has the ability to waive the development restrictions of the Clean Water Act; as a result, they've been battered by the press. Alan Dooley, public affairs officer for the St. Louis division of the Army Corps of Engineers, was on the defensive.

Weeks later, Dooley called me from the road; he was on his way to hurricane-ravaged Louisiana because levees had been breached and people were dying. Dooley sympathized with the duck-lovers.

"Look, I understand both points of view," he told me. "After all, this is one of the last major sections of the river that isn't levied off. From around Cairo, Illinois, to the Gulf of Mexico, the entire river is basically one big drainage ditch, because there are levees the entire way down.

And living behind a levee poses certain risks..." His voice faded out. He was thinking about where he was headed, about the horrors he'd see there, and maybe he was thinking that some day St. Louis could be another New Orleans.

Bureaucracy is bureaucracy, and the work they do often doesn't make sense even to the bureaucrats. Instead of just pointing fingers at bureaucracy, the Great Rivers Habitat Alliance was fighting to save the floodplain a smarter way.

Conservation easements ward off suburbia

Joan Fitzgerald, owner of the Donald Duck Club, lived in a house on stilts, and she lost everything but her land to the 1993 flood. "My husband and I always said we'd make this 123-acre farm into a duck club," recollected Fitzgerald as we walked her land. "We wanted to give something back to the native wildlife. When he passed away, I was down pretty low, but then I stood up and said, 'Why should I give up the dream of doing what's right for me and the environment?' Now I flood eighty acres for waterfowl and my members are my new family. And economically, it just makes sense."

The Great Rivers Habitat Alliance was helping Fitzgerald put her property into a conservation easement. When she did, she'd get a check and tax breaks for years to come. The best part is that after she signed the easement the land would be preserved forever. Wayne Freeman said he was working with a dozen landowners in the area who were interested in easements. Scott Manley, a regional director of conservation programs for Ducks Unlimited, said they'd signed landowners in St. Charles County to conservation easements as well, and so the rush was definitely on by hunters to save this fragile ecosystem.

Conservation easements are popping up all over the country. The National Trust Census found that in 2005 protective land trusts and easements totaled thirty-seven million acres, a 54 percent increase from 2000; in fact, such easements have been growing by about 2.6 million acres per year. Many of these lands are being purchased for hunting and are being put into conservation easements to reduce taxes.[4]

As my plane took off from St. Louis in the gloaming of a summer evening and swung northeast, I was melancholy. Thunderstorms were blowing in from the west, and the sun was peeking between the storms and the horizon, glinting off the Missouri and Mississippi up twists, turns, and oxbows north and west until the rivers met the sun at the horizon. Lights were coming on in St. Louis and up in St. Peters but trickled out in the farms and duck clubs of the flood plain between the two great waterways. The plane climbed higher, and the big picture was right there framed in the plane's window. Seeing the marshes and lush bottomland along the river that way, you just knew every subdivision and levee matters on such a unique piece of land. Marshes aren't just a place where ducks live; they suck up floodwaters by allowing rivers to naturally swell when rains fall heavily.

Then the horrible notion occurred to me that even if the land is developed and the ducks are forced to fly on, and hunters to stay home, that maybe some year the skies will open like in 1993 all over again and the great rivers will swell and violently reclaim their flood plain. It was a horrifying thought of biblical proportions, the type of thought we all watched come terribly true in New Orleans, but I knew as I winged higher, getting the ducks' perspective, that if we don't respect nature enough, someday nature will teach us another hard lesson.

A month later, the town of St. Peters did get its permit for a levee. While the tragedy in New Orleans was at its peak, when the waters were smothering most of the city and bodies were floating down the streets, the Army Corps of Engineers gave them their permit to build a levee and a development. The city soon began building an industrial park in the flood plain. But though one battle was lost for sportsmen to save a fragile ecosystem, the war wasn't.

The National Rifle Association (NRA) stepped in where the well-intentioned but politically naïve Great Rivers Habitat Alliance lost. In January 2007 the NRA sent four lobbyists to St. Louis to convince legislators to pass the Hunting Heritage Areas Protection Act (Missouri state senate bill 225). The bill would make it illegal for local governments to use tax increment financing in the hundred-year floodplain of the Missouri and Mississippi rivers. This way towns and cities wouldn't be able to subsidize development in the disappearing ecosystem. Mainstream environmental groups weren't interested in the issue, but the politically incorrect NRA managed to convince Missouri's legislators to pass the bill, so the state's hunters will be able to continue to preserve a critical part of America's waning ecosystems.

Myth Debunked

Africa's elephants are not endangered; in fact, many areas of Africa are overpopulated with elephants. Such overpopulated herds destroy habitat: a single mature elephant knocks down an estimated 1,500 trees per year and drinks thirteen gallons of water per day. If elephants are not hunted to keep their populations in line with available habitat, they quickly destroy the forests that all wildlife needs.

Rich Miniter, "Too Many Elephants," *Wall Street Journal*, July 17, 1997.

Chapter 12

HOW HUNTERS RECAPTURED
ENVIRONMENTALISM

In 2003, when the upcoming presidential election owned the headlines, hunter-conservation groups united to condemn a move by the Bush administration. "Specifically," said the Theodore Roosevelt Conservation Partnership, "we are concerned that the January 15, 2003, Advance Notice of Proposed Rulemaking on the Clean Water Act Definition of 'Waters of the United States' will ultimately lead to the elimination of Clean Water Act protections for isolated wetlands, lakes, and ponds. We do not believe the U.S. Army Corps of Engineers and the U.S. Environmental Protection Agency should proceed with a rulemaking to redefine 'waters of the United States' and ultimately narrow the scope of the Clean Water Act."[1]

Such policy hounding is something environmental groups have long been known for, but with the exception of the National Rifle Association, hunter-conservation groups have never been policy wonks. They're good ol' boys from Middle America who concentrate on specific conservation projects, get little national credit, and who've never understood how to shoulder into the Beltway to lobby on Capitol Hill. However, they were suddenly united and being heard: President George W. Bush invited the hunter-conservation groups to the White House to discuss the issue. He didn't invite the environmental lobby—the primary agenda item for Greenpeace and the Natural Resources Defense Council was Bush's defeat,

187

he knew, and there's no use sitting down with such partisans. But the possibility of losing the hunter-conservation groups before the 2004 election shook him all the way from his Stetson to his cowboy boots. After all, Bush was one of them; he managed a bass pond and made land management decisions to enhance quail habitat on his Crawford, Texas, ranch.

The hunter-conservation leaders gathered at the White House, and Bush buckled. Soon thereafter the Environmental Protection Agency and the U.S. Army Corps of Engineers announced they would not issue a new rule ceding federal Clean Water Act jurisdiction over isolated wetlands. This was a big conservation victory—over half of the ducks in North America begin their lives in the small prairie potholes that would have been affected by the regulatory change. But though the mainstream media outlets reported that Bush had reversed course, they didn't report the most amazing part of the story: hunter-conservation groups had taken the baton out of the hands of environmental organizations.

How hunters quietly took Capitol Hill

Jim Range, a Washington, D.C., lawyer and lobbyist for sportsmen-conservation organizations, founded the Theodore Roosevelt Conservation Partnership (TRCP) in 2000 to help gather together hunting and fishing conservation groups that by themselves couldn't make a single thing happen in a town dominated by special interests. Range had been one of the architects of the wetlands protections in the Clean Water Act when he was counsel to the Senate's Committee on the Environment and Public Works in the 1970s. He knows his way around Capitol Hill and has been at the center of moderating environmentalism.

Since its founding, TRCP has worked with Ducks Unlimited, Pheasants Forever, the Rocky Mountain Elk Foundation, Trout Unlimited, Quail Unlimited, and more than a dozen other sportsmen-conservation groups to get things done in Washington. These groups put more money and man-hours into preserving habitat, creating waterfowl nesting cover, fixing trout streams, removing dams, making sure elk have winter range, and funding wildlife studies than the "mainstream" environmental groups who get media attention and Hollywood adulation. In contrast, the environmental groups condemn logging, oppose the genetically modified crops we all eat, prophesize a global warming apocalypse, oppose hunting grizzlies, mountain lions, and alligators (even after these large predators are so overpopulated they begin eating people), fight to keep species on the endangered species list (even after the animals have legally recovered), and file lawsuits to halt natural resource development projects.

However, despite these differences, Range wanted to form a lasting alliance on issues the two groups could agree on. He wanted to moderate the environmental activists, to make them negotiate with hunters and stop them from unfairly demonizing sportsmen. Range wanted to work with environmentalists to bring rational game management, such as hunting, to the table in national debates. After all, he argued, "If mainstream urban America knew what hunter-conservation groups are up to, the clichéd hunter wouldn't be Elmer Fudd or a beer-swilling Bambi killer; he'd be a conservationist in camouflage busily building duck boxes."

To align forces, Range sat down with the Pew Charitable Trusts. Pew has funded Greenpeace, the Fund for Animals, Defenders of Wildlife, and other environmental—even anti-hunting—groups. Can you envision a mixer between these crowds? Even the moderate (by comparison) Sierra Club is comprised mostly of suburban soccer moms and environmental activists—people who are often ambivalent about hunting, if not outright hostile to hunters; whereas the hunter-conservation groups are mostly populated by Middle America males with pickup trucks and photos of the buck they killed last fall in their wallets.

Because of TRCP's growing strength, however, Range was able to convince Pew Charitable Trusts to fund the organization; as a result, a group that had long funded radical environmentalism and anti-hunting organizations began funding a hunter-conservation group as well. Things were sure changing in Washington and in environmentalism.

How environmental groups lost touch

Range had momentum behind him because the national environmental groups had lost a considerable amount of grassroots support. When activists gathered on the first Earth Day in 1970, they saw a nation beset with severe environmental problems. The Cuyahoga River in Cleveland was so polluted it caught fire. Automobile exhaust fouled the air. Species like the California condor and the bald eagle were vanishing. The resulting call to arms produced about one hundred major pieces of federal legislation during the next decade, including the Clean Water Act, the Clean Air Act, and the Endangered Species Act. As a result, great progress was made. Poisonous rivers were cleaned up and auto-related air pollution was reduced, and in 2007 the bald eagle was taken off the endangered species list. In fact, the progress was so monumental that it became difficult for environmental organizations to find new battles to fight, and without new battles, the public becomes apathetic and funding dries up.

In the 1970s, environmental groups thrived. Dozens of new organizations were formed and young activists who didn't start their own groups succeeded in slowly taking over established conservation organizations such as the National Wildlife Federation, which had been founded by sportsmen decades earlier. Though they had little interest in hunting, and many were opposed to hunting, environmentalists knew that controlling these organizations was the key to prestige, policy victories, and the political establishment. Follow the money into the 1980s and 1990s and you find that the environmental groups increasingly fell under the influence of multi-million, even billion-dollar, environmental foundations. And the foundations themselves were becoming more radical, which began to further marginalize the environmental groups.

You see, most of the foundations that fund anti-hunting and radical environmentalism were founded in the same way: An industrialist created a fortune, he passed away, and his children (or children's children) grew up guilty rich. These silver-spoon-fed idealists decided they had to do something for Mother Earth to stop horrible corporations interested only in profit margins (like the ones that generated the cash for their trust funds). All the children or grandchildren of the deceased industrial giant take seats on a board and each year they gather to dole out cash from the interest on the money in their foundation's pool. In the 1980s and 1990s such groups gave millions to Greenpeace to run campaigns against genetically improved crops—campaigns that succeeded in preventing people in Third World countries from eating

A Fact the Media Won't Tell You

NRA's Institute for Legislative Action has done a lot for wildlife:

➤➤ Fought to preserve Missouri's disappearing wetlands

➤➤ Supported conservation programs on farmlands to improve wildlife habitat

➤➤ Has been instrumental in the passage of "right-to-hunt" state constitutional amendments that are good for hunters and wildlife

what the rest of us do. These groups funded the Humane Society's campaign to stop "trophy" hunters from controlling the bear population in Maryland, and PETA's billboards that declare, "Beef: It's What's Rotting in Your Colon," while PETA covertly passed money to eco-terrorists like the Animal Liberation Front so they, in turn, could burn down vacation homes.

In fact, during the 2004 presidential campaign you might have heard that Teresa Heinz Kerry was one of these guilty rich, liberal idealists. She was then listed as the "chair" of Heinz Endowments, a foundation insti- tuted by Howard Heinz's widow in 1941. Howard's father was Henry J. Heinz, the condiment innovator who founded the Heinz food processing company. As of 2005 Heinz Endowments held total net assets worth $1.44 billion. Records for 1995 though 2001 show that Heinz Endow- ments gave $6,049,500 to Tides Foundation and Tides Center (a founda- tion that gives millions to extreme animal-rights groups), $2,570,767 to Environmental Defense (a group whose key issue is global warming), and $88,000 to the Sierra Club.[2]

The Pew Charitable Trusts, the group that began funding Jim Range's TRCP, had about $5.2 billion in assets in 2006. In 2007 Pew was expected to give out about $250 million for environmental projects and other ini- tiatives. So it could lobby for and against politicians and more freely spend its money, in 2004 Pew transformed itself from a foundation into a charity. Pew was originally seeded with various inheritances from the four children of Joseph N. Pew, founder of the Sun Oil Company. It has been a large, powerful voice for environmental causes. Here are just a few examples of where it has spent its money: Earthjustice (the Sierra Club's legal defense fund, which has fought to stop the delisting and hunting of grizzles and wolves) got $19 million between 1995 and 2003; the Natural Resources Defense Council (a group that grew famous when it accused apple growers of using cancer-causing agents—allegations that proved false, yet cost apple growers an estimated $250 million) pocketed $12 million from Pew between 1991 and 2000; and the Sierra Club, which often opposes hunting initiatives, was given $4 million by Pew between 1992 and 2001.

When these foundations grew large and began funding radical environ- mentalism, and as a generation of environmental do-gooders climbed the corporate ranks of the Nature Conservancy, the Sierra Club, and the HSUS—people who were professional environmentalists, not people who rose from the grassroots ranks—the old conservation ethos of the environmental movement was pushed aside and replaced by radical environmentalism.[3] Green preservation was replacing camouflage conservation. The greens had lost touch with the people and real-world issues. Their mission evolved from making sure our grandchildren could still enjoy wildlife to making sure nobody's children got too close to wildlife. An increasing anti-hunting stance was just one symptom of this lack of touch with most Americans (according to surveys conducted by the National Shooting Sports Foundation, 80 percent of Americans approve of hunting).

However, the environmental movement didn't lose its way just because its real issues were mostly solved (air and water quality and species protection) or because it was led by the purse strings of foundations. It had also sold out. Many of the big environmental groups and anti-hunting groups became corporate—they had become their one-time enemies. Presidents of environmental groups began making salaries on par with Fortune 500 CEOs, and environmental groups began dipping into the pockets of not just foundations, but also of big business.

In response, the ever strengthening hunting-conservation groups began to chip away at this corporate support in the 1990s. For example, in 1991, Sears, Roebuck & Company donated 8 percent of the wholesale price of selected stuffed animals in its *Wishbook* catalogue to the HSUS. The U.S. Sportsmen's Alliance (a sportsmen-funded hunter-activist organization) called for hunters to express their outrage; as a result, Al Mathes, assistant to the president of the catalogue division, issued a formal apology and stated, "Every customer ordering stuffed animals from the catalogue will be informed that the promotion is over."

Ace Hardware Corporation, a major retailer of hunting and fishing gear, refused in 1992 to sever its relationship with the HSUS. As a result, the Sportsmen's Alliance asked hunters to send Ace comments on its partnership with the anti-hunting group. Soon thereafter, John J. Cameron, corporate communications director for Ace, announced that the promotion had been cancelled.

General Mills in 2001 promoted the Humane Society by distributing free HSUS calendars in marked packages of Golden Grahams cereal. The cereal maker, however, soon heeded sportsmen's protests and the promotion was ended.

And FOX Sports Net, which provides regional sports programming to eighty-five million households, announced in 2007 after thousands of angry letters that it would no longer run anti-trapping advertisements produced by the HSUS.

The Congressional Sportsmen's Caucus

Meanwhile, as environmentalists were losing their way, a small group of hunters who happened to all be U.S. congressmen decided to band together. The Congressional Sportsmen's Caucus (CSC) was founded in 1988 as a way to temper the anti-hunting movement, according to Melinda Gable, the chief operating officer for the Congressional Sportsmen's Foundation (CSF), which manages the caucus.

Though it stayed small through the early and mid-1990s, it took off in the late 1990s, and today it's one of the largest caucuses on the Hill. Congressmen sit for two-year terms as co-chairs of the caucus, one from each party. Also, the CSC doesn't take a position on gun rights; a stance that has helped it grow larger and has also allowed a few anti-hunters to don sportsmen's clothing.

The result has been a bipartisan sportsmen's coalition that has helped to shape pro-hunting policy. The foundation holds annual events in which it takes members of Congress hunting, shooting, and fishing. This puts a gun in the hands of congressmen who might never otherwise experience the joy of the hunt. As a result, when a bill comes to the floor pertaining to sportsmen or conservation, congressmen are able to make educated, first-person decisions.

The result has been a much more sportsmen-friendly Congress, so much so that as of January 2007, 63 out of 100 U.S. senators and 254 out of 435 members of the U.S. House of Representatives—a majority in both houses of Congress—were members of the CSC and so had publicly stated support for hunting. And though members don't always vote together, since the CSC was founded it has changed the dynamic on Capitol Hill. It has helped to pass hunter- and wildlife-friendly bills (such as more funding for the Conservation Reserve Program); it has killed anti-trapping and anti-bear hunting legislation; it has ensured that important programs, such as Wildlife Services (the division of the USDA that deals with problem wildlife), are funded; and it has helped to make highway bills wildlife-friendly by funding wildlife underpasses and other initiatives.

Gable boasted of her group, "We have an annual budget of a couple of million dollars, while the anti-hunting Humane Society of the United States—our chief opponent—has a stated budget of $100 million, yet we beat them again and again on every issue. This is because we are telling the truth, while they have to skew the facts to pass their left-of-reality agenda. It's also because we are grassroots. Under the National Assembly of Sportsmen's Caucuses, there are now sportsmen's caucuses in twenty-one states. We have millions of hunters and fishermen behind us. Sportsmen are now—and this is new—a force on Capitol Hill."

Hunters turned the tables in 2000

Another major factor in this trend has been the lobbying efforts of the National Rifle Association (NRA). Long before the CSC was formed, the demonized NRA, which launched *American Hunter* magazine in 1973 (a magazine that currently has more than one million subscribers), had begun to do even more for sportsmen. The NRA's Institute for Legislative Action (ILA) was founded in 1975 by Harlan B. Carter to fight anti-Second Amendment and anti-hunting legislation. In the decades since, NRA-ILA has fought on the federal, state, and local levels for hunters and shooters.

As anti-hunting rhetoric and initiatives escalated in the 1990s during the Clinton administration, NRA-ILA met each challenge head on. Today, executive vice president Wayne LaPierre and NRA-ILA executive director Chris Cox, together with their team of lobbyists, aggressively represent NRA members in Washington, D.C., and in every state capital. They have had a huge impact. For example, in 1999, when the U.S. Fish and Wildlife Service (USFWS) misappropriated funds generated by taxes on hunters, the NRA alerted its members and lobbied Congress. Congressmen were soon so besieged by letters, phone calls, and e-mails that they passed legislation forcing the USFWS not to pilfer hunter-conservation funds. The NRA also passed shooting range protection laws in the majority of states so that hunters could sight in their rifles safely.

It was during this period that the NRA's reputation darkened. The "Cop-Killer Bullet Ban" in the mid-1990s would have outlawed virtually all center-fire rifle ammunition—the ammunition most used by hunters. The bill, as written, would have banned any ammunition that was capable of penetrating soft body armor—any cartridge designed to kill deer without excruciating pain can do that. Darren Lasorte, NRA's manager of hunting policy, explained, "The NRA was the only group opposed to the ban, which made us look like we were for killing cops. We did the right thing to protect hunters and the Second Amendment of our Bill of Rights, but we got a very bad image as a result. The mainstream media mischaracterized us and spun the issue. We won in the end, but at a high cost. Remember in those days FOX News Channel wasn't on the air, conservative talk radio was minimal, and the networks still had most of the power. The liberal point of view controlled the airwaves. We couldn't afford to fight that airtime war. So we lost the PC war.

"The NRA also got a bad rap for opposing the assault weapons ban that expired in 2004. We always argued that if a ban passed it would be expanded to include other classes of firearms in the future. We were proven right once again when John Kerry introduced a bill in 2004 that would have classified all semi-auto shotguns commonly used by waterfowl hunters as 'assault weapons' and therefore would have banned them. This included the Berettas, Benellis, Brownings, and Remingtons all hunters use. We've won on all those issues because the NRA has strong grassroots support."

In fact, though the mainstream media likes to insinuate that the NRA does behind-the-scenes chicanery to get its way, the truth is that the only reason the NRA is often called the most powerful lobby in the country is because of its grassroots support—legislators listen when large groups of people speak together. In a short amount of time the NRA can mobilize its three to four million members to flood a state wildlife meeting or to write congressmen. There is no environmental group that can match those numbers. (The Sierra Club and Greenpeace combined have about one million members.)

As a result, the hunter-conservationists grassroots strength has been unmistakable in national politics. Consider the 2000 and 2004 U.S. presidential elections. In 2000, anti-gunners within the Democratic Party grew bold. Moms marched under banners of Handgun Control, Inc. in the capital and a post-Columbine nation seemed poised to force gun owners to register all firearms in a national database. As a result, NRA membership hit a record high, and sportsmen flooded to the polls—fear is a great motivator. This reaction to the anti-gun rhetoric is why guns became a non-issue. Eric Howard, spokesman for the Brady Campaign to Prevent Gun Violence, said as much: "The modus operandi of the [anti-] gun lobby is to keep the discussion down." And Larry Pratt, executive director of Gun Owners of America, agreed. "The Democrats have decided that the stove is still hot and they don't want to get burned again," he said. If

Democrats can neutralize Republicans' advantage with gun owners, argued Mark Penn, a Democratic pollster who was a key architect of Bill Clinton's winning message in two presidential elections, as many as 21 percent of swing voters could come their way.

The 2004 election was very different from the 2000 election. In 2004, presidential candidates tramped around rural states thumping their chests and boasting they'd gutted more deer and bagged more pheasants than their rivals, and anti-gun congressmen suddenly became gun-shy. Just four years before, then candidate Vice President Al Gore, in an interview in *Outdoor Life*, wouldn't even answer the questions "Do you hunt? Do you fish?" On the eve of the previous presidential election, anti-gunners in the Democratic Party would never have stood by and watched as the 1994 assault weapons ban expired, as they did in 2004. As the election neared, Senator John Kerry made sure a camera caught him when he went pheasant and goose hunting, and President Bush appeared on *Fishing with Roland Martin* on the Outdoor Life Network. Such things would not have occurred just a few years earlier.

In fact, in the 2006 elections, Darren Lasorte says, "The only federal campaign we could find where gun ban or prohibition was a campaign issue touted by a candidate was in Illinois, and that candidate lost. This is a far different world than what we faced in 1994 and 2000. Hunters are recapturing environmentalism and standing together to protect their Second Amendment rights more than ever before."

What the future holds

In yet another sign of a trend toward more rational environmentalism, in January 2007, the Theodore Roosevelt Conservation Partnership formed a partnership with unions, which typically lean toward the Democratic Party. TRCP launched the USA Union Sportsmen's Alliance. At a press conference at the SHOT Show (the largest hunting/shooting trade show in the country) a group of trade unions, including the AFL-CIO, the International Association of Firefighters, and the International Association of Machinists and Aerospace Workers (IAMAW), seeded hunter-labor alliance with a $1.2 million check. They promised to bring 3.2 million unionized hunters to the table to push pro-hunting and conservation initiatives in Washington. Suddenly a previously untapped grassroots group of sportsmen would be helping to moderate environmentalism—people who typically vote for Democrats would be lobbying for hunting rights.

Tom Buffenbarger, president of the IAMAW, summed it up this way: "Quality places to hunt and fish are disappearing—threatening America's sporting heritage. The USA Union Sportsmen's Alliance will help turn the tide by unifying union sportsmen and women across the country to form a strong voice of influence."

Though the mainstream press won't say it, and may not even grasp it, this is yet another factor that will continue to moderate environmentalism and anti-hunting rhetoric from politicians. As a result of all this ever strengthening grassroots action, hunter-conservationists should continue to influence the dynamics of state and Washington politics, no matter who is in the White House. Of course, the mainstream media will surely continue to find this too politically incorrect to report.

Part IV

HUNTING FOR A FUTURE

Chapter 13

HUNTING IS GOOD FOR KIDS

W e cannot but pity the boy who has never fired a gun; he is no more humane, while his education has been sadly neglected," penned Henry David Thoreau in 1854 in his classic *Walden*.[1] Yet a common politically correct perception today is that it's not safe to put a gun in a young hunter's hands. Perhaps more people need to learn the facts.

Official statistics from the Centers for Disease Control and the U.S. Fish & Wildlife Services make it clear that the injury rate for hunters is well below almost every other sport in America, including sports considered to be very safe.[2] For example, soccer is eight times more dangerous than hunting. If your daughter's in cheerleading, she's about seven times more likely to get hurt than if she were hunting. What about the American pastime? Sorry, baseball is five times more dangerous than hunting. Even tennis is about twice as dangerous as hunting.

Crunch the numbers a different way. According to American Sports Data, Inc., 13.8 percent of sports injuries are from basketball, 8.2 percent are from jogging, golf causes 1.4 percent of sports injuries, and hunters comprise only 1 percent of sports injuries.[3]

So okay, hunting is statistically safer than other sports, but when someone gets hurt with a gun, they can die, right? Yes, guns have the potential to kill, and accidents do happen. All tragedies are heartbreaking and

Guess what?

- School gun violence is more likely to occur in urban areas where very few kids are hunters.

- Statistically, hunting is safer for kids than football, bicycling, and tennis.

should be avoided through diligence and education. But fatal injuries are rare: according to U.S. Fish and Wildlife Service studies, the chances that one of the 1,727,000 youths between the ages of six and fifteen who hunted in America in 2001 would be killed were five in a million.[4] Those odds drop to two in a million when you count youths who were supervised by an adult. Let's put these statistics into context: The National Sporting Goods Association estimates that 20.6 million people hunted in America in 2002, and 93 of these people were killed from injuries related to hunting, such as drowning, falling, and firearm accidents. This makes a hunter's odds of getting killed while in the field less than five in a million. In 2001, 21 people died as a result of playing organized football out of 1.8 million participants, making the odds of dying from football nearly twelve in a million. This means that someone playing football is more than twice as likely to be killed as someone who is hunting. And, fatalities aside, football injuries blow hunting injuries away. In the U.S. in 1999 more than 172,000 children ages five to fourteen were treated in hospital emergency rooms for football-related injuries, or 18.8 per 100 participants, while hunting had just 1.3 injuries per 100 participants.[5] If any sport in America is really dangerous, it's bicycling: 173 children ages fourteen and under in the U.S. died in bicycle-related crashes in 2002. No matter how you crunch the numbers, hunting is one of the safest recreational activities.

In fact, the number of fatal firearms-related accidents among both children and the population as a whole has reached an all-time low, according to the Centers for Disease Control, while the number of civilian-owned

Myth Debunked

Not all hunters are men. A 2006 survey by the National Sporting Goods Association (NSGA) found that 72 percent more women are hunting with firearms today than just five years ago. The NSGA survey estimated that more than three million women now hunt.

CNN Debate: Is hunting with kids safe?

On December 1, 2005, the following discussion took place on CNN's *Paula Zahn Now* show:

Miles O'Brien, CNN anchor: Heidi, what do you think about this? What is an appropriate age [for hunting]?

Heidi Prescott, Humane Society of the United States: Well, obviously, we have laws in this country stopping children from driving cars. We believe it should at least be that minimum age.

O'Brien: Okay. And what happens at sixteen? I mean…the difference here, of course, is…we're talking about supervised activities, right?

Prescott: Tragically, there are already five children dead this year. Obviously, we need to have laws in this country to stop children from being out in the woods under the age of sixteen.

O'Brien: Okay. But, you…say it's unsafe. But, if you look at the statistics, the thing that is most unsafe for kids to participate in is football, by a long shot.

Prescott: Well…

O'Brien: Look at the facts, injuries per hundred thousand participants. It's more than three thousand for football. Down at the bottom, below ping-pong, as we said, is hunting. So, it really is safe, statistically.

Prescott: Well, statistically, you are looking at accidents. We are talking about fatalities as well. When you have accidents with ping-pong or with football, children don't lose their lives.

O'Brien: Well, okay, but, sometimes, they…get paralyzed in football. I mean, we can talk about injuries. There are serious injuries that are associated with football. Ted, when you hear about these terrible incidents we just talked about at the top of the program, what *continued on 207* firearms and gun owners has never been greater—according to the National Rifle Association, eighty million American now own guns.

Why hunting is good for kids

Find a kid who has hunted, ask him about nature, and you'll see his eyes light up. Then you'll hear about how bucks grunt and turkeys gobble. Maybe the kid has sat with a parent in a duck blind and will tell you how a mallard makes a feeding chuckle. Kids who hunt have a real, active relationship with nature and with the earth. Take a kid who has never hunted (in 2001, only 4.23 percent of Americans between ages six and fifteen hunted)[6], ask him about nature, and he'll say, "Huh?"

Children who hunt learn how nature works. They understand why and when elk bugle and waterfowl migrate and bucks make scrapes. They also learn to play by the rules when they attend their state's mandatory hunting-conservation course and as they begin to follow their state's hunting regulations. Yet some people consider teaching a young person to hunt to be socially irresponsible—so much so that a culture war rages today in America's classrooms over hunting.

The anti-hunting propaganda

There is a real ideological war being waged in the schools over our children's conception of nature. On one side are the animal welfare and animal rights groups. Teaching materials from anti-hunting organizations such as Humane Education Programs, People for the Ethical Treatment of Animals (PETA), and the Humane Society of the United States are being used to teach "humane education" courses across America. Such courses are mandatory in some school districts in California, Florida, Illinois, Maine, New Jersey, New York, and many other states.

CNN Debate: Is hunting with kids safe?

continued from 205 do you say about that? Because, I mean, that's a tragic situation. And you don't want to see that kind of thing happen. And she does have a point. We're talking about lethal weapons here with very young people.

Ted Nugent, rock star, writer, hunter: Yes, but, still, the statistics do prove, irrefutably, Miles, that the death rate is higher in many, many other activities. Remember that these kids get to hunting camp in vehicles, in high-speed vehicles on highways using gasoline and hunting camps and knives at the kitchen table, that we will never be able to protect each other from ourselves. There's always going to be accidents. And they are always tragic and they are always heartbreaking. But, as you saw in the report, hunting is at an all-time safe level right now, with the fewest accidents, the fewest injuries, the fewest deaths in the history of the shooting sports. And let's be perfectly clear. Heidi Prescott and the Humane Society of the United States, they are on record to ban all hunting. So, I think she's quite disingenuous in her claim that she wants to change the age. She wants to ban hunting. It's come out of her mouth hundreds of times. And it's her official policy. So, let's call a spade a spade here.

O'Brien: Heidi, you want to say it again tonight?

Prescott: Well, again, you know, the Humane Society of the United States, obviously, considers hunting not part of a humane world. But, tonight, we're talking about…

O'Brien: So, so, I'm sorry. Let's get that straight. You would like all hunting banned?

Prescott: Well…

(LAUGHTER)

These materials typically spout feel-good platitudes, such as this quote from an article in a 1998 issue of the *Animals' Agenda*: "Humane education teaches about our relationships with each other, other species, and the Earth itself, and promotes respect, compassion, critical thinking, and positive, life-affirming, humane choices."[7]

Myth Debunked

America's hunters aren't going anywhere. Though the number of sportsmen shrank by 7 percent between 1991 and 2001, according to the U.S. Fish and Wildlife Service, hunter numbers actually rose from 14,740,188 in 2003 to 14,779,071 in 2004, a statistical hiccup, but it shows that though the number of American hunters has been falling slightly for decades, it isn't diving off a statistical cliff.

When you dig into these teaching materials, you start to scratch your head. They're spinning the facts about the natural world to suit a nonsensical ideology. They think compassion and kindness can stomp out nature's predator-and-prey system. They maintain that cougars and bears are attacking people because we're "invading their habitat," even when these attacks occur in areas that have been urban for decades. They refer to dogs, cats, hamsters, and the like as "companion animals," not *pets*, because in their anthropomorphic view, animals have the same rights as humans. They are against using animals for research to find cures for diseases that kill millions of people. They view any kind of meat eating by humans as "inhumane." They consider hunting as a control measure for wildlife overpopulations to be "irresponsible."

Here's the National Humane Education Society's official stance on hunting:

> NHES opposes the hunting of wildlife for either sport or trophy because neither serves any human survival need and is inherently cruel. Some hunting advocates argue that hunting

is necessary to control wildlife populations and to prevent wildlife from destroying the environment via overfeeding. NHES contends that in most instances ample forage exists to support the wildlife population, and nature has provided natural controls over population growth—as animals increase in numbers, reproduction decreases. If, however, nature fails to maintain adequate control over the wildlife population, NHES recommends that wildlife management officials implement programs to remove the overpopulated wildlife from growing urban areas and relocate them to less populated areas. In instances where such relocation efforts cannot be implemented and nature fails to provide ample forage and natural population controls; and there is a demonstrable need (starvation or disease) to kill some wildlife, then it should be performed by responsible persons who utilize methods that result in instantaneous death.[8]

A Fact the Media Won't Tell You

When given a choice, many young people chose hunting. Youth numbers are beginning to show signs of climbing because youth-only hunts are being implemented and age restrictions are being rethought. For example, more than eleven thousand new apprentice-hunting licenses were sold in Michigan and Ohio in 2006, after the states passed "Families Afield" legislation allowing youths to try hunting under direct supervision of an experienced adult hunter. The eleven thousand newcomers represented a 10 percent increase in young hunters age six to fifteen in those two states.

This Is Actually What They Think

A Humane Education lesson plan for teachers tries to humanize animals with these tips:

1. During nice weather take younger children on a walk to view birds, squirrels, and rabbits. Point out how the animals are enjoying the day just like the children. Would the animals want someone to hurt them? [Predators like foxes, coyotes, and hawks, would surely feel awful if they could understand this.]

2. Never refer to an animal as "it." Always use "she" or "he." [As in, "Look at that bullfrog, he looks just like you."]

3. Teach children that all animals have feelings just as people do. Get children thinking about how animals might feel in different situations. ["Kids, just imagine if a hunter were after you!"]

Source: http://www.theanimalspirit.com/AWE.html.

Like their logic, this is a muddled message. The last sentence actually voids the stance's main argument, because wildlife biologists already set hunting seasons and bag limits to prevent wildlife starvation and disease and hunters already utilize methods that result in instantaneous death. And the position's other main point is actually cruel—trap-and-transfer of wild game is prohibitively expensive and results in a large percentage of animals dying from stress. Also, biologists don't like to use this technique because deer and other wildlife taken from one habitat and thrust into another have a high mortality rate due to difficulty acclimating to their new environs. Besides, as any seasoned biologist would point out: who's going to take the dispossessed deer, cougars, or bears?

The entire humane education ideology is built on the false premise that nature only wants to be hugged and that humans can opt out of the food chain. They seem to think Mother Nature is a real entity, that Mother Nature has "natural controls" she'll sprinkle about like fairy dust to reduce pregnancies when animals overpopulate. Though the viewpoints touted by these animal welfare organizations promote a secular humanist view, they believe humans are separate from nature, not natural or divine, but just despoilers of the natural system who thwart nature's system of checks and balances. They believe wholeheartedly in evolution, but think that nature should be kept static—that it can be kept without change. They want to fence off the wild world and sit miles away in their offices in concrete metropolises and feel good that nature is out there, safe from evil humans.

When nature defies these false boundaries, the humane education zealots don't admit that humans are a part of nature and so can hunt to control wildlife populations. Instead, animal rights activists and animal welfare groups purport that we should feel guilty because we must be responsible for auto-deer collisions or gator attacks—after all, we, the invaders, are living in "their" habitat, so we can't do anything real to solve these human-wildlife conflicts.

Without exception, the anti-milk, anti-meat, anti–common sense, anti-hunting viewpoints of these humane education groups are outside the mainstream—according to the National Shooting Sports Foundation, surveys by the U.S. Fish and Wildlife Service have consistently shown that about 80 percent of Americans approve of hunting. The humane education groups themselves even admit they aren't mainstream; for example, a 2000 article in the *Animals' Agenda* said, "Unless we raise children with values that differ significantly from those that dominate our culture and school systems, we cannot expect to create a world in which all beings and the Earth they share are treated with respect, care, and justice." However, despite being in left field, these materials are used to teach millions of young children and are somehow seen as politically correct by many of the national media outlets.

On the right side of the issue

On the other side of the issue is the National Shooting Sports Foundation (NSSF), the National Rifle Association (NRA), the Sportsmen's Alliance, and other hunter-rights and hunter-conservation organizations. The NRA's Eddie Eagle GunSafe Program, for example, has taught more than nineteen million kindergarteners through fourth graders: "If you see a gun: Stop. Don't Touch. Leave the Area. Tell an Adult." The NSSF has published educational booklets and uses classes and programs to teach children gun safety, to give an honest view of nature, and to ensure a continued conservation ethic. The NRA's Youth Hunter Education Challenge teaches conservation and gun safety to about fifty thousand kids across the country each year. The NSSF's Step Outside program and state wildlife department summer programs teach many more (see Appendix D). But the real story is what's going on legislatively to make sure America's youth don't lose the real connection with the natural world that hunting fosters.

Despite opposition from the mainstream media and from anti-hunting organizations, the NSSF, the U.S. Sportsmen's Alliance, and the National Wild Turkey Federation, with on-the-ground lobbying from the NRA, are increasing youth participation in hunting. Called the Families Afield program, the initiative is designed to eliminate or reduce minimum age barriers and create hunter mentoring programs to introduce youths to hunting. State wildlife agencies have embraced the initiative because conservation money dries up without hunters, and wildlife biologists can't control deer and predator populations without their allies in orange.

Since Families Afield launched in 2004, at least eleven states have changed laws and regulations to create additional hunting opportunities for youths. As of January 2007, thirty states didn't have a minimum age restriction for hunting; as a result, parents, not politicians, could decide the right age to introduce their sons and daughters to hunting in more than half the country. According to research from the International Hunter Education Association, youths who hunt in states with no minimum age restrictions have slightly fewer accidents than those who hunt in states with age restrictions. The likely reason for this is that adults are able to teach children to hunt safely when they can take them afield at younger ages.

Also, at least twenty states now have adult-mentored youth hunting programs, which allow youths to try hunting before taking a conservation course. This dismantles a huge roadblock to hunting: many youths who are invited by friends to try hunting often can't go because they haven't taken the course. Under these looser rules, you can get the kid hooked first, so he's eager to fulfill the conservation course requirement.

In fact, a U.S. Fish and Wildlife Service study recommended that some hunting regulations be changed to make it easier for youths to try hunting.

A Fact the Media Won't Tell You

Kids who hunt don't do Columbine. In 2001, according to a *Journal of the American Medical Association* study, about 12 percent of the homicides in U.S. schools occurred in rural school districts where hunting participation is highest. About 58 percent of the murders occurred in urban schools and 30 percent occurred in suburban schools. According to *Youth Violence: A Report of the Surgeon General*: "Youths at greatest risk of being killed in school-associated violence are those from a racial or ethnic minority, senior high schools, and urban school districts." A basic conclusion drawn from this data is that students are not showing up at schools with their deer rifles looking to kill people. Kids who learn to hunt attain a respect for firearms. And Eric Harris and Dylan Klebold, the two murderers who killed twelve students and a teacher in 1999 at Colorado's suburban Columbine High School, were not hunters.

"School-Associated Violent Deaths in the United States, 1994–1999," *Journal of the American Medical Association*, Vol. 286, No. 21, December 5, 2001.

The study determined that some state laws actually make it too difficult for parents to introduce their young sons and daughters to hunting. Such state laws restrict those younger than twelve or fourteen from hunting and subject them to stringent coursework requirements when they do reach the minimum age. A few states even forbid parents to let their underage children tag along on a hunt. These barriers cause many youths to lose interest before they even have a chance to try hunting. Eventually, as participation trails off, hunting itself—and all its ties to conservation funding and wildlife management in America—is compromised.

In 2001, U.S. Fish and Wildlife data showed that for every ten adult hunters only six young hunters were taking their place, which is why conservationists are working hard to introduce youths to hunting. If hunting does fade away as an American pastime, that's bad news for songbirds, vegetarians, suburban drivers, and our nation's wildlife.

Chapter 14

HUNTERS AND GUN RIGHTS

"A well-regulated militia being necessary to the security of a free State, the right of the people to keep and bear arms shall not be infringed." The U.S. Bill of Rights yellowed in the National Archives for nearly two centuries before the meaning conveyed by the twenty-seven words in the Second Amendment became controversial. In recent decades, however, the mainstream media has decided that the Second Amendment doesn't protect an individual's right to bear arms. When the gun control issue came to the fore in the late 1990s, this became the politically correct reading of the Constitution. The record needs to be set straight.

First of all, the Second Amendment is still open to interpretation because the closest the Supreme Court has ever come to defining it was *United States v. Miller*, a 1939 Supreme Court decision so ambiguous that both sides of the gun control debate claim it as a victory. The defendants in *Miller* were indicted for transporting a sawed-off shotgun from Oklahoma to Arkansas, a violation of the 1934 National Firearms Act, which prohibited interstate transportation of certain types of firearms (such as machine guns, rifles, and shotguns with barrels shorter than eighteen inches) without registration or stamped order. The prosecutor's first argument in *Miller* was that the defendants weren't members of a militia and so did not have the protection of the Second Amendment (the "collective

Guess what?

- The Second Amendment protects every American citizen's right to bear arms, not just those in militias or the military.

- Washington, D.C., has a strict no-guns law and the thirteenth highest crime rate in the nation—just another example of the fact that when guns are outlawed, only outlaws have guns.

215

rights" interpretation gun control groups still tout today). However, the Supreme Court didn't rule on this particular question, thereby passing up an opportunity to define the Second Amendment. Instead, the Court decided that the sawed-off shotgun wasn't a firearm type "employed in civilized warfare." In so doing, the Court indicated that only military-type arms are constitutionally protected. As a result, the defendants lost the appeal. (However, gun control groups should be wary of rallying behind *Miller*; after all, if the Second Amendment covers arms used by the military, then handguns and sawed-off shotguns are the least of their worries.)

Now, because the Supreme Court hasn't settled this issue, on March 9, 2007, the D.C. Circuit of the U.S. Court of Appeals didn't have a clear precedent to follow when it decided *Parker v. District of Columbia*,[1] a lawsuit contending that the District of Columbia's gun control laws are unconstitutional. Specifically, *Parker* asserted that the District's near-total ban on handguns and its requirement that registered shotguns and rifles be disassembled or locked when stored at home preclude any chance of someone using a firearm for self-defense. Dick Heller, a D.C. police officer, was one of the plaintiffs in the case. Heller was permitted to carry a gun on duty, yet the District government denied his application to keep a gun at home for self-defense. This blatant usurpation of Heller's right to bear arms was upheld but then appealed to the D.C. Circuit of the U.S. Court of Appeals.

The following facts outlined in this important case will give you a retort every time an anti-gun zealot challenges your Second Amendment rights.

The truth about the Second Amendment

Judge Laurence Silberman's responsibility in hearing *Parker* was to review the district court's ruling against Heller and the other plaintiffs. In his ruling, Silberman wrote, "The court held that the Second Amendment does not bestow any rights on individuals except, perhaps, when an individual serves in an organized militia such as today's National Guard. WE REVERSE." Judge Laurence Silberman's majority opinion ruled that the Second Amendment to the U.S. Constitution is not limited to organized militias, but extends to the personal possession of guns for purposes such as self-defense and hunting. In other words, Heller and every other American citizen have the right to bear arms.

This case was important because its entire underpinning rested on whether the Second Amendment gives an individual the right to own a gun. The six plaintiffs argued that the District of Columbia's gun control laws, which forbade handguns or unlocked long guns, took away their Second Amendment rights. The defendant, the District of Columbia, asserted that the Second Amendment allows only a state militia to collectively own guns. The District's lawyers also argued that the Second Amendment's use of the phrase "a well-regulated militia" refers to organized militias of the founding era, which are no longer in existence. In this interpretation, the Second Amendment is now defunct.

However, this collective right argument stumbled when Silberman pointed out that the Bill of Rights is almost entirely a declaration of *individual* rights. Every other provision of the Bill of Rights, except the Tenth Amendment, which addresses the allocation of governmental power, protects rights enjoyed by individual citizens. To dance around this fact, the collective right advocates contend the first U.S. Congress tossed a state right into a list of individual liberties without explaining why. To this point, Judge Silberman wrote, "The Second Amendment would be an inexplicable aberration if it were not read to protect individual rights as well."

To muddle this fact, the District's lawyers argued that the Second Amendment was written in response to fears that the new federal government would disarm the state militias by preventing men from bearing arms. Thus, they argued, the Second Amendment should be understood to check federal power to regulate firearms only when federal legislation was directed at the abolition of state militias. Judge Silberman responded, "At first blush, it seems passing strange that the able lawyers and statesmen in the first Congress (including James Madison) would have expressed a sole concern for state militias with the language of the Second Amendment. Surely there was a more direct locution, such as, 'Congress shall make no law disarming the state militias' or 'States have a right to a well-regulated militia.'

"The District's argument—as strained as it seems to us—is hardly an isolated view," Judge Silberman continued. "In the Second Amendment debate, there are two camps. On one side are the collective right theorists who argue that the amendment protects only a right of the various state governments to preserve and arm their militias. So understood, the right amounts to an expression of militant federalism, prohibiting the federal government from denuding the states of their armed fighting forces. On the other side of the debate are those who argue that the Second Amendment protects a right of individuals to possess arms for private use. To

Books You're Not Supposed to Read

The Origin of the Second Amendment: A Documentary History of the Bill of Rights 1787–1792 edited by David E. Young; Ontonagon, MI: Golden Oak Books, 1995. This eight-hundred-page book reprints letters, speeches, and debates from the founding fathers on the Second Amendment. It also republishes newspaper editorials and articles on the right to bear arms that were originally run in the founding era. If you want to fully understand the Second Amendment, this is mandatory reading.

The Bias Against Guns: Why Almost Everything You've Heard About Gun Control Is Wrong by John R. Lott, Jr.; Washington, DC: Regnery, 2003. This is a thorough analysis of the Second Amendment and gun control today.

these individual right theorists, the amendment guarantees personal liberty analogous to the First Amendment's protection of free speech, or the Fourth Amendment's right to be free from unreasonable searches and seizures."

Silberman also noted that in 2004 the U.S. Department of Justice, under then attorney general John Ashcroft, upheld an individual right to bear arms and published a report titled "Whether the Second Amendment Secures an Individual Right,"[2] which lays out a clear history of how the Second Amendment was written.

However, because there was no clear precedent from the U.S. Supreme Court, Silberman decided to turn to the text of the Second Amendment itself. In doing so Silberman showed himself to be a strict constructionist. Rather than interpreting the Constitution as he might like it to have been written, as activist judges so often do these days, he interpreted it literally, in its original context.

Silberman wrote, "The most important word is the one the drafters chose to describe the holders of the right to bear arms: 'the people.' After all, that term is found in the First, Second, Fourth, Ninth, and Tenth Amendments. And it has never been doubted that these provisions were designed to protect the interests of *individuals*." Also, Judge Silberman noted that the "Tenth Amendment ('The powers not delegated to the United States by the Constitution, nor prohibited by it to the States, are reserved to the States respectively, or to the people') indicates that the authors of the Bill of Rights were perfectly capable of distinguishing between 'the people,' on the one hand, and 'the states.'"

Therefore, he ascertained, the natural reading of "the right of the people" in the Second Amendment would correspond with usage elsewhere in the Bill of Rights, meaning the right is an individual one. The District of Columbia, on the other hand, wanted the court to read "the people" to mean some subset of individuals, such as "the organized militia." Thus Judge Silberman concluded by saying, "There is certainly nothing in this history to substantiate the strained reading of the Second Amendment offered by the District."

In the dissent, Judge Karen Henderson mocked the decision for its length, but Judge Silberman could have called on even more historical evidence for his ruling. For example, he might have pointed out that though Thomas Jefferson was a proponent for drafting a bill of rights, the Second Amendment wasn't his own invention. The U.S. Bill of Rights was based primarily on the states' bills of rights, which found their origins in common law and in the British Bill of Rights of 1689. All of these states' bills of rights clearly supported an individual's right to keep and bear arms.

For example, in February 1788, the Massachusetts Convention was the first to include with its ratification of the U.S. Constitution a list of recommended amendments. Among the amendments, Samuel Adams proposed that the Constitution "be never construed to authorize Congress . . . to prevent the people of the United States, who are peaceable citizens, from keeping their own arms." New Hampshire's convention adapted some of Adams's proposals. Among others, it recommended that "Congress shall never disarm any citizen unless such as are or have been in actual rebellion." And the New York Convention included this proposed amendment: "That the people have a right to keep and bear arms; that a well-regulated militia, including the body of the people capable of bearing arms, is the proper, natural, and safe defence of a free State."[3]

In fact, every recommendation in the state conventions regarding the right to bear arms sought to protect an individual right, not a collective right. Therefore, with regards to gun rights, the first U.S. Congress simply followed the path marked by the state declarations when they assembled the U.S. Bill of Rights and, consequently, they proposed an individual right, not a collective right restricted to state militias.

What the Founders Said

Thomas Jefferson

"No free man shall ever be debarred the use of arms."

First draft of proposed constitution for Virginia, available at http://www.constitution.org/jw/acm_5-m.txt.

"And what country can preserve its liberties, if its rulers are not warned from time to time that this people preserve the spirit of resistance? Let them take arms....The tree of liberty must be refreshed from time to time, with the blood of patriots and tyrants."

Letter to William Smith, November 13, 1787, available at http://www.loc.gov/exhibits/jefferson/105.html.

George Mason

"...to disarm the people, that was the best and most effectual way to enslave them."

Debates on ratification of the Virginia constitution, June 14, 1788, 380, available at http://www.constitution.org/rc/rat_va_12.txt.

Patrick Henry

"Are we at last brought to such humiliating and debasing degradation that we cannot be trusted with arms for our defense? Where is the difference between having our arms in possession and under our direction, and having them under the management of Congress? If our defense be the real object of having those arms, in whose hands can they be trusted with more propriety, or equal safety to us, as in our own hands?"

"Guard with jealous attention the public liberty. Suspect everyone who approaches that jewel. Unfortunately, nothing will preserve it but downright force. Whenever you give up that force, you are inevitably ruined."

Quoted in *Jonathan Elliot's Debates in the Several State Converntions on the Adoption of the Federal Constitution. Vol. 3: Debates in the Federal Convention of 1787 as Reported by James Madison* (2nd ed., Philadelphia, 1836), 45.

The mainstream media gives in

The *Parker v. District of Columbia* decision caused a mainstream liberal media temper tantrum. The *New York Times* editorial page accused the U.S. Court of Appeals of striding "blithely past a long-standing Supreme Court precedent, the language of the Constitution, and the pressing needs of public safety."[4] The *Washington Post* called it a "radical ruling" and screamed, "In overturning the District of Columbia's long-standing ban on handguns yesterday, a federal appeals court turned its back on nearly seventy years of Supreme Court precedent to give a new and dangerous meaning to the Second Amendment."[5]

The "seventy years of precedent" refers to the *United States v. Miller* Supreme Court decision in 1939, an ambiguous ruling that actually favors an individual's right to bear military arms. As for people killed as a consequence, they might be right: as a result of the ruling, more violent criminals might have their obituaries featured in the NRA's "Armed Citizen" column. After all, while the District's violent crime rate has followed the national trend down from a bloody high in the early 1990s, its overall crime rate remains among the highest of U.S. cities, and in 2005 it was ranked as the thirteenth most dangerous city in the nation. In fact, D.C.'s crime rate surpasses those of Los Angeles and New York. Perhaps if the residents of D.C. had the right to bear arms in self-defense, some the 165 D.C. rape victims of 2005 could have driven off or killed their attackers.[6]

After the *Parker v. District of Columbia* decision, the Brady Campaign to Prevent Gun Violence (formerly known as Handgun Control, Inc.) turned up the heated rhetoric another notch, releasing a paper titled "Second Amendment Fantasy." The paper, they claimed, "exposes how the majority opinion in *Parker* is a tangled web of inconsistency, flawed reasoning, distortion of binding precedent, and misunderstood historical materials, all in service to the court's single-minded determination to rewrite the Second Amendment."[7]

Since the decision, the anti-gunner view has turned from reinterpretation to total repeal. Ten days after the ruling, Benjamin Wittes wrote an article for the online version of the leftist magazine the *New Republic*: "The simple truth is that the individual-rights view is in intellectual ascendancy, and not just among gun-loving wing nuts. . . . It's time for gun control supporters to come to grips with the fact that the amendment actually means something in contemporary society. For which reason, I hereby advance a modest proposal: Let's repeal the damned thing."[8]

A few months later, the *New York Times* had gone from rage to depression to acceptance: In May 2007 an article titled "A Liberal Case for Gun Rights Sways Judiciary," quoted liberal scholars like Harvard law professor Laurence H. Tribe who said they had come to believe the Second Amendment protects an individual right. The article even noted: "Several other leading liberal constitutional scholars, notably Akhil Reed Amar at Yale and Sanford Levinson at the University of Texas, are in broad agreement favoring an individual rights interpretation."[9]

The newest tactic: Divide and conquer

So have law-abiding gun owners won a fundamental debate? While the D.C. Circuit has come down on their side, the Supreme Court is closely divided on the issue. This is also another reason why presidential elections are so important: whoever is elected president in 2008 may get to pick one or even two Supreme Court nominees, who could swing the Court left or right regarding the interpretation of the Second Amendment.

Meanwhile, hunters and shooters are increasingly being treated as two different factions by politically correct anti-gun groups. Organizations like the Brady Campaign are trying the divide-and-conquer strategy on Second Amendment advocates. The latest example of this is the American Hunters & Shooters Association (AHSA), a group that says it's for "reasonable gun control" yet has been staffed with anti-gun activists.

The AHSA thinks the 1994 assault weapons ban was "reasonable." *Reasonable* is the wrong word for this legislation. There is no functional difference between the firearms banned by that law and a hunter's Remington 1187 duck gun or Winchester Super X Rifle. Banning a gun because it looks scary is neither reasonable nor harmless. It's the beginning of a ban on a type of firearm that is over a century old: the gas-operated semi-automatic firearm. The AHSA has also declared that .50-caliber rifles should be banned. (It's unclear if this ban would include Smith & Wesson's .500-caliber handgun or the .50-caliber muzzleloaders used by millions of hunters today.)

Meanwhile, the AHSA's central tactic is to wound the NRA. For example, AHSA executive director Bob Ricker told CNN, "It just became clear to me that the extreme positions the NRA was forcing everyone to take was really hurting hunters and shooters, like myself."[10]

NRA chief lobbyist Chris Cox smashed back by rattling off Ricker's anti-gun résumé: "Ricker hasn't been able to sidestep his history as a failed gun-industry lobbyist, then as a paid shill for the anti-gun lobby and its lawyers. Ricker was paid to give a sworn deposition in the baseless New York City lawsuit against the firearm industry on September 27, 2005. Ricker reports AHSA as merely another one of his clients in the deposition and that his services as executive director are compensated at the rate of $3,000 per month. Ricker stated his 'biggest' client was the Educational Fund to End Handgun Violence, which is the 'educational' arm of the Coalition to Stop Gun Violence, a gun-ban group."

The AHSA is undeniably staffed with gun control advocates. For example, AHSA's board member John Rosenthal was a founder of the anti-gun Massachusetts state group Stop Handgun Violence. AHSA's president, Ray Schoenke, has donated money to the Brady Campaign.[11]

"Reasonable gun control"

The perceived opening presented by the AHSA's "reasonable gun control" mantra hasn't been overlooked by anti-gun politicians. For example, consider Senator John Kerry's duplicity: Kerry's prowess as a hunter became a joke when he bragged to the *Milwaukee Journal Sentinel*, "I go out with my trusty twelve-gauge double-barrel, crawl around on my stomach. I track and move and decoy and play games and try to outsmart [deer]. You know, you kind of play the wind. That's hunting."[12] Anyone who has ever hunted knows deer hunters don't crawl around on their stomachs. It seems Kerry got his Vietnam "heroics" confused with his hunting hallucinations.

Now, there's certainly nothing new about a politician pandering, and hunters might even have considered Kerry's clumsy attempts flattering if he wasn't hiding so much hypocrisy. For example, when asked by *Outdoor Life* magazine if he was a gun owner, Kerry answered, "My favorite gun is the M-16 that saved my life and that of my crew in Vietnam. I don't own one of those now, but one of my reminders of my service is a Communist Chinese assault rifle."[13]

Kerry's duplicity blew up in the press. Kerry was simultaneously pushing for a renewal of the 1994 assault weapons ban and gloating in a hunting magazine that he owned a Communist Chinese assault rifle, a gun outlawed by the ban. When news organizations ran with the story, Kerry's first reaction was to blame his aides for fibbing—though he later admitted to owning the rifle.

As it turned out, Kerry's hypocrisy on guns ran deeper than his closet. Since his election to the U.S. Senate in 1984, he'd voted to ban guns, impose waiting periods on gun buyers, financially punish gun manufactures for operating a legal business, and restrict the free speech of Second Amendment advocates. Incredibly, Kerry co-sponsored Senate Resolution 1431, a bill that would have banned all semi-automatic shotguns, all detachable-magazine semi-automatic rifles, and many other guns (including his Chinese assault rifle). The bill would even have banned a shotgun he took hunting in front of television cameras as he ran for president.

As if all that wasn't enough, the Humane Society of the United States, the biggest anti-hunting group in the U.S., gave Kerry a 100 percent rating.[14] In a further attempt to have it both ways, Kerry boasted, "I've had my name on every piece of animal-rights legislation ever passed by Congress!" to the HSUS while telling hunters, "I do a better job of fighting for the rights of sportsmen than George Bush does."[15]

If Kerry had been elected president and had kept his word, he would have tried to ban all semi-automatic firearms, which are common in hunting. In fact, it could be easily argued that semi-automatic rifles are more humane than other models, because they make taking a second shot (when needed) fast. Semi-autos also reduce recoil because some of the energy is used to cycle the next round into the chamber. This makes them easier to shoot for women and smaller people who are sensitive to heavy recoil. So-called "assault rifles" are semi-automatics, and to claim otherwise is to differentiate by looks—as in, "Sorry, that gun's too dangerous for civilian use, 'cause it has a pistol grip!"

So during election cycles when organizations or politicians try to divide shooters from hunters, remember that hunters and shooters are one and the same.

APPENDICES

HOW TO GET STARTED

Not everyone has the chance to sit next to a parent on a crisp autumn dawn listening to the whistling wings of ducks descending. To wade through a field of tan, swaying grass behind a bird dog with the expectation of a pheasant flushing in a flurry of gaudy grandeur. Or to call in a rut-crazed bull elk in a high-country aspen grove. Not everyone—just 6 percent of Americans these days—gets to feel the thrill of not just watching nature, but of being an active player, a predator, a wolf, fully enraptured in nature's seasonal rhythms, connected through generations to our origins in the hunt.

Many pass through adolescence with no real connection to the wild, though many surely yearn to see and feel how irrevocably we are still linked with nature. Too many are trapped in the convoluted guilt of modern environmentalism, which tells us we shouldn't acknowledge our part in the natural cycle—that we should be ashamed of our past. Others fall away from that connection as college and careers send them running among responsibilities only to recall in melancholy moments the solace they once felt in nature.

Reaching out is hard. There's jargon in hunting, terminology and unique phrases—B&C bucks, scrape lines, strut zones, decoy spreads— that to the uninitiated are as confusing as ancient Greek. There are myths and mischaracterizations about hunters. And there's a learning curve.

Where do you find a mandatory hunting-conservation course? How do you meet people who'll gladly show you the way? How do you master the dense regulations? Where do you go? What firearm do you buy? How do you shoot? If you need answers to these questions, here is your guide.

Where can I find a hunting-conservation course?

Every state has a mandatory hunting-conservation course. Some states have exceptions that allow a licensed hunter to take a non-licensed hunter into the field to try hunting for the first time. Call your state game department for specific regulations pertaining to your state (see Appendix B). Most courses can be taken during one weekend and teach species identification, shot placement, regulations, and firearm safety. At IHEA.com, a Web site run by the International Hunter Education Association, you can take a sample hunter-education course.

Who will show me what to do?

Magazines and books will get you started—and will whet your appetite. A good first step is to join the National Rifle Association and subscribe to *American Hunter* magazine. There are also dozens of national and regional hunting magazines on the shelf in just about every supermarket and bookstore. Magazines and outdoor television will give you an idea of what's out there and will show you how it's done; however, the best way to learn is with a hunting mentor. If you don't have an uncle, brother-in-law, or friend who can show you the way, you can join your local hunting club or call your state's game department and ask about classes and instructors who can help—money generated from taxes on hunting equipment is often used for educational purposes. The Web site huntinfo.org will answer many of your questions. If you are a female or a teen, you'll find special programs just for you.

Programs for women

According to research from the National Sporting Goods Association, 72 percent more women are hunting with firearms today than just five years ago. And 50 percent more women are now target shooting. The statistics are from NSGA surveys spanning 2001 through 2005, and they show that more than three million women now hunt and more than five million now enjoy shooting.

A big reason for the surge in women's participation in hunting is Women in the Outdoors programs. Many state game departments now have such programs. They invite women to events where they will be shown how to shoot, hunt, and be ethical conservationists. In some cases these programs host women at a lodge or camp where they'll be taken hunting. The National Rifle Association's Women on Target program sponsors "women-only" hunts and instructional shoots. For a list of hunts and shoots, log on to NRAhq.org/women/wot.asp. The National Wild Turkey Federation has eighteen full-time Women in the Outdoors regional coordinators and a quarterly magazine dedicated to women's interests. They host hunts and shoots all over the U.S. To see a list of NWTF's Women in the Outdoors events, log on to womenintheoutdoors.org.

Youth mentoring programs

For a list of conservation organizations that have youth mentoring programs, see Appendix D. Groups from the National Rifle Association to the National Shooting Sports Foundation have a lot of events and programs to help youths get started. States also have youth programs and camps and many have special youth hunts and seasons, which allow young hunters to get the jump on everyone else. Call your state game department for details.

Where do I go?

The NRA has developed a database that will direct you to public lands open to hunting, located at freehunters.org. Just click on "Places to Hunt" and then choose a state. The National Shooting Sports Foundation has a Web site at huntandshoot.org that is also searchable by state. Both resources will lead you to public hunting areas near you. You can also call your state wildlife department; most states have maps and other resources available to show you where to go.

What firearm do I choose?

This is one of the first questions everyone asks. Before it can be answered, however, you have to decide what type of game animal you'd like to pursue. Next you need to check your state's hunting regulations to check restrictions—some states allow you to use a rifle when deer hunting, others require you to use a slug gun or muzzleloader. There are shot size and type restrictions for waterfowl hunting, and many other regulations designed to keep hunting ethical and safe. These parameters will be outlined in your state wildlife department's regulation booklet.

Once you've read the regulations and have decided what game you wish to hunt, it's time to select a firearm or a bow. There are a lot of books available that will help you weigh the tradeoffs for different firearm actions and shot types; for example, the National Rifle Association's *Hunter Skills* series of books teaches how to hunt and shoot and what firearms to chose. *Hunter Skills* books are available on upland birds, whitetail deer, waterfowl, bowhunting, and more. This subject is much too complex to cover authoritatively in this book, but employees at any sporting goods store, people who hunt, and various videos, books, and magazines cover the topic.

How do I learn to shoot?

Shooting courses performed by NRA-certified firearms instructors can be found at nra.org. There are also shooting schools available. If you would like to try upland bird or waterfowl hunting, you can go to places like the National Wing & Clay Shooting School (360-225-5000; shootinginstruction.com) or to one of Orvis's Wingshooting Schools, which are located in Florida, Georgia, Vermont, and New York (800-235-9763; orvis.com). Your local skeet facility likely has professional instruction available as well.

If you wish to hunt with a rifle, you'll have to look for a local rifle range. You may have to drive to find one, but most regions have shooting facilities available. Rifle instruction is harder to come by but can be found from NRA-certified instructors or from other professionals at some ranges. Log on to nrahq.org/shootingrange/findlocal.asp and you'll be able to search for a local range in your state and region. There are 212 ranges listed in New York State alone. The Web site rangeinfo.org will also direct you to local shooting facilities.

Appendix B

WILDLIFE DEPARTMENTS

USDA Forest Service
(202) 205-8333
http://www.fs.fed.us

U.S. Fish and Wildlife Service
(800) 344-WILD
http://www.fws.gov

Alabama Department of Conservation and Natural Resources
(334) 242-3467
http://www.outdooralabama.com

Alaska Department of Fish and Game
(907) 465-4100
http://www.adfg.state.ak.us

Alberta Sustainable Resource Development
(780) 427-2711
http://www.srd.gov.ab.ca

Arizona Game and Fish Department
(602) 942-3000
http://www.azgfd.com

Arkansas Game and Fish Commission
(800) 364-4263
http://www.agfc.state.ar.us

British Columbia Ministry of Environment Fish and Wildlife Branch
(800) 663-7867
http://www.gov.bc.ca/fw

**California Department
of Fish and Game**
(916) 445-0411
http://www.dfg.ca.gov

Colorado Division of Wildlife
(303) 297-1192
http://www.wildlife.state.co.us

**Connecticut Department of
Environmental Protection**
(860) 642-7239
http://www.dep.state.ct.us

**Delaware Department of
Natural Resources**
(302) 739-5297
http://www.dnrec.state.de.us

**Florida Fish and Wildlife
Conservation Commission**
(850) 488-4676
http://www.myfwc.com

**Georgia Department of
Natural Resources**
(770) 918-6416
http://www.gohuntgeorgia.com

**Hawaii Department of Land and
Natural Resources**
(808) 587-0166
http://www.state.hi.us./dlnr

Idaho Fish and Game
(208) 334-2920
http://fishandgame.idaho.gov

**Iowa Department of Natural
Resources**
(515) 281-5918
http://www.iowadnr.gov

**Illinois Department of Natural
Resources**
(217) 782-7305
http://www.dnr.state.il.us

**Indiana Division of
Fish and Wildlife**
(317) 233-4976
http://www.wildlife.in.gov

**Kansas Department of
Wildlife and Parks**
(620) 672-5911
http://www.kdwp.state.ks.us

Kentucky Department of Fish and Wildlife Resources
(800) 858-1549
http://www.kdfwr.state.ky.us

Louisiana Department of Wildlife and Fisheries
(225) 765-2350
http://www.wlf.state.la.us

Maine Department of Inland Fisheries and Wildlife
(207) 287-8000
http://www.state.me.us/ifw

Manitoba Conservation Wildlife and Ecosystem Protection Branch
(800) 214-6497
http://www.gov.mb.ca/
conservation/wildlife

Maryland Department of Natural Resources
(410) 260-8540
http://www.dnr.state.md.us

Massachusetts Division of Fisheries and Wildlife
(508) 792-7270
http://www.mass.gov/
masswildlife

Michigan Department of Natural Resources
(517) 373-1263
http://www.michigan.gov/dnr

Minnesota Department of Natural Resources
(888) 646-6367
http://www.dnr.state.mn.us

Mississippi Wildlife, Fisheries and Parks
(800) 5GO-HUNT
http://www.mdwfp.com

Missouri Department of Conservation
(573) 751-4115
http://www.missouri
conservation.org

Montana Fish, Wildlife and Parks
(406) 444-2535
http://www.fwp.state.mt.us

Nebraska Game and Parks Commission
(402) 471-0641
http://www.OutdoorNebraska.org

Nevada Department of Wildlife
(775) 688-1500
http://www.ndow.org

**New Hampshire Fish
and Game Department**
(603) 271-3422
http://www.wildlife.state.nh.us

**New Jersey Division of
Fish and Wildlife**
(908) 735-8793
http://www.state.nj.us/dep/fgw

New Mexico Game and Fish
(505) 476-8000
http://www.wildlife.state.nm.us

**New York Department of
Environmental Conservation**
(518) 402-8843
http://www.dec.state.ny.us

**North Carolina Wildlife
Resources Commission**
(919) 733-7291
http://www.ncwildlife.org

**North Dakota Game and
Fish Department**
(701) 328-6300
http://www.state.nd.us/gnf

**Ohio Department of
Natural Resources**
(614) 265-7040
http://www.dnr.state.oh.us

**Oklahoma Department of
Wildlife Conservation**
(405) 521-2730
http://www.wildlifedepartment.com

**Ontario Ministry of
Natural Resources**
(800) 667-1940
http://www.mnr.gov.on.ca/MNR

**Oregon Department of
Fish and Wildlife**
(503) 947-6300
http://www.dfw.state.or.us

Pennsylvania Game Commission
(717) 787-2084
http://www.pgc.state.pa.us

Quebec Ministry of Natural Resources and Wildlife
(418) 521-3830
http://www.fapaq.gouv.qc.ca/en/index1.html

Rhode Island Department of Environmental Management
(401) 789-0281
http://www.dem.state.ri.us

South Carolina Department of Natural Resources
(803) 734-3886
http://www.dnr.state.sc.us

South Dakota Game, Fish and Parks
(605) 773-3485
http://www.sdgfp.info

Tennessee Wildlife Resources Agency
(615) 781-6500
http://www.state.tn.us

Texas Parks and Wildlife Department
(800) 792-1112
http://www.tpwd.state.tx.us

Utah Division of Wildlife Resources
(801) 538-4700
http://www.wildlife.utah.gov

Vermont Fish and Wildlife Department
(802) 241-3700
http://www.anr.state.vt.us/fw/fwhome

Virginia Department of Game and Inland Fisheries
(804) 367-1000
http://www.dgif.state.va.us

Washington Department of Fish and Wildlife
(360) 902-2515
http://www.wdfw.wa.gov

West Virginia Division of Natural Resources
(304) 558-2771
http://www.wvdnr.gov

Wisconsin Department of Natural Resources
(608) 266-2621
http://www.dnr.state.wi.us

Wyoming Game and Fish

(307) 777-4600

http://gf.state.wy.us/

Appendix C

HUNTER-CONSERVATION ORGANIZATIONS

Association of Fish and Wildlife Agencies
444 North Capitol Street, NW
Suite 725
Washington, DC 20001
Phone: (202) 624-7890
Fax: (202) 624-7891
http://www.iafwa.org

Boone and Crockett Club
250 Station Drive
Missoula, MT 59801
Phone: (406) 542-1888
Fax: (406) 542-0784
http://www.boone-crockett.org

Congressional Sportsmen's Foundation
110 North Carolina Avenue, SE
Washington, DC 20003

Phone: (202) 543-6850
http://www.sportsmenslink.org

Delta Waterfowl
P.O. Box 3128
Bismarck, ND 58502
Phone: (888) 987-3695
http://www.deltawaterfowl.org

Ducks Unlimited, Inc.
One Waterfowl Way
Memphis, TN 38120
Phone: (800) 45-DUCKS
http://www.ducksunlimited.org

Izaak Walton League of America
707 Conservation Lane
Gaithersburg, MD 20878
Phone: (301) 548-0150
http://www.iwla.org

**National Rifle Association
of America**
11250 Waples Mill Road
Fairfax, VA 22030
Phone: (800) 672-3888
http://www.nra.org

**National Shooting
Sports Foundation**
11 Mile Hill Road
Newtown, CT 06470
Phone: (203) 426-1320
http://www.nssf.org

National Wild Turkey Federation
P.O. Box 530
Edgefield, SC 29824
Phone: (800) THE-NWTF
http://www.nwtf.org

**North American
Grouse Partnership**
P.O. Box 408
Williamsport, MD 21795
Phone/Fax: (301) 223-1533
http://www.grousepartners.org

Pheasants Forever, Inc.
1783 Buerkle Circle
St. Paul, MN 55110

Phone: (877) 773-2070
Fax: (651) 773-5500
http://www.pheasantsforever.org

Quail Forever
1783 Buerkle Circle
St. Paul, MN 55110
Phone: (866) 457-8245
Fax: (651) 209-4988
http://www.quailforever.org

Quail Unlimited, Inc.
P.O. Box 610
Edgefield, SC 29824
Phone: (803) 637-5731
Fax: (803) 637-0037
http://www.qu.org

**Quality Deer Management
Association**
170 Whitetail Way
P.O. Box 160
Bogart, GA 30622
Phone: (800) 209-3337
Fax: (706) 353-0223
http://www.qdma.com

Rocky Mountain Elk Foundation
5705 Grant Creek
Missoula, MT 59808

Phone: (406) 523-4500
Toll-free: (800) 225-5355
http://www.rmef.org

Ruffed Grouse Society
451 McCormick Rd.
Coraopolis, PA 15108
Phone: (412) 262-4044
Fax: (412) 262-9207
http://www.ruffedgrousesociety.org

Safari Club International
4800 West Gates Pass Road
Tucson, Arizona 85745
Phone: (520) 620-1220
Fax: (520) 622-1205
http://www.safariclub.org

**Theodore Roosevelt
Conservation Partnership**
555 11th Street, NW
6th Floor
Washington, DC 20004
Phone: (202) 654-4600
http://trcp.org

U.S. Sportsmen's Alliance
801 Kingsmill Parkway
Columbus, OH 43229
Phone: (614) 888-4868
http://www.ussportsmen.org

Whitetails Unlimited
P.O. Box 720
2100 Michigan Street
Sturgeon Bay, WI 54235
Phone: (800) 274-5471
Fax: (920) 743-4658
http://www.whitetails
unlimited.com

Wildlife Management Institute
1146 19th Street, NW
Suite 700
Washington, DC 20036
Phone: (202) 371-1808
Fax: (202) 408-5059
http://www.wildlifemanagment
institute.org

The Wildlife Society
5410 Grosvenor Lane
Suite 200
Bethesda, MD 20814
Phone: (301) 897-9770
Fax: (301) 530-2471
http://www.wildlife.org

Appendix D

YOUTH PROGRAMS

Big Brothers Big Sisters: The National Shooting Sports Foundation works with BBBS to introduce youth to hunting and shooting. Web site: www.ksbbbs.org/passiton

Delta Waterfowl: Delta Waterfowl and other pro-hunting organizations are battling the declining number of waterfowlers in Canada and the United States through active promotion of youth hunting. Web site: www.deltawaterfowl.org/waterfowling/youthhunting.php

Ducks Unlimited: Through its Greenwing Program for youths, Ducks Unlimited is educating the conservationists of tomorrow and offering information about waterfowl identification, hunting traditions and ethics, and the important role of hunters in conservation. Web site: www.ducks.org

Families Afield: The National Shooting Sports Foundation, in partnership with National Wild Turkey Federation and the U.S. Sportsmen's Alliance, uses the Families Afield program to increase opportunities for youths in the nearly two dozen states that currently restrict big game hunting by age. Web site: www.nssf.org/programs/FamiliesAfield

National 4-H Shooting Sports Foundation: This program teaches marksmanship, the safe and responsible use of firearms, the principles of hunting and archery, and much more. Web site: www.4-hshootingsports.org

National Rifle Association: The NRA Youth Education Hunter Challenge and other programs host an array of hunting, safety, and shooting programs for youths. Web site: www.nrahq.org

National Wild Turkey Federation: NWTF sponsors youth outreach through Jakes and Xtreme Jakes. Web site: www.nwtf.org

Pheasants Forever: At national and chapter levels, PF invests in young members through a growing variety of activities and events to youth members known as Ringnecks. Its Leopold Education Project provides conservation education to members. Web site: www.pheasantsforever.org/education/index.php

Quail Forever: Dedicated to the protection and enhancement of quail and other upland wildlife through habitat improvement, public awareness, education, and advocacy for sound land management policy, Quail Forever is involved in youth hunts. Web site: www.quailforever.org

Quail Unlimited: Founded in 1981 to battle the problem of dwindling quail populations and declining wildlife habitat, this is the oldest national, nonprofit conservation organization dedicated to the wise management of America's wild quail. Many chapters conduct informational and educational programs such as workshops and youth conservation days. Web site: www.qu.org

Ruffed Grouse Society: This organization works with youths to improve woodland habitat for ruffed grouse, American woodcock, and other upland birds. Web site: www.ruffedgrousesociety.org

Scholastic Clay Target Program/Scholastic Rifle Program: These programs provide regularly scheduled, adult-supervised events that emphasize sportsmanship, safety, and skills development. Web site: www.nssf.org/sctp

Step Outside: This is the National Shooting Sports Foundation's premier, award-winning outdoor mentoring program that introduces newcomers to traditional outdoor sports through its many partners. Web site: www.stepoutside.org

U.S. Sportsmen's Alliance: This hunter-rights organization hosts the Trailblazer Adventure Program developed for families. Web site: www.trailblazeradventure.org

Wingshooting USA: The National Shooting Sports Foundation launched this initiative in 2005 to increase hunter awareness of the convenient and high-quality experiences offered today by bird-hunting preserves around the country. Web site: www.wingshootingusa.org

NOTES

Chapter One: Hunting: When Killing Is Right

1. Quoted in John Burroughs, *Camping and Tramping with President Roosevelt* (New York: Houghton Mifflin, 1907), 110.

2. Archibald Rutledge, "My Friend the Deer," in *Tales of Whitetails: Archibald Rutledge's Great Deer Hunting Stories* (Columbia, SC: University of South Carolina Press, 1992).

3. William Faulkner, *Big Woods* (New York: Random House, 1931).

4. Ernest Hemingway, *Green Hills of Africa* (New York: Scribner, 1935).

5. Erich Fromm, *The Anatomy of Human Destructiveness* (New York: Holt, Rinehart and Winston, 1973).

Chapter Two: Why Florida Has Killer Gators

1. Tom Zucco, "Gator attack ends protection on island," *St. Petersburg Times*, September 20, 2004.

2. Florida Fish and Wildlife Conservation Commission, "Historic Alligator Bites on Humans in Florida," updated annually.

3. Author interview with Gary Morse, August 2006.

4. Michael A. Scarcella, "People 'going crazy' over attacks," *Sarasota Herald-Tribune,* May 16, 2006.

5. Laura Figueroa and John Simpson, "Gator permits gobbled up fast," *Miami Herald*, June 20, 2006.

6. Akilah Johnson, "Woman jogger killed by alligator after being dragged into Sunrise canal," *South Florida Sun-Sentinel*, May 11, 2006.

7. John Holland and Akilah Johnson, "Medical examiner confirms woman jogger was killed by alligator in Sunrise," *South Florida Sun-Sentinel*, May 11, 2006.

8. Shannon Pease, "Gator deaths rise to three," *Miami Herald*, May 15, 2006.

9. Kathy Waters, "Florida marks third deadly alligator attack in less than a week," Associated Press, May 15, 2006.

10. "Alligator Harvest Summary for 2004," Florida Wildlife Commission, December 7, 2005.

11. Figueroa and Simpson, "Gator permits gobbled up fast."

12. "Estimated producer value of wild alligator harvests in Florida during 1977–2004," prepared by the Alligator Management Team of the Florida Fish and Wildlife Conservation Commission, December 8, 2005.

13. Author interview with Noel Kinler, 2006.

14. "Louisiana's alligator management program," prepared by the Louisiana Department of Wildlife and Fisheries, Office of Wildlife, Fur and Refuge Division, December 2005.

15. "Lousiana's alligator management program gator notes," prepared by the Louisiana Department of Wildlife and Fisheries, November 2005.

16. Harry J. Dutton, "Alligator Management Program Review: A Progress Report," Florida Fish and Wildlife Conservation Commission, 2007.

Chapter Three: Why Bear Attacks Are Increasing

1. "Woman killed in bear attack in Alberta," CBC News, June 6, 2005.

2. "Grizzly Bear Management," a report compiled by the Alberta Sustainable Resource Development, February 24, 2004.

3. Stephen Herrero, Tom Smith, Terry D. DeBruyn, Kerry Gunther, and Colleen A. Matt, "From the Field: Brown bear habituation to people—safety, risks, and benefits," Wildlife Society Bulletin, 2005.

4. M. A. Haroldson, C. C. Schwartz, S. Cherry, and D. S. Moody, "Possible effects of elk harvest on fall distribution of grizzly bears in the Greater Yellowstone Ecosystem," *Journal of Wildlife Management*, 2004.

5. Author interview with Dave Moody, Wyoming Game and Fish Department trophy game coordinator, February 2007.

6. "Yellowstone Grizzly Bear Management Plan," prepared by Idaho's Yellowstone Grizzly Bear Delisting Advisory Team, March 2002.

7. "Successful Recovery Efforts Bring Yellowstone Grizzly Bears Off the Endangered List," U.S. Fish & Wildlife Services.

8. "Widow of man killed by grizzlies appeals to Supreme Court," Associated Press, March 5, 2006.

9. Herrero and Smith, "A century of bear-human conflict in Alaska: analyses and implications."

10. Stephen Herrero, *Bear Attacks: Their Causes and Avoidance* (New York: Lyons Press, 2002).

11. Author interview with Tom Smith, U.S. Geological Survey, August 2006.

12. Author interview with Lynn L. Rogers, North American Bear Center, August 2006.

13. Author interview with Ian McMurchy, January 2007.

14. "Canoeist stabs bear to death in Ontario," CBC News, July 22, 2006.

15. Author interview with McMurchy, 2007.

16. "Bear mauls and kills infant," Associated Press, August 19, 2002.

17. "6-year-old girl dies in bear attack," Associated Press, April 14, 2006.

18. Bill Poovey, "Hunt on for killer bear in Tennessee," Associated Press, April 15, 2006.

19. Tillie Fong, "Bear attack leaves two campers injured," *Rocky Mountain News*, July 15, 2003.

20. Author interview with Tom Shupe, wildlife biologist with the Florida Fish and Wildlife Commission, September 2006.

21. "Number of black bear complaints 1999–2005," compiled by the New Jersey Division of Fish and Wildlife, 2006.

22. Jim Lockwood, "Predatory black bear attack," *Newark Star Ledger*, August 12, 2003.

23. Author interview with Patrick C. Carr, a supervising wildlife biologist for the New Jersey Fish and Wildlife Bureau, September 2006.

Chapter Four: Predators Aren't Public Pets

1. John Ritter, "Cougar hunting doesn't lower fatal attacks," *USA Today*, August 8, 2006.

2. Ed Zieralski, "They protect lions, don't they?" *San Diego Union Tribune*, January 11, 2004.

3. "Verified mountain lion attacks on humans in California (1890 through 2006)," California Department of Fish and Game.

4. Author interview with Doug Updike, California Department of Fish and Game's senior wildlife biologist, 2006.

5. Nikolaus Olsen, "Missing boy may have been dragged off by mountain lion," *Rocky Mountain Collegian*, October 7, 1999.

6. "Shredded clothes tell a sad story," CBS News and the Associated Press, June 11, 2003.

7. Charley Able, "No human blood found on cat: Officials believe that mountain lion attacked 7-year-old," *Rocky Mountain News*, April 26, 2006.

8. Author interview with Lieutenant Bob Turner, California Game and Fish Department, 2004.

9. "Mountain lion killed after attack," CBS News and the Associated Press, January 9, 2004.

10. Author interview with Mark Dowling, cofounder of the Eastern Cougar Network, 2004.

11. Author interview with Mark Jakubauskas, research assistant professor with the Kansas Biological Survey, 2004.

12. Author interview with John Hobbs, Nebraska director of Wildlife Services, 2004.

13. Author interview with Rich Staffon, Minnesota Department of Natural Resources wildlife manager for the Duluth-Cloquet area, 2004.

14. Author interview with Brad Swanson, assistant professor of biology at Central Michigan University, 2004.

15. Zieralski, "They protect lions, don't they?"

16. Author interview with Debbie Dimmick, 2000.

17. "Coyote attacks 3-year-old boy on Cape Cod," July 30, 1999.

18. Author interview with Glyn Riley, a federal coyote trapper with the USDA's Wildlife Services, 2000.

19. Author interview with Professor Rex O. Baker of California State Polytechnic University in Pomona, 2000.

20. Professors Rex O. Baker and Robert M. Timm, "Management of conflicts between urban coyotes and humans in southern California," Agricul-

ture & Natural Resources Research & Extension Centers, Hopland (University of California), 1998.

21. Author interview with Jim Zumbo, 2007.

22. http://westerngraywolf.fws.gov.

23. Author interview with Tom Lemke, a wildlife biologist with Montana Fish, Wildlife & Parks, 2006.

24. Author interview with Ed Bangs, the U.S. Fish & Wildlife Service's gray wolf recovery coordinator, 2006.

25. Tim Mowry, "Woman recovering after wolf attack," *Fairbanks Daily News-Miner*, July 12, 2006.

26. Ron Malast, "Attacks on humans may not be so rare as claimed," *Chinook Observer*, November 22, 2006.

Chapter Five: Nature's Deadliest Animal

1. "Avoiding Deer/Car Collisions," a study by the Insurance Information Institute, February 5, 2007.

2. "Many deaths in vehicle-animal collisions are avoidable," a report from the Insurance Information Institute, November 18, 2004.

3. "The hunter in conservation," a booklet compiled by the Council for Wildlife Conservation and Education, Inc.

4. "State wildlife agencies say hunting not the reason for national increase in deer-related collisions," a report by the Association of Fish and Wildlife Agencies, October 20, 2006.

5. Dr. Brent J. Danielson and Dr. Michael W. Hubbard, "A literature review for assessing the status of current methods of reducing deer-vehicle collisions," a report prepared for the Iowa Department of Transportation, September 1998.

6. "Wildlife Reflector Program," a report from the British Columbia Ministry of Transportation and Highways, 2000.

7. T. T. Forman and D. Sperling, *Road Ecology: Science and Solutions* (Washington, DC: Island Press, 2003); "High-tech equipment may help reduce car-wildlife collisions," Three Rivers News Services, September 12, 2006.

8. Mark Watson and Jon Klingel, "Literature summary assessing methods for reducing deer-vehicle accidents," a study by the New Mexico Department of Game and Fish, May 15, 2000.

9. Robert Alison, "Road salt blamed for roadkill rise," *Toronto Star*, April 22, 2006.

10. Author interview with Phyllis Marchand, 2000.

11. Author interview with Anthony J. DeNicola, 2000.

12. Author interview with S. Leonard DiDonato, 2000.

Chapter Six: Hunting's Reformation

1. Lowell K. Halls, *White-Tailed Deer Ecology and Management* (Mechanicsburg, PA: Stackpole Books, 1984).

2. Jim Casada, "It was always our game," *Outdoor Life*, June/July 1998.

3. "Gray wolf—a history," Michigan Department of Natural Resources.

4. Shawn J. Riley, Genevieve M. Nesslage, Brian A. Maurer, "Dynamics of early wolf and cougar eradication efforts in Montana: implications for conservation," Montana Department of Fisheries and Wildlife, 2004.

5. John N. Cole, "100 years of conservation," *Outdoor Life*, June/July 1998.

6. "Journal of John James Audubon Made During his Trip to New Orleans in 1820-1821," American Philosphical Society, 2002.

7. "A Guide to the Laws and Treaties of the United States for Protecting Migratory Birds," U.S. Fish and Wildlife Service, May 21, 2002.

8. "The hunter in conservation," a booklet compiled by the Council for Wildlife Conservation and Education, Inc.

Chapter Seven: Hunting Is Better Than Birth Control

1. Bob Cooney, "Curbside sterilization could become a deer-control option for gun-shy suburbs," published by the College of Agricultural & Life Sciences, University of Wisconsin–Madison, April 16, 2002.

2. Author interview with Russell Mason, a biologist with the USDA's National Wildlife Research Center in Logan, Utah, July 2000.

3. Author interview with Dr. Allen Rutburg, professor at Tufts University, July 2000.

4. Author interview with H. Brian Underwood, research wildlife ecologist with the Biological Resources Division of the U.S. Geological Survey, July 2000.

5. Author interview with Dr. Michael Holland, an Australian biologist who has worked with the USDA Predator Ecology Center in Logan, Utah, July 2000.

6. Author interview with Anthony DeNicola, president of White Buffalo, 2002.

Chapter Eight: Why Vegetarians Owe Hunters

1. "Wildlife damage," research compiled by Wildlife Services, a division of the Animal and Plant Health Inspection Service.

2. "Agricultural secretary says deer damage costs commonwealth $75 million a year," PAPowerPort, April 4, 2006.

3. "How are white-tailed deer affecting agriculture in New Jersey?" Rutgers New Jersey Agricultural Experiment Station Center for Wildlife Damage Control, October 21, 1998.

4. Tom Brown, "Assessment of Wildlife Damage to Crops in New York State," Human Dimensions Research Unit, Cornell University, April 2003.

5. Dave Golowenski, "Farmers want Ohio's deer herd cut in half," *Columbus Dispatch*, December 12, 2006.

6. Janet Ginsburg, "A Deer-Slayer Crosses the Mississippi," *BusinessWeek*, April 8, 2002.

7. Shannon Dininny, "Feds offer new way to manage elk," Associated Press, November 28, 2005.

8. "Summary of the National Organic Program," Department of Agriculture, Agricultural Marketing Service, December 21, 2000.

9. "Potential costs of losing hunting and trapping as wildlife management methods," a report by the International Association of Fish and Wildlife Agencies, May 25, 2005.

Chapter Nine: Some Environmentalists Carry Guns

1. "USDA Wildlife Services protects people," United States Department of Agriculture, 2004. http://www.aphis.usda.gov/ws/introreports/people.pdf.

Chapter Ten: Why Songbirds Love Deer Hunters

1. Fred J. Aun, "Deer hunting needed to limit deforestation," *Star-Ledger*, May 2, 2006.
2. "New sport hunting programs on National Wildlife Refuges declared unlawful," press release from the Humane Society of the United States, September 1, 2006.
3. "Why are hunting, fishing and trapping allowed on national wildlife refuges?" U.S. Fish and Wildlife Service's official position on hunting on national wildlife refuges can be read at: http://www.fws.gov/refuges/faqs/hunting.html.
4. "NJ's forest health is threatened; immediate action needed," a report compiled by the New Jersey Audubon Society, March 2005.
5. "Summary of harvested deer in NJ, 1972–2005," research compiled annually by the New Jersey Division of Fish and Wildlife.

Chapter Eleven: Hunting Is Incentive-Based Environmentalism

1. "Net economic values for wildlife-related recreation in 2001," a report compiled by the U.S. Fish and Wildlife Service's Division of Federal Aid.
2. Author interview with Mike DiSario, president of Outdoor Expeditions International and OEI Properties, June 2006.
3. Marc J. Perry, "Domestic net migration in the United States: 2000 to 2004," a report by the U.S. Census Bureau, April 2006.
4. Patrick O'Driscoll, "Report: Conservation efforts offset land lost to sprawl," *USA Today*, November 30, 2006.

Chapter Twelve: How Hunters Recaptured Environmentalism

1. "President Bush Convenes Conservation Meeting Top Priorities of Hunting/Fishing Community Covered in Crawford, TX," press release from the Theodore Roosevelt Conservation Partnership, April 9, 2004.
2. Reports compiled by http://www.activistcash.com.
3. Michael Shellenberger and Ted Nordhaus, "The death of environmentalism: Global warming politics in a post-environmental world," a report compiled for the Environmental Grantmakers Association, October 2004.

Chapter Thirteen: Why Hunting Is Good for Kids

1. Henry David Thoreau, *Walden*, from *The Portable Thoreau*, Carl Bode, ed. (New York: Viking Press, 1947).

2. Centers for Disease Control, "Sports-Related Injuries Among High School Athletes, United States, 2005–06 School Year."

3. "New National Study First Since 1970s to Document Full Range of Sports Injuries," American Sports Data, May 15, 2003. http://www.americansportsdata.com/pr-sportsinjuries.asp.

4. "Families Afield," a report compiled by the National Shooting Sports Foundation, the U.S. Sportsmen's Alliance, and the National Wild Turkey Federation, 2006.

5. Frederick O. Mueller, PhD, Robert C. Cantu, MD, "Annual Survey of Football Injury Research 1931–2005," National Center for Catastrophic Sports Injury Research. http://www.unc.edu/depts/nccsi/SurveyofFootballInjuries.htm.

6. "U.S. Fish and Wildlife Services 2001 National Survey of Fishing, Hunting, and Wildlife-Associated Recreation," a study compiled every five years by the U.S. Fish and Wildlife Service's Division of Federal Aid.

7. Zoe Weil, "Humane education: Charting a new course," *Animals' Agenda*, September/October 1998.

8. The National Humane Education Society's "Mission Statement" on hunting can be read at http://www.nhes.org/articles.asp?article_id=30&section_id=60.

Chapter Fourteen: Hunters and Gun Rights

1. *Parker v. District of Columbia*, a majority decision by the United States Court of Appeals for the District of Columbia Circuit, March 9, 2007. The decision can be read in full at http://pacer.cadc.uscourts.gov/docs/common/opinions/200703/04-7041a.pdf.

2. "Whether the Second Amendment Secures an Individual Right," U.S. Department of Justice, 2004. The report is available at http://www.usdoj.gov/olc/secondamendment2.pdf.

3. Ibid.

4. "The Right to Ban Arms," *New York Times*, March 14, 2007.

5. "Dangerous Ruling: An appeals court ruling would put handguns back in D.C. homes," *Washington Post*, March 10, 2007.

6. "Crime in the United States 2005," a report by the U.S. Department of Justice Federal Bureau of Investigation. http://www.fbi.gov/ucr/05cius/index.html.

7. "Brady Center Lawyers Launch 'Rolling Critique' of Ruling on D.C. Gun Laws," press release by the Brady Campaign to Prevent Gun Violence. http://bradycampaign.org/media/release.php?release=893.

8. Benjamin Wittes, "Ditch the Second Amendment: Gun Shy," New Republic Online, March 19, 2007.

9. Adam Liptak, "A Liberal Case for Gun Rights Sways Judiciary," *New York Times*, May 6, 2007.

10. "Could Andrea Yates Go Free? Should Jury System be Changed? Group of Hunters Wants Common Sense Brought Back to Gun Use," CNN, June 26, 2006. http://transcripts.cnn.com/TRANSCRIPTS/0606/26/gb.01.html.

11. Federal Election Commission records, available at www.OpenSecrets.org

12. Craig Gilbert, "Bringing the candidate to life," *Milwaukee Journal Sentinel*, July 5, 2004.

13. "Bush vs. Kerry," *Outdoor Life*, October 2004.

14. "Protecting the Environment & Improving Our Quality of Life," press release on Senator John Kerry's Web site. http://kerry.senate.gov/text/congress/environment.html.

15. John R. Lott Jr., "Misfires: John Kerry aims all over the map on guns," National Review Online, September 14, 2004.

INDEX

Index